HEALING *from* WITHIN

Dennis T. Jaffe, Ph.D.

HEALING
from
WITHIN

 Alfred A. Knopf   New York   1985

THIS IS A BORZOI BOOK
PUBLISHED BY ALFRED A. KNOPF, INC.

LIBRARY OF CONGRESS CATALOGING IN PUBLICATION DATA
Jaffe, Dennis T
Healing from within.
Includes bibliographical references and index.
1. Medicine and psychology.   2. Holistic medicine.
3. Health.   I. Title.
R726.5.J33   1980   613   79-23831
ISBN 0-394-41032-7

Manufactured in the United States of America
Published April 2, 1980
Reprinted once
Third Printing, May 1985

For Yvonne, Oren and Kai,
Who teach me daily about love

Did you ever observe that there are two classes of patients in states, slaves and freemen; and the slave doctors run about and cure the slaves, or wait for them in dispensaries—practitioners of this sort never talk to their patients individually or let them talk about their own individual complaints. The slave doctor prescribes what mere experience suggests, as if he had exact knowledge, and when he has given his orders, like a tyrant, he rushes off with equal assurance to some other servant who is ill. But the other doctor, who is a freeman, attends and practices on freemen; and he carries his inquiries far back, and goes into the nature of the disorder; he enters into discourse with the patient and with his friends, and is at once getting information from the sick man and also instructing him as far as he is able, and he will not prescribe until he has at first convinced him. If one of those empirical physicians, who practice medicine without science, were to come upon the gentleman physician talking to his gentleman patient and using the language almost of philosophy, beginning at the beginning of the disease and discoursing about the whole nature of the body, he would burst into a hearty laugh—he would say what most of those who are called doctors always have at their tongues' end: Foolish fellow, he would say, you are not healing the sick man but educating him; and he does not want to be made a doctor but to get well.

PLATO

Contents

PART III   WORKING FOR YOUR HEALTH:
            A SELF-HELP PROGRAM

Foreword by Robert A. Aldrich, M.D.

Professor of Preventive Medicine, Pediatrics and Anthropology, University of Colorado.

We are the last of the hominids. After millions of years of evolution, *Homo sapiens* remains, the sole survivor of man-like creatures on this planet. We have within us, each one, the proven characteristics for successful companionship with the natural environment in which we have evolved. Among the major factors contributing to this human achievement, health must rank very high. Historians, archaeologists, philosophers, and social scientists have provided us with much insight into how our early ancestors lived. Ancient wisdom, at first communicated by memory and verbalization, is today readily available through electronics, so that we can be instantly informed, providing we have learned how to listen. The message from our ancestors is consistent. The great religions all provide us with similar instructions about food, rest, privacy, meditation, family, friends, and the values by which we should conduct our lives. Throughout these teachings, one can find health, in the broadest sense of this word, as a central theme.

In this regard, I have often speculated about the high prestige assigned to elders in primitive tribes. Why should they be so respected and admired? My belief is that it is because they survived many years longer than others and were the repository of the tribe's history as well as the ancient wisdom and values which were to be transmitted to the younger generation. They combined longevity—usually an outcome of good health—with experience, knowledge, and wisdom. In this sense then, health has always been basic to human development and will continue to be the most influential of major factors in the evolution of modern man. It is in this context that Dennis Jaffe's *Healing from Within* may be regarded as an important contribution to the growing movement toward wellness and holistic medicine.

Our minds and bodies are not greatly different from those of human beings who lived in Stone Age cultures. Modern man functions with a Stone Age brain in an environment entirely foreign to his earlier evolutionary surroundings. Much of our present environment, built by human technologies, consists of urban structures and functions that are lacking in human scale and that exceed our ability to adapt. Stone, steel, and glass high rises are a shocking contrast to small dwellings on the land surrounded by trees, flowers, streams, and the shaping contours of hills or plains. Transportation by automobile in a large, congested city like New York at midday is slower than one can walk; yet after 10:00 P.M, a stroller is in danger on the streets, by then virtually uninhabited. There is a growing discrepancy between the human endowments fostered by evolution and the conditions that we are creating for ourselves. Urban, industrial culture may be diverging from our previous evolutionary path, and we may be deaf to crucial inner messages from mind and body warning us of danger ahead. One is reminded of the canaries taken into coal mines by miners to warn them of toxic gases. The little birds' sudden death showed the presence of lethal fumes well before the miner was affected. Modern people living out their life span in an urban setting exhibit unhealthy manifestations, both physical and behavioral, that could be warnings similar to those given by the canaries.

Individuals born in the United States now have a statistical life expectancy of approximately seventy years, females having a clear advantage over males. The factors that would allow us to understand this difference between the sexes in regard to mortality are unknown, and as often is the case, there are dozens of speculative theories in the absence of conclusive proof. This matter alone could justify expanded research into the characteristics of the two sexes, their differences and similarities. I believe, however, that an even wider concept is open to us as the direct result of this greatly increased longevity. Since life expectancy is usually quite long today, what can we do to make the middle and later years of high quality and fill them with good health? Is this matter of good health in late adult life the result of multiple factors operating throughout the entire life span? Are these factors known, and, if so, how can they become a part of the culture we live in? In other words, is it possible to transmit to the generation being born at the beginning of this new decade an array of reasonably sound cultural practices that will assure good health in childhood on the basis of which adult good health can be achieved? I believe that this is possible by the end of this century. In the area of childhood, we have much of the knowledge we need to start with, and we can anticipate gaining critical new information about the adult stages of the life course that when fitted together will provide a pattern of factors operating together throughout the life span that favor, or cause, health.

We are indeed in a new era for human beings. World shortages of essentials are beginning to be felt. At the present time, one could mention energy, food, and probably clean water. The time of plentiful raw materials has ended forever, and we human beings will need to draw upon all the wisdom we have. The long-range view will have to replace the short-range view, competition must be tempered by cooperation, the maintenance of health should take precedence over the treatment of disease, and human habitation will have to be designed and constructed well within the limited adaptability of human beings of all ages. In his book *Survival of the Wisest,* Jonas Salk has addressed this new era upon which we are already embarked, stressing the sweeping changes in values and attitudes that will be required of modern man. Yet these "new" ideas and standards are remarkably close to the ancient wisdoms handed down for thousands of years. The ancients knew the importance of family, community, and individual respect for self that modern man may have forgotten, but is now beginning to rediscover.

The examination of the causes of health and of the impact of health over the life span will have some predictable economic consequences. The contemporary "health care delivery system" in the United States is not attuned to promoting health, let alone a certain amount of responsible self-care. Capital investments in facilities such as hospitals, clinics, institutes for research, and medical schools are aimed at treating illness, diagnosing disease, and studying and teaching about diseases and disease processes. Any major shift in public focus such as that from disease diagnosis and treatment toward health promotion and counseling could easily redirect the flow of money away from the sectors, both public and private, that support the present system. The re-investment of capital must be done wisely. Since maintaining health by using existing and future knowledge of health-causing factors in our daily lives will probably be less capital intensive and at the same time more effective in raising the level of public health, one can expect to see increasing pressure on the present system to engage in the practice of health maintenance and to utilize a large number of alternative healing modalities to complement modern medical practice. Some economic incentives are overdue from the health and life insurance industry. Here the concept of a variety of factors operating to cause health throughout the human life span could provide a basis for new forms of coverage by either life insurors or health insurors that would reward good health practices and longevity by bonuses, reduced premiums, or other means. One can only imagine what response state-supported medical schools might expect if strong, well-led, comprehensive wellness centers became separate major programs complementing the traditional centers for diseases. I am convinced that a great many among the public would be attracted to such centers on a pay-as-you-go basis, especially where such centers were staffed by professionals whose attitudes, orientation, philosophy, and expertise were in health. Possibly our educational institutions can start preparing men and women as doctors of health whose task would be the study of the epidemiology of health and its relationships to the stages of the human life span. Unlimited opportunities are visible in the immediate future if we are prepared to exercise change with wisdom. People can be encouraged to assume much greater responsibility for their own health, and a vigorous effort should be made to raise the level of knowledge about personal health at all levels in schools and colleges.

I commend Dr. Jaffe for this lucid, responsible, well-written book. He has added the best features of health practice from his experience to the sound base we have gained from years of studying disease and its causes. Joining an equal understanding of the causes of health with the causes of disease will mark an attainment in human development worthy of the new era we have entered.

Preface

Take a few minutes to assess the state of your personal health and well-being.

Sit comfortably in a quiet place and relax your entire body as much as possible. Then let your imagination weave a mental picture of yourself in perfect health. Spend some time examining every facet of this idealized image. How is the person you see different from the present you? How would the healthy you look and move? What can he or she do that you can't?

Despite its simplicity, this brief exercise will force you to recognize the difference—which may be great—between your present health and what you would like it to be. It usually raises some important questions: Why aren't you as healthy as you'd like to be? What are the obstacles to good health, and why do they exist? Might you be susceptible to a serious illness in the near future? If so, what can you do to prevent it from developing? Can a chronic or recurring illness or stress symptom be eliminated, or is it inevitable and permanent?

All of us have internal powers to protect and maintain our own health, yet through ignorance and neglect, many of us fall ill unnecessarily. If you become sick, you very often need to rejuvenate your innate abilities to heal yourself and preserve your future health.

This book is designed to help you mobilize yourself on that road to well-being. It is intended not only to be read, but to be used actively. Although I will cite case studies and research to support my theories, the real proof will lie within your own experience. As you proceed through each chapter, I hope you will see how this book can apply to your own life and how personal changes might improve your health and well-being.

This book contains questions and exercises to help you integrate the research and clinical information into your own life, create a personal health-promotion program, and experience the important role you can play in your quest for better health. If you approach them with an earnest and open mind, you will derive significant benefits. The questions and exercises and personal inquiry are not, however, intended as substitutes for medical care and treatment. Rather, they are meant to encourage you to follow a comprehensive health-enhancement program that not only can help you work with your physician to heal specific illnesses when they strike, but can prevent many common and serious but largely unnecessary ailments.

I hope that this book will be useful for health professionals as well as laypeople—that it will introduce physicians, nurses, psychologists, social workers, and rehabilitation and allied health specialists to a broader perspective of the nature and treatment of illness, enabling them to see it as a process with psychological, interpersonal, social, and spiritual aspects as well as physical ones.

It is difficult for health professionals to incorporate these methods and techniques into practice until they have tried them on themselves. A personal health exploration is the first step in professional training and growth, and likewise, is a starting point in patient education and preventive medicine.

The book is divided into three parts, following the Learning for Health program that has been developed in my clinical practice:

Part I explores the question "What is illness?" from the perspective of the physician, the health-care system, the psychologist, the poet, the sociologist, and the family. It suggests that the familiar concept of illness as merely a localized physical phenomenon is inadequate and inhibits a successful treatment program.

Part II examines the research and offers clinical examples of how an individual's illnesses may be intimately connected to his or her life-style, personal relationships, feelings, life history, response to stress, family dynamics, and community citizenship. Throughout this section, I will offer ways to assess the possible role of these factors in your illnesses or chronic stress symptoms.

Part III presents specific exercises and behaviors that can reintegrate mind and body. It describes several methods, including body awareness, biofeedback, relaxation, self-hypnosis, and meditation. It outlines a self-help program aimed at creating and maintaining health. Rather than interfering with or deprecating your physician's medical treatments or medication, this program invites you to mobilize your own internal healing powers to augment the healing process, using specific techniques of healing imagery, behavior control, and stress management to overcome common psychological health hazards.

How can you best prepare yourself to absorb the material in this book? I recommend that you commit yourself to spend between a half hour and an hour a day practicing exercises and reflecting on the various influences surrounding your specific illness and stress symptoms. Use a small notebook as your personal health journal. Here you can write your responses to the questions in Parts I and II, and the results of experiences and exercises in Part III. If you actively participate in this journey, I believe that your personal health, and your power to maintain it, will increase dramatically.

Acknowledgments

I do not claim originality in this book. What I have done is to synthesize the theory and clinical practice of scores of health professionals who represent a growing voice in health practice. Many of these people are close friends; others have influenced me as much by their writing, or by my observing them in workshops and seminars. I consider this book an effort emerging from that community of interest, and I want to offer credit to those who have helped me create my own synthesis.

First there is the immediate circle of those who have directly assisted me. Richard Trubo, a fine writer on health, rescued me after I had completed several drafts of this book by taking the manuscript in hand and showing me how to recast it so that I could communicate what I wanted to say. Mike Hamilberg, my agent, and Ashbel Green, my editor, both took on this project when it was a one-page outline, and had the faith to encourage me to complete it.

Then there are my closest colleagues, who have worked with me to develop a clinical style and practice. Yvonne Jaffe, my wife, is an immediate and daily source of reflection upon all my clinical work. Nancy Solomon, M.D., my partner in creating the clinic Learning for Health, in West Los Angeles, has co-directed health groups with me and aided me at each step of the way. David Bresler and others associated with the Center for Integral Medicine in Los Angeles have helped me develop imagery techniques and tapes and other educational materials, and disseminate them to other health professionals. Lawrence Allman, who brought me from Connecticut to work at UCLA toward the establishment of a family therapy program at the Veterans Hospital in Sepulveda, California, stimulated me to develop the theories about family processes and systems that underlie the conceptual model in the book. All of them have made essential contributions in every stage of writing this book.

Among others I must thank are Marilyn Ferguson, editor of *Brain/Mind Bulletin*, a tireless organizer, and a rich source of research and clinical material which I have drawn upon countless times in this volume. Jim Gordon, a psychiatrist at the National Institute of Mental Health, and Rick Carlson have also been supportive, have kept me in touch with the medical establishment, and have helped me address broad social-policy concerns in my writing. Some of the pioneers whose writing and example have been important to me in pursuing my own program include Carl and Stephanie Simonton, Ken Pelletier, John Travis, Lawrence LeShan, Mike Samuels, Hal Stone, Irving Oyle, Ross Speck, Barbara Brown, Bob Swearingen, Emmett Miller, Lynn LeCron, Brugh Joy, John Knowles, Eugene Gendlin, Don Johnson, and Norman Cousins. Milton Greenblatt, Simon Sayre, Andrew Lewin, Norman Cousins, David Wellisch, Jim Gagne, and Larry Allman, all of UCLA, plus Jerome Spitzer and Philip Kresky, read and commented on the manuscript.

I would also like to thank the following journals, newsletters, and periodicals for printing drafts of chapters, which enabled me to receive feedback: *Holistic Health Review*, *Hospital and Community Psychiatry*, *New Realities*, *Imagery*, and *Alternatives*. The National Institute of Mental Health partially supported the writing of chapters on the family, on self-management, and on imagery.

Finally, I have worked in many clinical settings that have influenced me. These include the Center for Health Enhancement at UCLA, the Center for Integral Medicine, the Holistic Health Center in Los Angeles, Pressure Partners Medical Clinic, and the Center for Healing Arts, as well as my own Learning for Health clinic. I would like to thank the hundreds of clients and participants in my classes, groups, and workshops and in family therapy and individual counseling whose response to me, and whose sharing, really forms the core of this book. Of course, when I present their stories, their names and life circumstances have been carefully disguised. Without their encouragement, responsiveness, commitment, and example, I would have had nothing to write.

Part I

THE
MANY FACES
of
DISEASE, HEALTH
and
HEALING

1 *The Healing Partnership*

*To ward off disease or recover health, men as a rule
find it easier to depend on healers than to attempt the
more difficult task of living wisely.*

RENÉ DUBOS

Most of us take our good health for granted. We tend to pay
little attention to our physical condition until pain or discomfort signals us that something has gone wrong. Our reaction usually consists of surprise and frustration at such an
unwarranted intrusion, accompanied by anxiety and helplessness. We are uncertain what has gone wrong, why it
happened, and how to heal it. We consider the inner workings of the body as a mystery that can be probed and re-
paired only by a physician.

I believe that many of our common assumptions about illness are inaccurate and sometimes dangerous. Most of us regard illness as an external invader, attacking a body that was
previously healthy. Illnesses are typically blamed on defective genes, bad fortune, last night's meal, or something in the
air. Using this logic, we assume that physical disorders cannot usually be prevented. There is a dim awareness that our
bodies have needs and require care, but such care is nevertheless rather low on our list of priorities. If you're like most
of us, you probably expend more energy on your house or
car than on your own self-preservation.

Such attitudes ignore our own power to influence health
or illness. In reality, most diseases stem from not one but a
long chain of contributing factors, which intensify and multiply over a period of months or years. Our behavior, feelings, stress levels, relationships, conflicts, and beliefs con-

3

tribute to our overall susceptibility to disease. In essence, everything about our lives affects our health. By improving these dimensions of ourselves over which we have control, we can maximize our well-being and our ability to resist illness. Our power to prevent and heal illness is far greater than most of us realize.

Consequently, no one should remain insensitive to his state of health or illness. If you are ill, it is essential for you to become an active participant in the therapeutic process. If you are healthy, you must be willing to work actively, every day, to maintain your well-being. While it may be reassuring to imagine that medical technology will eventually deliver you from illness, modern medicine has reached a point where it cannot guarantee good health unless you work in conjunction with your physician. Today, the key to enduring health and healing often lies in your own behavior.

This idea is not as radical as it may seem. A growing number of physicians and health professionals have arrived at the same conclusion. They agree that if an individual is to remain healthy, and avoid premature death or unnecessary disease and suffering, he must change his attitudes both toward himself and toward the health-care system. They regard disease not just as a crisis within the body, but as a process involving every aspect of life. Each person can help determine his own health status, using his physician or other health professional as an educator and guide. This book is an inquiry into this new perspective, the research that supports it, and the health-inducing behaviors that it requires.

Healing, Harmony and Wholeness

Two thousand years ago, Plato observed: "The great error in the treatment of the human body is that physicians are ignorant of the whole. For the part can never be well unless the whole is well."

Ancient physicians, lacking modern diagnostic techniques

and potent drugs, viewed a patient's illnesses as representing something gone awry with his or her entire life and place in the community. To these early doctors, physical diseases were intimately related to feelings and personal relationships. To facilitate healing, they mobilized the powerful restorative energies of the minds of the patient and of the people close to the patient.

We can learn a lot from the ancient physicians. Good health—in its broadest sense—occurs when we live in harmony with ourselves and our environment, maintaining a balance in the face of changes, growing with challenges, and developing our innate healing powers. In essence, to be healthy is to be integrated and whole.

But in this modern era of medical specialization, doctors are trained to concentrate on specific organs or physical systems. Their expertise is narrow and intense, and thus it is not surprising that they may fail to look at each patient as a whole person who is part of a larger environment that might have contributed to his or her illness. They see each patient only once or twice, typically when he is seriously ill, and often don't gather information about his living situation. Medicine has become separated from the community. It exists primarily in hospitals. Too often, organs and diseases, not people, are the objects of treatment. The approach of this book recognizes the value of medicine as it was practiced in earlier eras—approaching the patient as a whole person and as part of a community.

The most common name for this perspective is "holistic," or "wholistic," health. The term was introduced by biologist-explorer Jan Smuts to refer to nature's tendency to synthesize and organize toward greater wholes. The meaning of the whole organism was always more than merely the sum of the parts, because the merging process itself contained certain properties within it. According to Smuts, each person, and his health and illness, can be understood only in reference to his or her total functioning—physical, psychological, social, and spiritual.

Other terms used to describe this new perspective are "integral" or "psychosocial" medicine, referring to the integration of ancient and modern principles, and of psychological and physical methods, into the healing process. The terms "humanistic" and "person-centered" medicine are also sometimes utilized, indicating that the whole person, not simply the body, is the concern. No matter which term is used, be assured that none implies a rejection of modern medical science. Rather, this perspective represents an incorporation of physical medicine into the broader realm of a person's psychological, social, and even spiritual and religious functioning.

The Doctor's Dilemma

Why do we need a new approach to medicine? After all, aren't we a healthier society now than ever before?

To explore these questions, let's examine the role of the contemporary physician. For many decades, doctors have been revered as godlike figures. Most people entrust their physicians with almost full responsibility for their health. Time after time, at the first sign of illness, the doctor is called upon to deliver a miracle cure.

Despite this faith and reliance on medicine—reflected in the 12 percent of the gross national product spent on health care—doctors do not always provide remedies for our ills. And when they don't, we are usually bitterly disappointed. Given the past successes of medicine—control of infection, subtle diagnostic tools, delicate surgical procedures, chemicals to compensate for our body's deficiencies and difficulties—we have come to expect medicine to solve all our present and future health problems.

However, the common health problems we face today are often not ones which modern medicine is equipped to handle effectively without our help. Lewis Thomas, president of the Sloan-Kettering Cancer Center, notes that despite impressive advances in medical technology, currently accepted methods of care are ineffective in treating the leading fatal and nonfatal ailments.[1] Tragically, while physicians have learned to control the infectious diseases that accounted for most illness before 1900, new ones have developed in their place. Heart disease and cancer, which were once rare (and remain rare in underdeveloped countries), have evolved into our most prevalent killers, with few reliable treatments to combat them.

The new diseases of the late twentieth century have been called "diseases of civilization." They are not the result of outside invaders—germs, microbes, bacteria, viruses—but are caused by the gradual breakdown of the body's structure. Contemporary diseases such as cancer and heart, lung, and digestive failures cannot be cured by even our most sophisticated medical approaches. Treatment can smother some of the symptoms or the pain, and perhaps retard further damage. But patients are not "cured" in the traditional sense. Instead, they face continuous treatment, chronic disability, and perhaps even premature death.

Unlike the infectious (and often childhood) diseases which caused the fatalities of earlier eras, the diseases of civilization develop slowly and strike primarily older, mature people. They are often produced by an individual's abuse or neglect of his or her own body. Lung cancer, for instance, was almost nonexistent before smoking became widespread. Other modern diseases are related to the stresses and pace of contemporary living, the deficiencies of our fast-food diet, or environmental contamination.

Inventions designed to enhance the quality of life have sometimes simultaneously impaired our health. The automobile, while convenient and seemingly indispensable, not only deprives us of important exercise, but kills or injures nearly as many people as died of infectious diseases in earlier times. In fact, it is our leading cause of death, injury, and hospitalization. Alcohol abuse, while not unique to contemporary man, is now so widespread as to cause thousands of accidents each year, and it destroys both internal organs and family relationships.

And how does society respond to such evils? Instead of policing our behavior and our environment to minimize or eliminate damage to our health, we instead look to physicians to repair the injury, often only when it is too late for effective treatment.

So with our unrealistic expectations and demands, we've placed the physician in a difficult position. Less than a quarter of the patients he sees have ailments he can effectively treat. Another 30 or 40 percent of them suffer from long-standing, chronic, degenerative illnesses that are already in such an advanced state of development that all he can offer at best is palliative treatment to reduce the symptoms or control the pain.

Doctors are similarly ill equipped to cope with even minor pains and disorders. In trying to treat vague aches, a lack of energy, and negative emotional states such as depression, anxiety, and worry, physicians are frequently as frustrated as their patients. David Rogers, president of the Johnson Foundation, reports that more than 60 percent of the complaints brought to general practitioners are diffuse, generalized symptoms for which only comforting care is available.[2] Typically, unless the doctor can pinpoint a specific, acute illness, his treatment consists primarily of sympathy and concern and an assortment of tranquilizers and pain relievers (which account for over 25 percent of all medications prescribed). Fortunately, most of the complaints that come to a physician's office are self-limiting—that is, they will eventually disappear on their own, cured by the body's own self-healing powers. And these successes buttress our faith in our doctors.

The contemporary physician faces still another dilemma, stemming from the setting of his training. In medical school, he tended to see illness as almost purely a biological and physiological event, occurring in a hospital. He saw largely serious, critical episodes of illness outside of the context of the patient's family and environment. He learned crisis medicine. Yet in practice he must grapple with the reality that perhaps three-fourths of the physical ailments he encounters are less serious, have no clear, specific physical cause, and sometimes, as with chronic pain, have not even a specific physical locale or damage to accompany them.

He labels these "psychosomatic" ailments, but he is largely unschooled in how to treat them effectively. He cannot refer all of these people to psychiatrists, and it is doubtful that even psychiatry could be of much help. So even when doctors accept that psychological and social factors play a role in creating illness, they have difficulty dealing with them. For example, while they understand that management of many illnesses depends upon cooperation and commitment of the patient, they often find themselves unable to obtain such cooperation and commitment. If we were fairer to our doctors, perhaps we would call upon them only to treat the illnesses which they in fact can cure, and we would rely primarily on preventive measures for other types of ailments.

Taking Responsibility for Your Health

In your quest for optimum health, you must look beyond the doctor to yourself. Unless you work along with the physician, becoming an active partner in the healing process, he may not be very helpful. As social critic Ivan Illich notes, our continued reliance solely on the medical establishment to provide health has itself become a health hazard—a "medical nemesis"—because it has led us to neglect ourselves and even forget how to take care of ourselves.[3]

Thomas McKeown, a world leader in preventive medicine, reports that physicians can rightfully take credit for only about 10 percent of our collective health.[4] There are other, far more important factors in maintaining good health—the quality of nutrition, the environment, work, personal hygiene, and, most important, decisions about how we will live and treat our body. The LaLonde report on health problems of Canadians supports this hypothesis that our behavior is the primary cause of serious illnesses.[5]

The late John Knowles, who was president of the Rockefeller Foundation, offered two blunt conclusions about health:

> Over 99 percent of us are born healthy and suffer premature death and disability only as a result of personal misbehavior and environmental conditions.[6]
>
> The next major advances in the health of the American people will result from the assumption of individual responsibility for one's own health. This will require a change in lifestyle for the majority of Americans.[7]

The majority of civilization's diseases, while not curable when they reach advanced stages, are preventable if we would take better care of ourselves. Clinical signs of almost every serious illness surface years before irreversible damage occurs. That is when the most effective intervention can take place.

By accepting reponsibility for your well-being, you need not assume blame for your illnesses. If you are sick, you need not feel guilty. Guilt will not change the past or the present, or enhance your chances for a healthy future.

Your energies should instead be focused upon acquiring an understanding of the factors that may have helped cause or aggravate your illness, and changing them. Rather than feeling helpless, hopeless, or guilty when you become ill, you must begin to explore what you can do to make yourself healthier. While some elements that help cause illness may be beyond your control, by changing the factors within your influence, you can maximize your chances for recovery. In our clinic, we refer to this active, positive, committed attitude as "responsible health care." It implies that both the physician and the patient have detailed and demanding responsibilities in the treatment process. They form a working partnership, which demands the skills and energies of both to create optimum health.

Reclaiming Our Bodies

Too many people regard the body as an alien being, not really part of them. They behave as if they barely have bodies, ignoring most of the messages, sensations, and warnings the body sends them. They often push the body to the limits of its endurance, as if they could exchange it for a new model if it breaks down.

Lewis Thomas suggests that our current dependence on physicians and medication is evidence of a decrease in our confidence and faith in our bodies.[8] We act as if we expect something to go wrong at any moment. A generation ago, more people had confidence that their bodies could combat illness and return to health. But today, influenced by an onslaught of advertising suggesting that medication is the key to feeling good, we have come to believe we can't remain healthy without outside help. Drugs or surgery, we think, are the only means of safeguarding or regaining good health.

The holistic perspective requires us to become more comfortable with our bodies and aware of their ability to stay well. Throughout this book, you will learn how to mobilize the self-healing powers of your body. Many illnesses can be healed only by built-in mechanisms of the body. A physician can set a bone, administer a useful antibiotic, or remove a severely damaged organ that no longer functions. But the body's natural self-healing mechanisms—its self-protective powers—are the primary agents to accomplish the necessary healing. Medicine prods and aids the magnificent work of the body. Indeed, every day we are saved from countless illnesses by the body's vigilance and protectiveness.

As your search for self-healing proceeds, you will find it increasingly difficult to separate the roles played by your

body and your mind. For centuries, physicians and philosophers alike assumed that the mind and the body existed in
distinct, largely parallel worlds. This dualism, which dates
back to the seventeenth-century speculations of René Des-
cartes, was a useful distinction because it allowed physical
and biological science to evolve, unhampered by subjective
biases. But current research is breaking down the boundaries between mind and body, as it explores the connection
between them.

We cannot understand the creation of diseases of civilization, which are suffered primarily by human beings, without
noting that our mind's thoughts and feelings affect our physiology, and vice versa. Our physical health problems cannot
be treated only physically, because our psychological state
can also contribute to our illness or well-being. Treatment
may be far more effective if it utilizes mental powers as a
way of affecting the body. Holistic medicine frequently
relies upon an interchange between the mind and the body.
Within this perspective, the mind and body are perceived as
a unified whole, not two separate realms to be treated by different practitioners.

Biofeedback researcher Elmer Green has proposed that
every mental event is accompanied by a simultaneous corresponding physical event, and vice versa.[9] Thus, when you
experience a change in feeling or in thought, there is a related change in your physiology. Conversely, a change in
your body affects your psychological state. For example, if
you are feeling anger or depression, there is an accompanying change in your physical state—perhaps an increase in
muscle tension, or in the secretion of some hormones. When
your mental state improves, your physiology changes as
well, also for the better.

A goal of holistic medicine is to help people recognize and
take advantage of the connection between mind and body.
For example, once you understand that your mind can
change your body more effectively than most drugs, you
will feel more confident about your body and its ability to
maintain your health. If your psychological feelings—such

as anger, frustration, or depression—can cause illness, then perhaps more positive feelings may help you become and remain well again. If you can raise your blood pressure through worry, or create a headache with stress, you can also lower blood pressure and stop pain through mental techniques. Once you learn to accomplish such feats, you will have acquired a health tool of inestimable value.

A Personal Health Program

When I originally developed my Learning for Health program, it was in response to the need for a psychologically oriented and family-oriented treatment program. I was joined in this venture by Nancy Solomon, a physician with advanced training in both internal medicine and psychiatry. Our foremost goal was—and still is—health education and counseling, rather than primary medical or psychiatric care. Every individual we work with is also a patient of a primary physician, and we consider our program an adjunct to that treatment, not a substitute for it.

In the Learning for Health program, as in this book, patients are first asked to explore possible connections between (1) their lives, relationships, emotions, needs, feelings, and environment, and (2) their past, present, and potential future health problems. For several weeks they spend some time each day reflecting on their feelings and behavior and the relation of these to their health. They thus become acquainted with the demands and responsibilities of the holistic perspective and learn the reasons why they must become active in their treatment and health processes.

After a few sessions of self-assessment and education, each patient creates a personal health contract and strategy, committing himself or herself to make certain changes within specific time frames. Individuals are also required to make appropriate use of the medical resources available to them, agreeing to become knowledgeable about their physicians' recommendations and treatments and to comply fully with them. For example, our program is not a substitute for insulin or hypertensive medication. Rather, we try to get the body to help the medication work, and to release stress which can undermine or interfere with effective disease management.

The techniques of holistic medicine are vehicles to build greater sensitivity to the body and to help harmonize the individual's mental and physical functionings. But, contrary to popular belief, specific modalities alone are not the entire process. While meditation, relaxation, imagery, biofeedback, and behavior control are all components of the holistic inventory, they are not holistic in themselves. Only a comprehensive multidimensional health program is holistic. In essence, each person develops his or her own overall, active pathway to optimum wellness, which may include some of these techniques, but which must also integrate the individual's particular experience, style of living, values, and needs.

Interestingly, some physicians, nurses, and other health professionals are beginning to recognize the limits of their own traditional methods. In the holistic orientation these medical practitioners are seeking—and often finding—a more comprehensive and effective style of treatment for patients suffering from the diseases of civilization. Even more important, they are discovering a preventive approach to help people avoid these modern-day illnesses. Sadly, traditional medicine today spends less than 1 percent of its resources on prevention and education. But to resist disease, I believe that we all must constantly maintain self-awareness, self-care, and personal integration for the rest of our lives.

This book is intended to guide you, step by step, through the ways that you can enhance and participate in the healing process, no matter what your physical difficulty. If you have a chronic physical condition, you need to understand what is wrong, and how you can specifically minimize that condition. If you are well, a self-care program can help keep you that way. Your physician should be glad to have your help, because your assistance can only benefit his treatment—and your own well-being.

2 Disease as Adaptation

Illnesses hover constantly above us, their seeds blown by the wind, but they do not set in the terrain unless the terrain is ready to receive them.

CLAUDE BERNARD

Every new vaccine or surgical breakthrough generates the fantasy that disease can someday be completely eliminated. As appealing as that seems, life without any disease would actually be as much of a handicap as life without thumbs, and as frustrating as life within a plastic bubble. True, disease can be painful, frightening, and disruptive of our lives, but it is also a complex, effective, and essential adaptive process that allows us to remain alive and productive in a difficult, stressful, and often dangerous environment. When we are ill, our body is engaged in a determined struggle to protect us from an external threat or invader, or to repair internal damage, either of which could claim our life.

The fever, pain, redness, swelling, loss of appetite, and lethargy we experience during illness are messages from our body that we need to withdraw our attention and energy from outside involvements and allow the body to use all its strength to combat the disease. When any body cell begins to break down or is unable to function, the body, automatically and outside of consciousness, senses the situation and promptly begins corrective action. Except when we react to the experiences of pain, lethargy, and discomfort, there is no conscious participation in the mechanics of this extraordinary automatic self-healing process.

Because the body's defense system operates so automatically and usually so effectively, you could spend your entire lifetime without the slightest awareness of the ongoing, difficult inner struggle to keep you alive and intact. As you move through the outside world—encountering various dangers and stresses, risking accident, taking in food that may be damaging or poisoning your internal organs—it is essential that the body sustain a constant temperature and internal milieu to allow the natural healing process to occur. Claude Bernard, a nineteenth-century French physician, gave the name "homeostasis" to the efforts of the body to maintain a stable internal environment of correct temperature, circulation, movement of energy sources, elimination of toxic wastes, and reaction and protection against external changes.

Disease, then, is a central aspect of the body's struggle to preserve homeostasis. When the adaptive responses by the organism to stimuli are inappropriate in kind or amount or both, disease is the result. Whenever something breaks through our body's defenses, or some part of the body fails in its defensive functions, the disease process begins. Disease is not a static event, or simply an alien presence within us, but a conflict of opposing forces of differing strengths. Your task is to make certain that your body is optimally prepared for this struggle. *The healthy person is not someone who is never ill or who avoids disease, but someone whose healing powers are strong enough to combat any threat or breakdown.*

It's important to separate a disease from its symptoms. If, for example, you have a particular symptom such as elevated blood pressure, that is not a disease in itself. Rather, the disease encompasses a long behavior pattern of eating, exercising, reaction to stress, and self-care—all of which create a strain which is experienced as added pressure within the circulatory system. No single element of this system is the disease; rather, it is a result of the dynamic interaction between the various inappropriate stresses and the body's attempt to compensate for them.

Why is this distinction so important? If you understand it, you will not be so apt to associate the removal or suppression of your symptom with a cure. In reality, a cure involves a transformation of the entire system which initially created the undue strain, so that the hypertension is no longer necessary.

Of course, disease-producing microorganisms are always present, but usually they can be fought off successfully. However, some individuals never get sick, while others pick up every cold in the neighborhood. So although the germ may be one of the essential and contributing causes, it alone is not sufficient to produce illness.

The same dilemma exists with environment and heredity. One person can be exposed to food additives for a lifetime, or smoke a pack of cigarettes a day, and never become ill. Another can have a hidden hereditary weakness of the stomach or lungs, which becomes apparent after years of a poor diet or habitual smoking. Only then does the weak link break down.

Theorists distinguish several types of specific causes that play a role in illness. There are *predisposing* causes, such as weaknesses or genetic deficiencies, which are the soil in which a later illness can take root. Still, with knowledge and understanding of these predispositions, a person can guard against that illness.

There are also *contributing* causes, which are factors increasing the likelihood that an organ or area of the body will become ill. These include chronic stress of an organ, such as a baseball pitcher's use of his arm, smoke from cigarettes, or the increased secretion of acid in the stomach when under tension.

In a bodily area that is either hereditarily weak or abused by stress, a precipitating incident may trigger an illness. This event could be a sudden psychological strain, a serious injury, or a virus attack in a body whose reserves are already weakened by previous illness or anxiety. Although this episode typically receives most of the blame for an illness, a more objective perspective suggests that if the bodily area was weak enough, the disease was almost inevitable.

Finally, there are *maintaining* or *continuing* causes, which keep a person in ill health or prevent him from getting better. These influences can range from poor mental attitudes (such as a feeling of hopelessness), to unsuitable behavior (such as refusing to take medication), to irresistible social benefits (such as large disability payments, or the attention and sympathy of other people). In some cases, the treatment itself may become a maintaining cause, as when tranquilizers keep a person from identifying and overcoming the real sources of his worry, anxiety, or muscle tension.

Philosopher David Bakan, in defining the nature of disease, has noted that disease may be conceived of as a manifestation of a deeper disorder involving the total condition of the individual and that a specific disease from which any individual appears to be suffering may be regarded as its manifestation.[1] Bakan is suggesting that if a person has a disease—whether it be cancer, hypertension, schizophrenia, neurosis, or any other—it can be regarded as a sign that there is a split, an alienation or a disconnection, within the whole person. This statement echoes the ancient wisdom that disease was a sign of disharmony and lack of balance of an individual's entire life.

According to Bakan, disease may be expressed not only through various organs, but also on different levels—the physical, the psychological, the social, or the spiritual. Depression and a heart attack may both be symptoms of the same inner conflict within an individual. Treatment, therefore, must be aimed at both the physical and the emotional dimensions of the patient.

Of course, some may express most or all of their illnesses primarily on a psychological level, while others lean toward a physical or somatic manifestation. As yet, we don't know precisely why. Interestingly, several types of well-defined psychological illnesses, notably schizophrenia, are found in individuals with few physical disorders in their medical history. This has led psychologists Claus and Marjorie Bahnson to theorize that certain people, like schizophrenics, tend to exhibit their conflicts primarily in mental/emotional terms, while others, such as cancer patients, often express few psychological distress symptoms despite their severe inner conflicts.[2]

Even so, all physical illnesses have psychological components, and vice versa. Think about your own ailments for a moment. Whenever you have been ill and in pain, there was probably also some accompanying depression, frustration, and even guilt, which affected the people around you. We behave differently when we're sick, and expect to be treated differently. Our feelings about illness, the manner in which we experience it, and the way others react to it can have considerable influence on the healing process. Compare the person who feels hopeless and depressed and does not want to live with the person who has important goals in life. If they are afflicted with identical life-threatening diseases, their mental attitudes will surely affect the course of their illness.

When sickness is expressed on a social level, it is often difficult to define. Accidents and suicide, for example, are socially manifested problems, as might be warfare, racism, and other forms of violence and aggression. Perhaps those who can project their personal conflicts onto other people in these ways may therefore prevent illness or imbalance from manifesting itself in other dimensions. We can speculate that these social mechanisms may allow people to express or handle their inner conflicts and keep themselves healthy.

Once you recognize that disease is not simply a physical struggle but may also involve psychological, spiritual, and social dimensions, then it becomes clear that the appearance of any physical symptom—especially a serious or chronic one—ought to evoke a deep personal inquiry into your life.

Medicine: Helping the Body Maintain Health

Think of the treatments your doctor has prescribed for your own illnesses. Most of them focus upon augmenting the healing environment or aiding the body's natural adaptive defenses. When you were ill, you may have been told to rest and been placed in the care of others, at home or in the hospital. This created a receptive healing environment. Other environmental modifications may have been added, such as supplemental oxygen, special diet, warm baths, heating pad, splint, or bandage. All of these changed the environment so that the healing process could take place more smoothly.

From a psychological viewpoint, you may have been told to avoid stressful situations, and to avail yourself of the solicitous and caring people around you. The physician's genuine concern and bedside manner were also important, because you could relax and place your faith in the wisdom and ability of the healer.

The major medical interventions, then, consist of aiding the body in its struggle to maintain itself. In some cases, treatment is directed at turning the body off when it is fighting a harmless threat. Other times, drugs are administered to help the body kill invading microbes and infection, surgery is performed to remove harmful growths or deposits, or injections are relied upon to replace or replenish hormones and other vital body chemicals. All these measures help the body maintain and protect itself. But essentially, the body repairs its own damage. The swelling, redness, pus, and fever are more than signs of illness; they signal the body's energetic and total mobilization of its internal healing armies.

The treatment for many of today's diseases of civilization is likely to become more complicated. Unlike ailments of earlier eras, these illnesses are not contests against powerful external invaders, but involve the breakdown of some bodily function, typically because of years of stress and abuse, or because of a hereditary weakness. For instance, a hole may develop in a stomach or intestine, deposits may be formed on an artery, or a group of cells may begin to multiply and smother the normal tissue around them. Or perhaps the arteries or joints may lose their elasticity, or the back or head may be in continual pain.

What can be done for these degenerative diseases? Treatment often involves artificial means to keep the body functioning. Sometimes a poorly operating organ needs to be supported by daily doses of medication. The most common treatment is simply to cover up the symptom—usually pain—and tell the person to function as well as possible. Only rarely, as in the case of some tumors, can the difficulty be removed or treated so that the person can return to complete good health. The treatment process can also attempt to ease the stress and the psychological response to the world that may be contributing or maintaining causes of these ailments.

The many influences that can contribute to illness—emotional, psychological, attitudinal, family, and social factors, as well as the hereditary and environmentally caused weaknesses in the body's self-healing apparatus—are called "host factors." When Claude Bernard talks of the "terrain" in which illness takes root, he is referring to these host factors.

Recent medical research has shifted from the intensive study of the disease-producing microorganisms to the examination of host factors. What, for instance, makes a particular person healthy, or extraordinarily long-lived? In certain pockets of the globe, such as the Soviet Caucasus Mountains and parts of South America, some residents live for over a century. These people, who do not seem to have unusual constitutions, enjoy such long lives despite primitive medical treatment, poor diet, heavy drinking, smoking, and hard work.

Researchers have suggested that such longevity may be related to the way these men and women respond to stress, and their mental attitudes about age. We all have friends who are models of health. Perhaps an examination of their lives and psychological makeup can help us understand the host factors that enable them to resist illness.

Frankly, we don't know precisely to what extent a person

can affect his body and his health. But indications are that this self-healing power is greater than most of us dream, and many physicians are devoting more energy to taking advantage of it.

3 The Personal Message of Illness

*Considering how common illness is, how tremendous
the spiritual change that it brings, how astonishing,
when the lights of health go down, the undiscovered
countries that are then disclosed, what wastes and des-
erts of the soul a slight attack of influenza brings to
view, what precipices and lawns sprinkled with bright
flowers a little rise of temperature reveals, what ancient and obdurate oaks are uprooted in us by the act
of sickness, how we go down into the pit of death and
feel the waters of annihilation close above our heads
and wake thinking to find ourselves in the presence of
the angels and the harpers when we have a tooth out
and come to the surface in the dentist's arm-chair and
confuse his "Rinse the mouth—rinse the mouth" with
the greeting of the Deity stooping from the floor of
Heaven to welcome us—when we think of this, as we
are so frequently forced to think of it, it becomes
strange indeed that illness has not taken its place with
love and battle among the prime themes of literature.*

VIRGINIA WOOLF

Like most holistic health practitioners, I developed my beliefs and ideas from my contact with patients in a hospital
setting. Trained as a clinical psychologist and sociologist, I
had been taught that my expertise would be relevant only to
people with emotional conflicts. Physical illnesses belonged
to a completely different world, to be cared for exclusively
by physicians. Unless I was called in to consult with a patient who the physician felt had a "psychiatric" problem, I
assumed I had no business in a medical clinic.

But my experience ultimately led me to change my thinking. I had helped coordinate a family-therapy program in the UCLA psychiatry department and was invited to the medical clinic to determine whether my program might be useful to the families of the patients. So much family stress, tension, and anxiety are associated with illness that a support and counseling program seemed likely to be useful. I began by sitting in the waiting room and asking the confused, anxious, concerned patients and their spouses about themselves. They needed little encouragement to open up; in fact, they were surprised and gratified that a member of the staff would listen to them.

They told me about personal crises and employment difficulties, economic pressures, sexual and emotional conflicts, children leaving home or getting into trouble, recent deaths, and other concerns. As they talked, despite my ignorance about physiology and medicine, I began to see obvious connections between their chronic and recurrent illnesses and their life situations.

I soon hypothesized that some people might express their emotional conflicts and struggles via illness. Their illnesses could be due, at least in part, to the pressures of their life situations. Not surprisingly, I discovered that their aches and pains, strokes and heart attacks, ulcers and asthma, and even cancers all had personal and emotional meaning to them. Each family connected its illnesses to other life events, and was trying to make sense of them and cope with their consequences.

I became certain of a real need for the kind of services I could offer a medical clinic. As well as giving guidance and support, I felt that I might have a positive impact on physical symptoms. So I began to develop a health program, and in the process I investigated past research and clinical work concerned with the connection between psychological difficulty and physical illness.

The program I designed for these patients is detailed in this book. But initially, I simply helped the ill people and their families to make personal connections between their feelings, their life stresses, and their illnesses. This process of reflection and self-exploration was therapeutic in itself. As often happens with purely psychological problems, when a patient becomes aware that there may be inner meaning behind his symptoms, he can spontaneously create a personal strategy for combating it.

Unraveling Meaning from Symptoms

How would you react upon learning that you have a life-threatening illness? Most people initially sink into a state of anger and despair. They cry "Why me?" as a protest against the seeming injustice of it all. Physicians find it difficult to answer this desperate question.

Ask yourself, or someone you know, how people become ill. Review your past illnesses and write down what factors you think played a role in your own sickness. The tendency is to stress external, or fixed, factors. For example, in grade school we learn the truism that disease is caused by germs. We assume that when a virus or bacterium hits us, we will get sick, unless we have been vaccinated against it.

With this defensive attitude that externals are to blame for illness, it is no wonder that many individuals are chronically worried about their health. If people believe they live in a germ-filled, polluted environment and that they are weak because of inherited psychological and physical deficiencies, they will perceive themselves as helpless and victimized when they become ill. If our imaginations are not enough to make us insecure, disaster movies and tales of supernatural possession reinforce the feelings of weakness and inadequacy against a malevolent and unsafe environment.

On the other hand, poets and novelists, who create by looking within themselves, have often suggested that illness, like accidents or twists of fate, is the vehicle that brings justice to a character. Many a nineteenth-century novel concludes with the child of an evil or ill-matched couple dying of the plague or tuberculosis, bringing their lives to a sort of metaphorical finality. Weakness of character or will is often reflected in the ultimate submission to illness. Did these authors twist illness to suit their needs, as Susan Sontag hypothesizes,[1] or is there some basis for this common literary device?

Tolstoy provided the classic commentary on the multi-layered meanings of illness in his story "The Death of Ivan Ilyich." A minor civil servant and a petty person in a loveless marriage, Ivan had always done what was expected and proper. But one day he awoke with an undetermined illness that got progressively worse. As his suffering increased, his family began to resent it as an intrusion on their lives. His sickness—eventually diagnosed as cancer—led him to recognize the isolation and aloneness that had existed all his life. And his doctors, in their concern to establish a correct diagnosis, ignored Ivan as a person and were unsuccessful in treating him.

Cancer allowed Ivan to realize the truth about his family and his life, which he had denied until then. The illness was a reflection of his existence, and it motivated him to change. The suffering forced him to confront his life as he had never done in health. Just before he died, he was able to grasp the inner, spiritual truth which at last gave his existence some meaning and purpose.

In Tolstoy's story, we see how illness can both illuminate essential aspects of our lives and also point the way, or create the conditions, to learn some important, central truths about ourselves. We may speculate that if Ivan had learned these truths earlier, he might have been spared his premature death.

Liza, a cancer patient I worked with, exemplifies how illness can carry an important message about the victim's life. According to Lawrence LeShan, cancer often strikes people who are extremely well mannered, helpful, and loving, while ornery, self-centered, and demanding people either escape the illness or recover from it. This particular patient was typical of the first type. She had spent her life taking care of a succession of husbands, children, and bosses—always self-less and never showing resentment.

In my discussions with Liza, it soon became clear that the person she took the least care of was herself. The cancer was a powerful indicator of her inattention to her own needs. As a way of directing some energy to caring for herself, I asked her to think each morning of five positive things she could do only for herself. Then she was to spend that day accomplishing as many things for herself as she did for her husband. In the following weeks, she regained much of her vitality and zest for living. It was as if the cancer were a message to take care of herself; it was a visible symbol of neglect.

Your Own Self-Inquiry

As you may have presumed by now, a basic principle of holistic medicine is that with each illness, an inquiry into its full subjective meaning must be initiated. While pursuing appropriate medical treatment, it is also essential to define the personal messages or meanings that may lie within the illness. This inquiry may help clarify some of the basic questions that plague physicians, such as "Why is this person ill with this particular ailment at this time?"

Over a century ago, the British physician Sir William Osler told his students, "Ask not what kind of illness the patient has, ask what kind of patient has the illness."[2] In a similar vein, philosopher Charles Péguy noted, "When a man dies, he does not just die of the disease he has . . . he dies of his whole life."[3]

Adhering to this philosophy, I approach self-healing without concentrating too heavily on the distinct causes of specific illnesses. After all, your technologically oriented physician is without peer in this area, offering specific treatments tailored to particular diseases. Instead, I prefer to address the causes, cures, and meaning of illness from the perspective of the individual who is sick.

A complete medical history is a good starting point for
your own self-inquiry. It can be as specific as a fingerprint,
revealing considerable information about your character and
the stress, conflict, and difficulty in your life. These data are
not only useful for understanding yourself better, but also
will offer clues to the proper way to treat an illness.

A mundane incident from my own life will demonstrate
how such an inquiry can lead to valuable personal insights. I
have always suffered from an assortment of colds, sneezes,
and allergies, blaming them on pollen or dust. I finally noticed that for about five consecutive Sundays—my one day
off—I had colds. At first I told myself that it was probably a
coincidence. I joked to my wife that even though I believed
in holistic medicine, I was still entitled to have a simple cold.

The next Sunday, right on schedule, my cold returned.
After lunch that day, a colleague came over and we began to
work. In ten minutes I noticed that my nose and head were
clear. Yet a half hour earlier, I had been suffering in bed!
Clearly, like so many men raised in our culture, I was trou-
bled by not working. I could no longer deny that my cold
and my internal conflicts were connected. I began to examine my feelings whenever I felt on the verge of a sneeze. I
discovered that when I was angry with myself for not meeting a deadline or with others for demanding things of me,
and I did not express this anger, I would sneeze. However,
by simply accepting my feelings, and not even necessarily
venting them, I was often able to avoid colds.

Symptoms, then, can serve as a warning or a message that
something needs to be explored or changed in one's life. And
because illness is a message, if we treat only its physical
manifestations, it can linger on or recur until the message is
heeded.

Unfortunately, modern medicine not only is skeptical that
illness can have an existential, personal meaning, but often
denies patients the opportunity to investigate the possibility.
Some of my holistic colleagues believe that hospitals cater
more to technological requirements than human experience.
By isolating the sick, we rob patients and their families of a

suitable environment to explore these questions. Hospital staffs are often uncomfortable with feelings, talk of death, or exploration of personal issues. With the heavy medication so common in hospitals, we also effectively remove a person from any direct experience of his or her symptoms and feelings. In a modern hospital, Ivan Ilyich might never have acquired his insight, because his pain and feelings would have been drugged until he slipped unconsciously into death.

The Basic Split and the Hidden Truth

The most likely message of an illness is that we need to pay attention to an aspect of our lives that we have ignored. Our body seems to be aware of the need before our higher consciousness. Walter Cannon coined the phrase "the wisdom of the body," to indicate that it takes responsibility in many situations where the rational, conscious mind is not aware of what is good for the whole person. The biographies of many noted people reflect the wisdom that can emanate from serious illness.

Psychologist Rollo May may have saved his own life, while learning something basic about humanity, in his recovery from tuberculosis. When he placed himself wholly in the hands of doctors, May's physical condition deteriorated. Finally, he admitted to himself, "Maybe I know more about it than my doctors." Rather than a rejection of their medical advice, this was a realization that his illness had more than physical components.

May felt depressed, but realized that his attitude was a realistic one under the circumstances, as opposed to the false optimism projected by his physicians. He believed his depression indicated that he was facing the disease for what it was, that he was taking responsibility and accepting his actual feelings about it. He notes:

After becoming aware of my body and its disease, I began to get better. I experienced a new kind of freedom, invented a sort of meditation for myself, which was a capacity to actually sense what was happening in my body. Things came in a flood. I wouldn't trade that moment for any others in my life.[4]

May's concept of responsibility for his disease did not consist of blaming himself, self-pity, or hopelessness. In the end, he used his illness as an opportunity for change. He learned to tune in to his body, and a spontaneously created meditation process became an important component of his self-healing. By turning inward, he was able gradually to guide himself toward good health. This is the holistic concept of personal responsibility.

Time after time, my patients have told me that their illnesses or injuries made an important life transition or growth period possible. I recall a middle-aged engineer who suddenly found himself unemployed for the first time in his life. This led to a state of terrible depression. A few days later, he had a serious auto accident. His agitation and depression were probably contributing factors to the car crash. During his long convalescence, he spent time talking to his family and began to read and think in ways that were new to him. This soul-searching eventually led him into a different career as a counselor, in which he worked less and made his own family a more important part of his life.

Whenever you are ill, it is wise to ask yourself if changes are necessary in your life. The hard-driving individual who experiences a stroke or heart attack should recognize that he must develop a new attitude toward his life and his work. When a man becomes ill just as he is about to retire, perhaps his illness is suggesting that he must soon decide how to spend his time.

One message of nearly every illness is that we need to pay more respect and attention to the demands of our body. However, our culture teaches us that meeting our needs before those of others is selfish. Women in particular, via traditional sex-role training, have been taught to ignore themselves emotionally and sexually, as well as intellectually. Men tend to ignore their need to relax and to turn inward, and their emotionality, as they seek power, money, respect, and admiration. The common illnesses of men and women reflect these gross differences, and can facilitate learning about a side of the self that has been ignored.

The Will to Live a Meaningful Life

It is a truism of medical practice that a person's "will to live" is central to healing and recovery. At a certain point most physicians have done all they can, and they proclaim, "It's in God's hands now." When someone they expected to die hangs on or even recovers, it is often because he or she has a powerful sustaining faith or will for living, or because some life task still needs to be accomplished.

Why do some patients have a strong will to live, while others seem to have none at all?

Psychologist Lawrence LeShan notes that it cannot simply be attributed to the demoralization resulting from illness. Rather, "the patient whose will to live is very weak in a catastrophic situation is almost invariably an individual whose will to live was weak before he became ill." He also believes that the will to live is not simply a response to a fear of death:

Clinical experience seems to indicate strongly that, in serious physical illness, the fear of death is not a very powerful tool. It does not seem to bind the resources of the individual together and to increase host resistance to pathological processes. The wish to live appears to be a much stronger weapon for this purpose and to bring more of the total organism of the patient to the side of the physician. In mobilizing this wish to live, we must have goals in the future that are deeply important to the patient.[5]

LeShan conducted intensive psychotherapy with hundreds of patients suffering primarily from terminal cancer. He asked them to examine how fully they had lived their lives, and to formulate and act upon a set of goals that clearly

reflected an inner purpose. This reflection, he found, promoted personal integration and usually had a positive effect
upon illness.

LeShan's patients often discovered that their lack of en-
thusiasm for life before illness could be ascribed to their
choice of goals, which reflected what others wanted them to
do, or expected of them, rather than their own desires. Both
he and I have noted that after a period of forced reflection
caused by illness, patients may decide to redirect their lives
along very different paths. They may choose different
careers, spend more time with their families, or leave unful-
filling relationships.

Despite a scarcity of evidence to support it, I believe that
the speed and extent of recovery for such people may relate
to their unearthing a new direction, and a commitment to it
for the future. The choice and anticipation of renewed goals
may help them mobilize healing resources.

But what happens when an individual's response to illness
is to remain aimless, going through the motions of whatever
he is doing, very uninvolved or uncommitted, without clear
values, goals, or purpose? Might we not expect that resistance to disease would lower? I believe so. When a person
denies some part of himself—a talent, a desire, an impulse, a
goal—he is in essence at war within himself, and hence ripe
for invasion from without.

I once treated a middle-aged woman with advanced
cancer. When I met her, she told me of being depressed
since her teenage years. In her twenties, she had had no idea
of what to do with her life, or where she might be headed.
By contrast, her older sister had married and had become
successful in a career.

My patient married at age thirty, primarily because she
felt she ought to. She reasoned that since nothing else
seemed to be working for her, perhaps marriage and mother-
hood would be the answer. Her husband was distant, and
when a child arrived, rather than being a source of energy
and inspiration, he was merely another disappointment and
burden.

This woman wanted to battle her cancer through therapy not because she felt there was something to live for, but because she was terribly afraid to die. As LeShan predicted, this was not a good motivation for healing. In her therapy sessions, I tried to find some way to involve her in an enjoyable project or guide her toward a relationship with a person with whom she felt good. But nothing worked. Her condition worsened, and she told me she wanted to die. She finally passed away at home, very suddenly and before her doctors had expected her death. My belief is that the therapy helped her clarify her feelings to the extent that the only option she desired was death. Clearly, the forces toward dying were operating in her life long before her cancer diagnosis; the cancer was merely the culmination of a long chain of internal conflicts.

Two other patients had both had serious cervical illness necessitating surgery after the birth of their children. Although these women had been healthy before, both acknowledged feelings of being burdened and suppressed in the role of mother. Upon becoming sick, each began a painful period of reflection on her life, her future, and her role. During therapy, each realized she had been denying her inner self, her own needs and unique qualities, in accepting the role of housewife and mother. Each decided that her health depended on making changes that would provide more meaning in her life.

One of the women, although intellectually recognizing the need for change, felt increasing anxiety over the implications of these alterations. Although she had separated from her husband, she decided to return to him, and became ill again. She felt incapable of doing what she knew she needed.

By contrast, the other woman spontaneously experienced intense, overwhelming, lovely sensations relating to her own beauty and worth. She was also overwhelmed by previously unfelt impressions of self-acceptance and self-love. For the first time, she felt she was important. On the strength of this experience, she began to make changes in her life, which affirmed her as the person that she now knew herself to be.

With her child attended by a babysitter, she renewed her training for a professional career, despite her husband's anger and opposition. Her symptoms disappeared, and she has been healthy ever since. The discovery of and commitment to a life goal seems to have been the key difference between these women.

An Exercise of Self-Inquiry

One way to determine the usefulness of this doctrine of self-exploration is to initiate your own intensive inquiry into your current or most serious ailments.

To begin this exercise, first write down what you feel are some of the predisposing, contributing, and maintaining causes of your symptom or illness. At the time you were sick, and in the months before, what were your feelings, attitudes, expectations, personal and family relationships, and sources of anxiety or stress? Note some of these factors that may have contributed to your illness.

I usually ask patients to suggest about ten causes that may have influenced their ailment. These often include stressful events around the time of its onset, such as an impending school exam, a visit from parents, or anger at having to complete a report for the boss. The list of maintaining causes frequently includes the attention received from a spouse when illness strikes, or the attractiveness of taking time off from work.

While doing this exercise, you'll probably face some uncertainty over whether a particular feeling or event really contributed to your sickness. This dilemma is understandable. It is hard to know precisely the role that a specific episode or emotion played, if any. There is no way to measure objectively the influence of, say, a pressure-filled business trip or a marital conflict on a subsequent case of high blood pressure. But this exercise is still valuable, because it will begin to make you aware how every aspect of your life may influence your health. Once you start to explore these connections, you will begin to appreciate your own role in your health and illness and be willing to take a more active part in making the changes necessary for a life of better health and greater control over your well-being.

Here is how you can further investigate the relationship of illness to your life experience. Take a sheet of paper. From left to right across the bottom, list the years of your life, using five-year intervals. In the space above the appropriate year, fill in the ailments you suffered at that time. Insert as many as you can remember, beginning with the most severe or memorable.

Next, above each illness, write the significant events— both positive and negative—for that period. Record the conflicts, emotional traumas, life transitions, and various events that contributed to the fabric of your life. Do you see patterns developing as you complete this lifeline? Did your sicknesses occur in periods of stress, difficulty, or other personal crises?

Most people who do this exercise discover that their serious or chronic illnesses are intimately connected with their life events. While sickness can occur without any obvious triggering event or emotion, most often there are personal and behavioral causes preceding it.

Let's now carry this exercise one step further and try to uncover the hidden meanings behind your ailments. Take each illness in your lifeline, beginning with the most recent. To elaborate on the reasons and meanings behind each one, sit in a comfortable position and ask yourself why you became sick at that time; then, without trying to force yourself to arrive at an answer, see what ideas spontaneously come into your mind. When these thoughts emerge, write them down, and contemplate their significance and possible validity. Think about each potential meaning to see if it feels right.

In the case of chronic illness, there are two specific questions you need to ask. You can first try to discover a set of personal reasons for its initial appearance. But since an ailment does not continue unless there are maintaining or con-

tinuing conditions which prevent the body from healing itself, next ask yourself why the symptom remains.

These two sets of reasons will interact. For example, a
woman suffered her first headaches when she began to work,
as a message that she was frightened and uncertain about her
abilities. The headaches remained even after she became effective in her job, because she pushed herself to accomplish
things she really didn't want to do and did not allow herself
to form satisfying or close emotional relationships. The
headache was telling her, "You can't do it all alone."

In seeking these causes and meanings, you might imagine
your life unfolding in front of you like a play or novel, with
yourself as an observer trying to perceive events and discover their hidden significance. It often helps to do this with
another person.

When I conduct this inquiry with a patient, I ask about
the meaning of illness in a variety of ways. I may ask, "Why
now?" Or more specifically, "What does this illness permit
you to do that you would not ordinarily let yourself do?"
Very often a patient says that it gives him a chance to rest,
sit back, and give up his burdens, and accept some care, nurturing, love, and comfort. Such people seem to have much
smoother recoveries than those who regard illness as an intrusion or resent its place in their lives. Another question
might be "What was your illness warning you against?"

What are some other reasons that people come up with?
Let me relate what I discovered in myself for a rare eye disease that necessitated two corneal grafts several years ago.
My physician told me a genetic defect caused this particular
illness. But in my own exploration, I noted that I regarded
myself as a scholar, and my eyes were obviously the most
overworked part of my body. I remembered I had been embarrassed in grade school by having to sit in the front row
because I could not see the blackboard, and was teased because of my glasses. I felt inferior because of the weakness of
my eyes.

At the time I became ill, I was under the stress of running

a chaotic community agency and had just been married. I was not accustomed to intimate relationships, to seeing and being seen in that way by another person. In response to my discoveries, I began to try to rely less on my eyes and to substitute more interpersonal activities and work, which in turn made me feel better about myself and allowed me to get closer to other people. I became more active and less of an introverted scholar, and have had no further difficulty with my eyes. I feel I have placed them in perspective. Further, I did not neglect medical treatment and proper eye hygiene in this process. Whether these factors were causal or not, the personal inquiry resulting from my illness enriched and re-balanced my life.

Many factors combine to create illness, and in conducting this kind of personal inquiry, it is important to recognize as many potential causes as possible. You can thus move beyond thinking of illness as simply the result of physical events within your body, to an awareness that anything in your life might affect your health.

4 The Benefits, Responsibilities and Consequences of Being Ill

The actual presentation of the syndromes of disease, as apart from the factors facilitating their eruption, is determined to a large extent by the type of community in which the symptoms appear. . . .

Disease is essentially an attempt on the part of the individual to communicate with the world from his own position of aloneness.

ARTHUR GUIDHAM

Illness is more than a state of the body. It incorporates a life-style, a way of perceiving yourself, and how you ask others to see and respond to you. In a sense, it can be thought of as a journey into another kingdom, another way of life, which can influence us in many ways. Susan Sontag writes:

> Illness is the night-side of life, a more onerous citizenship. Everyone who is born holds dual citizenship, in the kingdom of the well and in the kingdom of the sick. Although we all prefer to use only the good passport, sooner or later each of us is obliged, at least for a spell, to identify ourselves as citizens of that other place.[1]

Comparing illness to a kingdom suggests the need to inquire about the rights and responsibilities of that form of citizenship. Our decisions about our obligations can, in turn, affect our health, and our desire to remain well or ill.

Responses to Illness: Acceptance, Denial and Amplification

Some people immediately presume that every small ache is a sign of sickness. Others must experience a major catastrophe like a heart attack to concede that something is wrong. The same major or minor ailment can provoke many differing responses, depending on psychological makeup, prior experiences, and personality.

The best possible reaction to illness is for an individual to consider it an unwanted intrusion into an otherwise active, fulfilling, and meaningful life. He recognizes the reality of his illness (thus is labeled an "acceptor"), but rather than capitalizing on its side benefits, the first question to his physician is "What can I do to help make the best possible recovery?" He informs himself, and does everything possible to get better. This ideal patient would be a perfect complement to a holistic physician, but the former is currently as rare as the latter. Most people need further education before they can play such a helpful role in the healing process.

Ideally, the acceptor has always been quite aware that every human being is prone to illness, and thus he has long been active in maintaining his health by adhering to an active preventive-medicine program. Since illness is always possible, a daily program designed to maintain good health is very necessary. The body is too precious to be left to fate. The acceptor is alert to the early-warning signs of possible danger and learns not to give up or give in to them, but to take sensible steps in response to them. He knows when it is time to seek medical help.

Unfortunately, not only do most people ignore preventive care, but they delay seeking treatment as long as possible once symptoms start surfacing. They don't want to be regarded as hypochondriacs, nor do they wish to waste money or time, or to bother doctors with minor complaints. So they tolerate discomfort until it reaches a serious level.

Are there other reasons for the long delay in seeking treatment? Delay may be related to a feeling of omnipotence, a denial of mortality, or a distrust of physicians. Certainly none of us likes to face mortality or physical frailty, and sometimes we may fear the pain and the results of treatment as much as the illness itself. Additionally, most illness does go away by itself because of the body's self-healing powers, so many people say, "Why bother seeking professional help?" They gamble to avoid confronting their fears.

Seeing a physician is not usually taken lightly by the patient. He doesn't typically make an appointment until after he has checked with others around him and concluded that he is probably sick. In consulting with family and friends, he discusses his symptoms and asks for an informal consultation, diagnosis, and referral. This "lay referral network," according to sociologist Eliot Friedson, is much like ancient folk healing methods.[2] Other people offer their own experiences, make suggestions about treatments (e.g., herb tea, a certain kind of oil), and recommend the type of healer to visit—ranging from the witch doctors and shamans of other cultures to Western-trained physicians, osteopaths, chiropractors, Christian Science practitioners, faith healers, psychologists, and nurses.

What other responses are there to illness? There are denial and amplification, but neither attitude contributes much to the health of the individual.

The "denier" refuses to acknowledge his possible illness, and consequently does not take the necessary steps, or does not do enough, to regain his health. He sometimes appears similar to the acceptor in that he acts as if he were not ill at all. He may push himself to return to work earlier than is sensible, fearing that subordinates or co-workers can't do without him. He thinks that if he were to admit to illness, this would be a sign of weakness. He is afraid to confront his sickness and its possible consequences.

In a compulsive drive to resume activity, deniers reject many of the advantages (the rest and the care) of being sick, but in so doing, they also refuse to allow themselves to get well. When they return to work, telling everyone they are "as good as new," they ignore the body's urgent messages of need, protest, or despair. Deniers often succumb prematurely to ailments such as heart disease and cancer.

By contrast, the "amplifier" responds to each illness by making it seem more lethal than it really is. He worries chronically, he places himself under intense stress, he expects the worst, and/or he becomes addicted to and dependent upon the helpful and caring responses of others. This type of complainer makes his illness a way of life in order to control the people around him and meet his own needs. He dwells upon his symptoms, speculating about their ominous implications, and makes demands on physicians for help or special consideration. Despite seeking medical treatment, he does not respond to it positively, much to the chagrin and frustration of his physician. He thinks that responsibility for his illness rests outside of himself, and therefore he does not accept or utilize his own power in overcoming his sickness.

Others sometimes assume that the amplifier's illness is imaginary. Yet his pain is real, and by a kind of reverse causality, his focus on symptoms actually tends to create and maintain real illness. Also, his treatment, which usually consists of a daily regimen of pills, or exploratory and elective surgery, can add to his difficulties with serious side effects.

The irritation with which we react to an amplifier is reflected in the many nicknames we assign him: physicians refer to him as a "crock"; laypeople use terms like "kvetch" or "complainer" to indicate how draining and burdensome he can be. Because he cannot exist in a vacuum, the people around him are the keys to extricating him from his dilemma. He cannot continue his destructive life-style without solicitous, self-denying relatives to care for him, as well as cooperative physicians to diagnose and treat a continuing series of symptoms without responding to the basic causes of his illness. If these other people do not play their parts "properly," the amplifier will feel isolated, and illness may no longer serve much purpose.

Before you react too angrily to an amplifier, keep in mind that almost all of us have occasionally exaggerated our symptoms as a way of getting love, care, attention, or pity from others. But in the process, we only complicated healing. Although chronic illness may begin as an acute episode, it can become a regular part of one's physiological response because of the positive advantages it offers the sufferer.

Of course, a person's response to illness is not inborn or unchangeable. He may respond dissimilarly at various times in his life, or in different situations. For example, some people with a history of denying illness finally acknowledge it when it becomes very serious. They then use their illness to motivate themselves to finally make changes necessary in their lives—reducing workload, retiring, or learning to relax. In these instances, illness can be a lifesaving warning.

Take a few moments to explore your own reaction to illness at various times in your life, and how others responded. Did you like being sick, and did you enjoy feeling cared for? Or were you angry and frustrated, wanting to conquer your illness as quickly as possible? How do you react to doctors? Do you avoid them or overuse them? Your answers to these questions should provide some valuable insight about your health, which is independent of the state of your body.

The Sick Role: Rights and Responsibilities of Illness

It is impossible for the physician to perform his job properly without the cooperation of his patient. The physician needs the patient's presence at office visits and the patient's information about his body, and he expects the patient to take medication and perform other prescribed actions to maintain or recover health. Sociologist Talcott Parsons described these obligations and expectations as the "sick role."[3] From a social perspective, these expectations take effect when a physician certifies that the person is indeed physically impaired in his functioning.

And what are the patient's other responsibilities in his relationship with the physician? According to Parsons, he must consult the doctor when sick, and follow his instructions in order to get well. Otherwise he might be accused of malingering. In return for this minimal cooperation, the patient is relieved from many of his family, work, and social responsibilities. Instead he is taken care of as though he were a child. From my perspective, the way a person plays the patient role, discharges his responsibilities, and responds to the benefits is a critical factor in how well and how quickly he heals.

Unfortunately, Parsons' description represents ideal rather than actual patient behavior. In fact, the ill often do not approach their obligations seriously. They subtly act as if some part of them does not want to get well. Although most patients claim they are eager to follow their physician's therapeutic program, their behavior may be quite to the contrary.

Barry Blackwell, reviewing hundreds of studies of patient adherence to medical treatment, reports that less than half of all physicians' suggestions are followed.[4] Patients tend not to comply, particularly when their physician suggests a behavior change other than bed rest and taking a pill several times a day. If the treatment involves altering diet, exercise, or stress in their lives, they often ignore the instructions. Thus, the illness may linger on indefinitely, or will almost predictably recur even if it does temporarily disappear. Could this rejection of the doctor's instructions, then, represent a reluctance to abandon the attractive side benefits of illness?

Consider the gallant behavior of the executive who returns to work shortly after an operation. Despite his apparent speedy recovery, he may soon suffer a relapse. Was his quick return to the job a way to ensure his relapse, a choice (perhaps unconscious) to remain sick rather than stay at work? For treatment to be complete and effective, our deepest feelings, and the way that they can be indirectly expressed via illness, must be addressed.

This dilemma leads us back to the issue of responsibility for illness. Conventional thinking places no blame upon the individual for his physical illness, contending that sickness is in no way related to feelings, psyche, or life events. So when a man takes much longer than usual to recover from the flu, or when he catches every cold in his vicinity, and thus avoids some onerous responsibility, he can try to justify his situation with "It's not my fault."

Interestingly, an individual's responsibility for his own illness has always been a much more acceptable concept with mental illness than with physical illness. When a person is in emotional turmoil or distress, friends and doctors readily assign him at least part of the blame. We tend to avoid those who have emotional symptoms, visiting them only irregularly in mental hospitals and not offering them the same spontaneous outpouring of sympathy as those with physical symptoms. In treatment, psychotherapists look within the patient and ask him to participate in the treatment process by examining himself, discovering how he became distressed and how he may have contributed to his illness. Thus, the assignment of some personal responsibility for psychological illness is similar to the attitude I believe is relevant to physical illness.

It is more socially acceptable to experience a physical illness than a psychological one. Within Parsons' traditional framework, a physically ill patient is neither blamed nor expected to cooperate more than perfunctorily, by following orders. When an individual perceives this, it is quite possible that through some complex and poorly understood mechanism he may express an inner conflict through a physical illness rather than an emotional one. To escape blame and to avoid confronting what lies behind an illness, many individuals choose to take a physical route in expressing the tensions, pressures, uncertainties, and difficulties of their lives. Emotional illness is socially suspect, so it's better to have an ulcer than a neurosis.

But the emerging, holistic interpretation of the patient's

role in illness demands that the sick person confront himself. It asks each patient to explore his participation in his illness, whether he is psychologically or physically ill.

This self-inquiry can be very revealing if it is approached without self-deception. It can help a patient to understand not only why his illness has manifested itself as it has, but also the way it has been influenced by the entire environment (job, family, pollution, and other factors that affect our bodies every day).

Although some sick people do not avail themselves of the advantages, or "secondary gains," that accompany illness, the existence and habit-forming tendency of these benefits add to the complexity of the nature of disease, treatment, and the ill individual's power to get well. When we take advantage of the benefits of illness, whether consciously or unconsciously, they must be considered among the forces that undermine health. Sick people are consistently excused from work, school, appointments, tests, family obligations, and social responsibilities. From the first time a child discovers that by reporting a stomachache he may be able to stay home from school and watch television, he learns that sickness is a graceful, socially acceptable way to avoid doing things. Eventually, many people become almost addicted to these advantages. When physicians are unable to account for a failure to get well or the unexpected chronic nature of a usually self-limiting illness, these benefits may be culpable.

So the generally accepted belief is that we "can't help" being ill, and thus should not be blamed or penalized for sickness or denied its attendant side benefits. But that isn't necessarily true. If our desire for the accompanying advantages is strong enough, an unconscious network of processes within us may actually get our body to cooperate. Physiological functions influenced by mental suggestions and emotions can actually facilitate illness and retard the healing process. Thus, it's possible to "learn" to become ill as a way of meeting some of our needs or desires.

Because of the peculiar causes of these ailments, symp-

tomatic treatment is rarely effective. If you have developed
certain physical damage or pain in order to compel others to
treat you in a certain way, your physician will have a difficult time treating your symptoms successfully, no matter
how powerful his medication. That is because a root
cause—the benefits (such as the supportive behavior of
others)—is not being treated.

Chronic pain, for example, is notoriously difficult to treat,
although people consult physician after physician in a desperate search for relief. Medication, surgery, physical rehabilitation, and scores of visits to different specialists are often
futile. But some psychologists and physicians who have recently created treatment programs that employ different approaches are enjoying unprecedented success.

In their pain clinic, Fordyce, Fowler, and DeLateur have
discovered that when family members and hospital staff
react to patient discomfort with caring, nurturing, and at-
tention-giving responses, the patient is actually motivated to
experience more and more pain. As an example, Fordyce
and his group treated Mrs. Y, who had an eighteen-year history of back trouble, including four operations. Her pain
persisted, although no neurological problem could be pinpointed. The team decided that her pain might be a result of
the attention and care she received from others. They instructed the hospital staff to ignore Mrs. Y when she com-
plained, but to praise her and give her attention when she
was active or talked about something else. Instead of offering
her medication when she said she hurt, she was given pain
pills at regular intervals, and no longer rewarded for discomfort.

Mrs. Y's condition gradually improved, and she soon felt
good enough to go home. Her family had been asked not to
reward her for reporting pain, but for being active. Her affliction continued to decrease, and her activity was soon at a
normal level. Her doctors concluded that her pain had begun
because of an early injury, but had developed into a bad
habit because of the positive response it aroused from
others.[5]

Another surprising source of secondary gain is our health-care system. Physicians are often kind and caring people, and for patients who are lonely and lack comfort from those around them, a doctor can be a source of emotional support. But to receive the physician's attention, the patient has to manufacture or create symptoms. Caring and emotional support is one of the primary uses of physicians. Considering the training and expertise of doctors, this additional responsibility might more appropriately be transferred elsewhere.

Still another problem revolves around our medical-insurance program, which pays for many forms of treatment, but offers no incentives to remain healthy. In my clinic, we cannot bill for any preventive or educational programs, but only for psychiatric care or group therapy. So, in order to help our patients get well, we have to define their problems as psychiatric illnesses.

At times, it seems that we have a *disease*-care, not a *health*-care, system. I see few hospitals that run classes in self-care, or that help a patient recover emotionally from an operation or serious illness. I believe that insurance companies should provide incentives for preventive medicine by demanding that hospitals provide educational programs and that claimants participate in them in order to be reimbursed for health costs. At present, there is no personal or financial incentive for people to follow their doctor's orders, or to remain healthy. Recently, several corporations have started paying bonuses to workers for staying well; not surprisingly, their sick calls have dropped over 50 percent.

Through my clinical experience, I have become convinced that these secondary gains of illness are one of the major obstacles to health. I have never met a person with a serious malady whose treatment was not made more difficult by the many ways that his ailment was catered to and rewarded. Even so, I am not suggesting that we quickly dismiss the pains of sick people, or that we add to their pain by telling them that they are to blame for their illness. But as long as sickness remains the all-purpose excuse, and as long as so

many rewards are attached to it, good health will never be as
highly valued as it should be.

The Family Crisis of Illness

Perhaps the most serious crisis in the life of a family
occurs when one of its members is hospitalized with a serious illness. At such times, the stress upon the entire family
unit is immense, and in fact, the family may suffer as much
as or more than the patient himself. Psychologist Henry
Lennard reports that the family members of an ill individual
encounter many difficult fears and uncertainties, including
anxiety over the possibility of death or permanent disability.[6] To complicate matters, these apprehensions are ex-
acerbated by the information provided by hospitals and
physicians, which is typically confusing, cautious, and pur-
posely ambiguous so as not to instill false hope, and also to
avoid potential liability. Consequently, the fears of family
members grow, often out of proportion to the actual danger,
creating a curtain of isolation and disconnection between the
family and the ill relative. No forum exists for the family to
share information and explore the feelings and issues which
sickness raises.

When the ill person is in the hospital, the family at home
is frequently in crisis. Often, its members fear the dependency that convalescence may entail. Or they resent or feel
constrained by having to assume the responsibilities of the
sick member. A hospitalization can also bankrupt a family.
Sometimes children alter their decisions to marry, seek
higher education, or move out of the house when sickness
strikes a parent. Meanwhile, guilt often keeps the family
members from sharing their frustration, anger, or discomfort, and they never make demands or share any of their negative feelings. In some families, the strain of this behavior
causes other members to become sick as well. A family conference and counseling program sometimes helps people
respond to these problems more effectively, enabling them

to care for an ill relative without undue resentment and anxiety.

An atmosphere in which true feelings are suppressed is not the caring, supportive environment needed to recover from illness. Instead, it is upsetting and stressful, and can hinder healing. I have had patients who, when confronted with a negative home environment, suffered relapses and had to be rehospitalized.

The healing process, then, is affected by the response to illness of every member of the family, as well as the reaction of employers, physicians, insurance companies, and friends. Sickness can be both a personal transition and a family crisis. Unless all family members are included in the healing process—and are encouraged to express their feelings and help one another cope with their problems—medical treatment to cure the sickness can be inhibited or undermined.

Death

When a person is in the hospital, the specter of death is always felt by both him and his family. Illness is a reminder of human mortality and impermanence, but this message is often so feared that the patient and his family deny it. While everyone eventually must face his own death, the experience of dying—to be shared by a patient and his family—has not traditionally been incorporated as part of the healing process. Rather, death is perceived as a failure of healing, and therefore is rarely shared or discussed.

As Ernest Becker has written, the denial of our own death, and of death in general, pervades our culture.[7] We praise youth and fear growing old. We indulge ourselves in immediate pleasures without thought of consequences. As much as possible, we remove all reminders of death and suffering from hospitals, administering tranquilizing drugs to patients to keep them from feeling. Psychologically, we often act as if death didn't exist.

Thanks to the tireless work of psychiatrist Elisabeth

Kübler-Ross, death is less a taboo topic in hospitals and among physicians. When she first began talking with dying patients, she encountered scorn, resentment, and fear from hospital staff. Yet she demonstrated that her conversations were comforting and valuable to her patients. Indeed, these individuals and their families often welcomed the opportunity to talk about death openly and share their feelings. By contrast, the hospital staff avoided discussions of death with patients, putting on a facade of false optimism to mask their anxiety.[8]

When one of my patients is seriously ill, I talk to him about death. I ask how serious he believes his illness is, what he has heard about it from his physician, and whether he has discussed it with others, including family or a clergyman. I have not yet encountered one person who has talked about death with his physician, except in the context of the average time a person could expect to live. Nevertheless, I find that people near death are aware of it, and that open discussion of death and its effects on others is important to them and critical for the emotional stability of their families. The relatives of a patient are in great pain, and their own recovery and grieving demand that they share feelings with their dying member or they will be paralyzed by guilt.

The belief among physicians that death signals a failure of medicine needs to be challenged. Everyone eventually will die. If we accept death as real, then the question is "When is death appropriate?" This is a spiritual question that has invaded the boundaries of medicine. By communication with a patient about the meaning and purpose of his life, a physician can often determine when it is appropriate for death to occur.

Until the actual moment of death, every person must give each day as much meaning and importance as if he were fully involved in life. For me, working as a therapist with the psychological aspects of illness, the criterion for success is not how many people I have "saved," as if health professionals were servants of the gods. Rather, I evaluate my work according to the quality of the life that a patient and his family live, up until the time of death.

Finally, the continuity of life and death suggests that there must be more exploration of ways to support the entire family during and after the dying process. If you have experienced the death of a relative in a hospital, you know that institutional medicine leaves little room for the human side of the process. The pain of death is often accompanied by anger and resentment against the hospital for limiting the amount of sharing between patient and family.

The new hospice movement has begun to alter this grim reality. It creates special environments suited to the dying process and makes experienced counselors available to families.[9] All health professionals must go beyond their own anxieties about patient death and begin to reassume the responsibility for the psychological consequences of death that is usually either ignored or passed on to clergymen.

So we have discovered what most of us were only dimly aware of—that illness is not something merely inside an individual. It is a response to the circumstances of life, and it affects everyone around the ailing person. A holistic treatment process must take note of this social dimension of illness, because the environment and family relationships may hold the key to getting well. Very often, when a patient's family relationship or his approach to meeting his needs is restructured, his physical problem or pain disappears.

5 Placebo Power: Beliefs, Expectations and Self-Fulfilling Prophecies

When I asked Dr. [Albert] Schweitzer how he accounted for the fact that anyone could possibly expect to become well after having been treated by a witch doctor, he said that I was asking him to divulge a secret that doctors have carried around inside them ever since Hippocrates.

"But I'll tell you anyway," he said, his face still illuminated by that half-smile. "The witch doctor succeeds for the same reason that all of us succeed. Each patient carries his own doctor inside him. They come to us not knowing that truth. We are at our best when we give the doctor who resides within each patient a chance to go to work."

The placebo is the doctor who resides within.

NORMAN COUSINS

Several years ago, Dr. Philip West, one of the pioneer researchers of psychological factors in illness, was treating a man with severe cancer who begged to be given the experimental drug Krebiozen. At that time, Krebiozen was being touted by its proponents as a miracle cancer "cure." After only one dose of the seemingly worthless drug, the patient's tumor masses "melted like snowballs on a hot stove." Whereas he had once needed an oxygen mask to breathe, he soon became so active that he even began piloting his own plane.

Shortly thereafter, the same man read about studies indicating that Krebiozen was ineffective. Immediately, his cancer began spreading again, and he was hospitalized. His doctor, reacting to the dramatic turn of events, decided to test a hunch that he hoped would save his patient's life. He lied, telling the patient not to believe the studies, and promised treatment with a new, more potent Krebiozen. In fact, the man was given only water, but nevertheless, his condition improved significantly. His recuperation continued until he read in an article that the American Medical Association and the Food and Drug Administration had conclusively proved the worthlessness of Krebiozen. Several days later, the man died.[1]

This case, widely reported in the medical literature, continues to perplex the health-care profession. A few words and some water apparently reversed the cancer process for one patient, at least temporarily. Could the same happen for others? If so, why? By what physical mechanism do suggestions, and the patient's belief in them, affect diseases, even advanced cancer?

Throughout the history of medicine, the major cause of healing has probably been the patient's positive expectations and his belief in the healing powers of the physician. Psychiatrist Jerome Frank calls this "the power of expectant faith,"[2] which he regards as a major stimulus to the patient's own recuperative powers. Few, if any, of the medical treatments or medicines used before the last century had any positive physical effect on the body or illness. So healers relied heavily on suggestion, even when they were unaware they were doing so. They were also aided by the body's capacity for self-renewal and the self-limiting nature of most diseases.

The therapeutic effect of faith has been labeled the "placebo" effect (*placebo* is Latin for "I shall please"). Positive suggestion can create beneficial results from useless drugs, or it can have a negative impact by limiting the potency of a usually helpful drug.

Research studies document that placebos have some effectiveness in one-third of all cases. But even when they mea-

surably reduce pain, hasten recovery, heal tissue, and mimic
the actions of drugs, they are seldom taken seriously by
physicians, including those who use them.[3] The way in
which the placebo works has never been precisely defined,
nor is its effectiveness consistent. Thus, some doctors consider its cures unreliable or inauthentic. Medicine tends to
ignore or rationalize away the successes of the placebo. For
example, physicians usually describe the unexplained rever-
sal of cancer as a "spontaneous remission." Often when patients unaccountably survive a near-fatal illness or accident,
no explanation is offered at all by the attending physicians.

Very little research has been directed at these unexpected
cures. The National Institutes of Health have never funded
a study of spontaneous remissions, miracle healings (religious or otherwise), the effects of suggestion, or the "will to
live" phenomenon, despite their frequency. "Miracles" don't
seem to arouse scientific curiosity.

I believe that the mystery surrounding placebo healing
continues largely because the medical community does not
accept or is unaware of the impact that psychological processes have on the self-restorative capacity of the body.
Many doctors assume that spontaneous remissions occur
merely by chance and hence could not be introduced systematically into the treatment process. But what if researchers could prove that these cures are attributable to
specific psychological processes? If that were the case,
couldn't physicians incorporate them into their therapeutic
programs? Wouldn't beliefs then become an important aspect of treatment, and make "miracles" routine and ex-
plainable?

Placebo Power: The Physician's Suggestion

All medicine, both past and present, consists largely of
magic and suggestion. As in ancient times, the drug is still
the main symbol of the physician's healing power. In earlier

eras, healing mixtures were natural herbs and potions; today, although drugs are manufactured by chemical laboratories and prescribed by doctors with years of scientific training, they are no less mysterious than their ancient predecessors. Only the physician can prescribe them, and the patient is rarely entrusted with information on what the drug does and how it works. Still, if the patient believes that the drug will help him, its chances of doing so are greatly enhanced.

In most medical research, placebo effects and the power of belief systems are considered a distraction that interferes with the study of the actual physical mechanism of drug action. Attempts are actually made to minimize or eliminate the impact of positive expectations, usually by arranging the study so that neither the patient nor the researcher knows who receives the real experimental drug and who receives a sugar-pill placebo.

Henry Beecher, in reviewing studies of placebo treatments for dozens of ailments, found that 35 percent of over a hundred patients experienced satisfactory relief with placebos that they thought were their regular medication.

These placebo-induced cures are not merely imaginary or subjective, but are often the result of real physical changes. Stewart Wolf discovered that a placebo could produce abnormal numbers of a type of blood cell in the immune system, or reduce the amount of fat or protein in the blood.

In another study, a group of medical students were told that they were being given "stimulants" or "depressants." Actually, the "drugs" were placebos. Nevertheless, 50 percent of the students experienced physiological changes common to stimulants or depressants, such as increases or decreases in pulse and blood pressure, and side effects such as dizziness and watery eyes.[4]

In still another startling study, Beecher divided patients scheduled for a heart-bypass operation into two groups. One group underwent the complete operation, while the members of the other were merely cut open and sewn back up immediately. Both groups were told they had received the entire surgery. Follow-up studies indicated that all patients fared equally well in postoperative evaluations of their symptoms. The simple suggestion that the full operation had been performed was apparently enough to improve the condition of the second group. The positive expectations engendered by the modern healing ritual of surgery may produce healing just as the ceremonies of the ancient shamans did.[5]

Physicians have just begun to speculate about what physical mechanisms in the brain might initiate physical changes as a result of mental suggestion. The placebo effect may be activated in part by naturally occurring substances in the brain called endorphins. These molecules are the body's own pain-relieving materials; they allow the nervous system to turn off pain when it is appropriate to do so. In essence, the brain can release its own narcotic.

Endorphins were first identified in 1975, and scientists are still not certain precisely how they work. But early studies already indicate that they have a chemical structure identical to morphine. And when secreted by the brain, they may maximize the body's ability to respond to a variety of healing techniques—including the placebo effect.

Other research suggests that the placebo operates on a principle very similar to hypnosis. In the special hypnotic state of consciousness, a person is more than usually amenable to suggestion from an authoritative source. Hypnotists can make people sweat, itch, achieve physical rigidity, stop pain and bleeding, or create or cure physical symptoms such as boils. The authority of the physician and the needs of the patient make their relationship very conducive to hypnotic effects. Thus, because the doctor's expectations or suggestions, even when posed unwittingly as hypothetical probabilities, can be translated into physical actualities, the physician should make careful and positive use of this power.

Hypnotherapists David Cheek and Leslie LeCron suggest

that a person in a highly emotional state is very susceptible to suggestions, especially from people whom he respects or regards as authorities. If an ill person, especially a child, hears an authority figure make a statement such as "Nothing will do any good" or "You'll have to learn to live with this condition," he makes this part of his reality. Interestingly, the individual ordinarily has no conscious memory of the suggestion, although hypnotherapy or imagery work can bring it back to awareness. This process, called imprinting, may explain many somatic and emotional symptoms.

Cheek and LeCron relate the story of a young woman who had had a chronic cough for as long as she could remember. In a state of deep relaxation, she recalled having had whooping cough at age four. She remembered being in bed, with her mother nearby, distressed and crying, and her physician saying, "She'll never get over this." Once she recollected this event, her coughing ceased.[6]

In a study by Cheek, patients who were actually under anesthesia unconsciously picked up the expectations related by their surgeons during operations. Gallows humor, negative or questionable references, or expectations voiced during the operation ("He'll never survive the month") became in essence posthypnotic suggestions, which the patient often followed to his or her detriment.[7]

The most notable study on the effect of suggestibility and beliefs, that conducted by psychologist Robert Rosenthal, has been repeated by many researchers in different settings. Rosenthal randomly divided elementary school students into two groups, similar in every respect (IQ, grades, sex, ethnic group). He then told their teacher that one group was composed solely of "fast learners," while the other consisted of merely average learners. Within a year, the performance of the students in the so-called fast group dramatically surpassed that of the average section.[8]

This tendency to conform to the expectations of authorities, christened the "Pygmalion effect," illuminates another aspect of the power of the placebo. It suggests that the patient/student need not even be aware of the negative or positive expectations of the physician/teacher to be affected by them. If, for instance, your own physician is pessimistic, he may communicate that feeling by the tone of his voice or the brusqueness of his diagnosis. In turn, your health can be negatively influenced.

Don Johnson, a therapist who helps people discover the limberness of their bodies, has collected many case histories in which physician's pronouncements have become life sentences for people, leading them to avoid meaningful treatment. He writes:

> Susie is nine years old, born with cerebral palsy. She prefers to use her left arm and hand more than her right, with slightly more exaggeration than most of us might prefer. There is a slight rotation in her spine which twists her shorter right leg around to her right. This makes it hard for her to do jumping jacks. But she still does them. She also writes with her right hand. She has lots of friends whose games she plays. She does well in school. In fact, she is exceptionally bright. When she was an infant, Susie's mother, who had incurred measles during pregnancy, was reportedly told by her physician, "Susie has no sense of her right side because of brain damage." Perhaps he said, "a diminished sense of her right side." But Susie's mother heard "no sense," and has communicated the weight of that diagnosis to Susie for nine years. This diagnosis fed the guilt and frustration Susie's mother felt about contributing to Susie's brain damage. The fact is that she has a slightly diminished sense of her right side which, from my viewpoint, is open to virtually unlimited improvement through such measures as rolfing, patterning, autogenic training, and Feldenkrais techniques (methods of physical repatterning). Diagnosis by a physician is a linguistic tool of incredible power not only because of the esteem in which the physician is held, but also because of the vulnerable state of the troubled patient. When a mother is dealing with the emotional pain of bearing a child with brain damage, she is often feeling a great deal of self-hatred and inadequacy. If a physician tells her something which can be interpreted, "You're in a terrible mess," she may easily hear it that way.[9]

The patient's level of trust in his physician helps determine the extent of his suggestibility. Thus, if you perceive your physician as wise and caring, your hopes of getting better will rise with his own expectations. However, the Pygmalion effect also can work in the opposite direction: If your physician is pessimistic, believing that nothing can help you, this attitude can retard the healing process and keep you from "miraculously" or "spontaneously" getting better. For example, oncologist Carl Simonton reports that the physician's negative expectations about cancer often reinforce and confirm the fears of the patient. The physician assumes "that the disease comes from without, that it's synonymous with death, that the treatment is bad, and that the patient has little or nothing he can do to fight the disease."[10] While such potentially lethal attitudes may be based on statistical probabilities and research, they do not allow for the patient's self-healing abilities or the potency of positive expectations.

Not long ago, a woman with advanced cancer came to see me. She had experienced anxiety symptoms after living beyond the six months her physician had predicted she would survive. She felt she had let him down! She was also hesitant to go back to him because he was so discouraging ("Nothing more can be done for you"). But she could not find another doctor who would treat her because she was already under one physician's care.

This woman was in a deadly bind; she was not being allowed to maximize her ability to combat the cancer. Nevertheless, with my help, she was able to attain significant pain relief, and even stop taking her pain medication. She is still alive today.

Beliefs and Self-Fulfilling Prophecies About Illness

I find the evidence confirming the healing power of suggestion and expectations very convincing. But despite the studies supporting this theory, many of my patients remain skeptical. Perhaps you still have misgivings of your own.

In a sense, such doubts are understandable. Our own belief systems about health and illness have developed over
many years from all types of medical and pseudomedical information. We hear homilies such as "Germs cause illness,"
or "Going out without a jacket causes colds." Or we're told
misleading medical information, such as that tranquilizers
cure tension, back pain is actually located in one's back, or
cancer is incurable. We have learned gross oversimplifica-
tions of medical truth, and possess deep-rooted ideas about
how people get sick and well.

If we observe a situation that runs contrary to our belief
system—like an unexpectedly quick and complete recovery
from illness—we tend to ignore it or try to explain it in the
context of our existing system. It is easier to adapt reality to
our prevailing beliefs than to alter our beliefs to fit reality or
experience.

Much of the information in this book contradicts conventional assumptions about health, illness, and medical treatment. For instance, I dispute the belief that a patient is a
passive, helpless spectator in the healing process, or that
medicine is purely a physical process. Yet because so many
people believe they are powerless to heal themselves, they
run the risk that this belief system can become reality—that
is, their belief becomes a self-fulfilling prophecy.

Perhaps this concept of self-fulfilling prophecies can best
be explained by relating the story of a woman patient of
mine who grew up in a family in which every minor ache or
pain was a matter of grave concern. Each family member
seemingly suffered from one exotic disease or another and
spent much time bemoaning his or her own physical health.
Such complaining was the way in which each of them acquired attention from the others. Illness was almost essential
in order to fit into the family unit.

Imagine being raised in such an environment. Almost
from birth, my patient's mother told her she was sickly and
frail; consequently, she learned to regard her body as un-
trustworthy. Every pain or physical change, no matter how

slight, was interpreted as a sign of illness. While hereditary factors might have been involved in her later ailments, her perception of herself as sickly and a target for infection and illness certainly contributed to her severe health problems.

This patient's encounters with physicians only supported her beliefs. She visited doctors regularly with her assortment of aches, indigestions, allergies, fevers, and lethargies. In an attempt to be cautious and thorough, the physicians ordered a seemingly endless series of tests, which substantiated her belief that something was certainly wrong. The tests in turn had physical side effects, which she perceived as further signs of illness and cause for worry. In her own mind, she was ill until proved healthy.

If a doctor conducts enough tests, a small physical abnormality will almost inevitably be found. One of this woman's physicians eventually seized upon a test revelation as the possible cause of her illness. "You have a malfunctioning thyroid," he told her, validating her own belief that she was indeed sick. Further, the subsequent attention upon the gland may have magnified the actual weakness there; the patient was placed on a continual drug regimen that gradually altered the functioning of a previously adequate thyroid. Prescriptions for such patients of tranquilizers, allergy medication, hormones, and other drugs simply confirm to them what they had already assumed—that they are indeed ill.

I have encountered similar situations many times, in which an individual's negative beliefs about himself or herself were inadvertently reinforced by a physician. For such patients to become well, changes are necessary not only in their physical condition, but also in their attitudes about themselves and their health.

The physician's approach is critically important. If my patient's doctor had probed sufficiently into her family background, he might have decided to give her a placebo, along with calm reassurance that it would offer the relief being sought. However, although this approach could have improved her condition, it would have supported her assumption that something was indeed wrong that only a physician could cure. Instead, he might have tried to change her negative beliefs with a detailed exploration and explanation of how she had learned to see her body as unhealthy. He could have taught her ways to develop confidence in and positive expectations about her body. This latter approach could have led to lasting change, enabling her to experience fewer physical complaints in the future.

Take an inventory of your own beliefs and knowledge about the illnesses you, or members of your family, have experienced. What role could your beliefs about health and illness be playing in your sickness?

I grew up suffering from asthma and hay fever. I sneezed and wheezed at appropriate times, usually when I was outdoors in the country, or participating in sports. My doctor told me I needed constant treatment, including allergy shots, and that I should always carry my medication with me. I was usually excused from hikes and campouts, and running in gym class. I grew to think of myself as a partial invalid, dependent on my medication. My symptoms were never explained to me as connected with anything but heredity, nor was I led to believe I could have an effect on them, other than by taking the prescribed medication.

However, when I entered college, I consulted a different allergist. He told me I would probably outgrow the symptoms and suggested that I stop taking the medication for a while. After I did, the symptoms disappeared, and never returned.

Returning the Placebo Power to the Patient

Several specific steps can be taken to transfer and maximize the placebo effect. The physician ought to create a positive expectancy in his patients by actively providing clear, accurate medical information about the illness. For his part, the patient must start honestly examining his expectations and beliefs, and resolve to change those that seem to hinder the treatment process. He must work determinedly to alter negative mental patterns (guilt, worry, fear of the future) into positive, health-enhancing patterns.

The patient must be guided toward discovering the healing powers that lie within him. Faith in pills and external treatments can be replaced by faith in oneself. The billions of dollars spent for impotent over-the-counter remedies, for painkillers and tranquilizers, and for solace from physicians can be saved by a medical system which restores faith and hope not in drugs and physicians, but in each individual and his body.

Accurate information about the body's potential can counter a patient's fears and pessimism. For example, Simonton effectively uses his authority as a cancer expert to explain how the disease actually manifests itself and progresses. He shows slides and tells the patient how the illness develops and how his treatment works. In essence, this educational approach is a frontal assault on the confusion and the potentially negative ideas that people have about their illnesses. Patients react positively when Simonton shows them graphic slides of other people whose cancer responded to treatment and whose condition dramatically improved. Once a patient sees cancer progressively shrinking, he no longer considers the disease as a death sentence, and the healing process can begin.

Information, then, can be therapeutic, for it can calm the anxiety and tension that add to stress. Doctors who create an open dialogue with their patients soon learn that, as much as anything else, many ill people are seeking a sense of hope and the belief that they themselves may be able to effect change in their condition. By furnishing this information, much of their patients' confusion, feelings of neglect, and noncompliance with recommended treatment dissipates. The patients feel better knowing their exact condition, identifying the ways they can help their treatment, and understanding why it is important to do so. The healing process can begin in earnest.

6 Stress: How Self-Protection Can Become Self-Destruction

The three most obvious lessons derived from research on stress are: (1) that our body can meet the most diverse aggressions with the same adaptive-defensive mechanism; (2) that we can dissect this mechanism so as to identify its ingredient parts in objectively measurable physical and chemical terms, such as changes in the structure of organs or in the production of certain hormones; (3) that we need this kind of information to lay the scientific foundations for a new type of treatment, whose essence is to combat disease by strengthening the body's own defenses against stress. . . .

In other words we have learned that the body possesses a complex machinery of checks and balances. These are remarkably effective in adjusting ourselves to virtually anything that can happen to us in life. But often this machinery does not work perfectly: sometimes our responses are too weak, so that they do not offer adequate protection; at other times they are too strong, so that we actually hurt ourselves by our own excessive reactions to stress.

HANS SELYE

You probably expend your greatest amount of life energy in the protection and regulation of your own physical boundaries. That tough, durable, flexible skin separating your fluid interior from the arid exterior is constantly at work, fighting off invading forces that could harm the body. If something does injure you, usually all other activity is stopped while healing and regeneration take place. But even during healthy periods, much of your energy is spent channeling materials in and out of your body to maintain your defenses and thus your well-being.

This process, in which the body is continuously involved in self-protection or self-healing, is one of the most complex phenomena in the universe. Within each of us lies a remarkable diversity of interconnected cells, organs, and chemical and energy systems. This intricate network operates during every second of our lives to maintain our integrity and livelihood, and it requires a constant supply of nutrients (air, water, food). Chemical factories in each cell—and in the organ systems, on a larger scale—break down, store, convert, exchange, transport, and utilize the energy from these nutrients. Each cell also has physical centers for repair, reproduction, awareness, control, and integration of internal activities.

These self-preservation processes occur within an internal salt sea under our skin, which is not much different from the world of our early protozoic ancestors. This liquid environment maintains a constant cellular temperature, making possible the necessary energy transformations, regardless of the vicissitudes and threats of the outer world.

A lifetime of study could not unravel all the complex procedures that keep us alive. Maintaining homeostasis—a stable, consistent, and protected inner physical environment—is a monumental task, demanding thousands of simultaneous, ongoing, delicately calibrated responses to stimuli and change. Every cell is being periodically regenerated, and in the process, we technically become a new person every few years, at least chemically. Of course, in another very real sense, we are also still the same person, and so to maintain this constant identity, we must employ an instant restorative response to every expenditure of energy.

Our Internal Self-Preservation Systems

Health, as I define it, is your adaptive capability to meet the demands posed by your environment. Since health is so central to productive life and includes so many types of protections and responses, it is not surprising that there are not one but several bodily systems endowed with the responsibility of maintaining, or restoring, health when it is threatened.

Essentially, each of us relies on three complex and highly interconnected bodily systems to maintain our well-being—the nervous system, the general adaptation syndrome (or stress response), and the immune system. The *nervous system*, which is the seat of our conscious awareness, consists of the many parts of the brain, the spinal cord, the receptor and motor nerves, and the nerve passageways that extend to all parts of the body and to the major sense organs. It is our communication and command network for both external and internal changes, and also the regulator of our internal and external responses. It keeps track of the current state of each physical system—and the world—and turns on and off various responses. It also serves as mediator between each individual's consciousness and his physical body, and is the final integrator of his wholeness as a unique conscious person.

Within the nervous system are two major subsystems—the conscious or voluntary nervous system, and the visceral or autonomic nervous system (ANS). These systems developed at different stages of man's evolution. The ANS has two basic operating modes or patterns, called the sympathetic and parasympathetic responses, that adapt the body to nearly opposite but equally essential functions. The parasympathetic response is a condition of rest, relaxation, healing, and physical repair and regeneration. Food is digested, muscles relax and replenish energy supplies, tissues regenerate, and our awareness remains comfortably focused either on our existence in general or on whatever specific task is at hand.

The opposite pattern, the sympathetic response, is a pattern of general alarm, arousal, and readiness to operate physically against external threat or dangers to the body. The sympathetic response is triggered instinctively, without conscious direction. It is like putting on battle dress and preparing for sustained, energetic, forceful reaction to the limit of one's capacities.

Physiologist Walter Cannon first described this sympathetic mobilization process, which also seems to include a deep emotional arousal. He notes:

> It is remarkable that most of these reactions occur as the accompaniment of the powerful emotions of rage and fear. Respiration deepens, the heart beats more rapidly, the arterial pressure rises, the blood is shifted away from the stomach and the intestines to the heart and central nervous system and the muscles, the processes in the alimentary canal cease, sugar is freed from the reserves in the liver, the spleen contracts and discharges its content of concentrated corpuscles, and adrenalin is secreted from the adrenal medulla. The key to these marvelous transformations in the body is found in relating them to the natural accompaniments of fear and rage—running away in order to escape from danger, and attacking in order to be dominant. . . . The emotional responses just listed may reasonably be regarded as preparatory for struggle. They are adjustments which, so far as possible, put the organism in readiness for meeting the demands which will be made upon it.[1]

The body can live in such a state of extreme mobilization for only a brief period before it needs to relax and regenerate via the parasympathetic response. If it does not do so, it soon begins to break down.

The sympathetic response is also called the alarm, or fight-flight, reaction. It, in turn, is one of the triggers that activates the second of our three self-protective systems—the *stress response*, or general adaptation syndrome. The GAS responds to external or internal sources of stress with a wide

range of productive, regenerative, self-protective reactions,
all of which are regulated by free-circulating body chemicals
called hormones. Various neurological and immunological
changes also occur during the onset (or alarm stage) of the
GAS.

After the GAS is activated, the body initiates a process of
resistance, calling into action the specific defenses appropriate for the danger or threat, either within a single organ or
throughout the entire body. Resistance cannot continue indefinitely, however, and eventually a stage of exhaustion sets
in and remains until the adaptive reserves dissipated in the
struggle are replenished. (A more detailed explanation of
the GAS appears later in this chapter.)

The final self-protective bodily network is the *immune
system*, which is our internal army that searches out and destroys invaders and enemies and protects us from danger.
Like an actual military force, it has its own intelligence
units, and various forms of artillery and infantry to coordinate its mission.

The immune system has been mapped only within the
past two decades, largely because it is such a decentralized
bodily system, with parts throughout the body, including
the circulatory system, the lymph system, and certain glands
and specialized areas, as well as in the fluids which surround
every cell.

Good health depends on the coordinated, constant effort
of all three of our protective agencies—the nervous system,
the stress response, and the immune system. Each of them
works reasonably well without conscious effort on our part.
But under modern societal conditions, and because we abuse
our bodies, these systems can malfunction. And if the vigilance against external invaders (such as germs) collapses, serious illness or injury can result.

As we are quickly learning, we do have the ability to consciously modify and enhance the effectiveness of each of
these protective systems. The possibility of a medicine
based on conscious self-regulation could not have been envi-

sioned even a decade or two ago, but now we know that it can be a reality.

Evolutionary Origins of the Mind/Body Split

Much of the blame for the diseases of civilization lies with a deceptively simple enemy: stress. The fast pace of our lives, the continual change that Alvin Toffler called "future shock,"[2] our polluted food and environment, our sedentary life-styles, and the ambiguous, interpersonal nature of threats to ourselves—all are implicated in the dramatic rise in new, stress-related diseases.

But we make a mistake if we envision stress as an external entity, like an attacker or a germ. Stress is rather our own psychophysiological *response* to external changes and difficulties. Our excessive or misplaced reaction to these external stressors (stimuli that cause stress) takes a severe physiological toll on the body over time, and in the presence of an existing weakness in part of our body, causes physical disease.

As we begin to understand stress as a reaction to our environment, and when we recognize and amplify the conscious control we have over our stress response, our chances of achieving a state of good health improve significantly. No longer must we see ourselves as helplessly victimized by an environment which makes us sick. Instead, to some extent, we can take the steps necessary to change the way we respond to stressors, in order to adapt more effectively.

Unfortunately, most people react poorly and even self-destructively to the seemingly lethal nature of modern life, largely because we are ill equipped, in terms of our evolution, to respond properly. Our early ancestors lived under far different environmental conditions than we do. Prehistoric society bore no similarity to the man-made, machine-dominated, urban-centered world of today. While the world has changed rapidly (in evolutionary terms), human physiology has not kept pace. Physical evolution takes eons, and thus

today, we still possess the physical structure and human responses of the caveman, pressed into service in an environment that makes demands very different from those of
thousands of years ago. Perhaps this explains why the
body's previously adaptive responses are no longer as protective, and often even seem harmful and counterproductive,
themselves producing many of the diseases of civilization.

For a moment, let's explore how evolution may have failed
us in our attempts to adjust successfully to our modern environment. To begin with, human beings think of themselves as separate from the rest of the animal kingdom,
because they have developed conscious self-awareness and
the ability to think, plan, reason, and imagine independently
of the environment. But the basic physiological functions—
breathing, digestion, circulation, maintaining a constant internal environment and protecting it against threat—are all
apart from our conscious awareness, and are controlled unconsciously by the visceral, or autonomic, nervous system,
which we share in common with most other animals.

In our own bodies, this autonomic system is regulated by
the structures in the brain stem, located at the top of the spinal cord and the base of the brain. These structures are collectively known as the diencephalon, or the reptilian
brain—named after the animal ancestor that first possessed
this type of automatic, integrated nervous-system organiza-
tion. In addition to controlling our vegetative functions, this
reptilian brain also contains the tiny hypothalamus, which is
the central switchboard for activating emotional responses.
(That is why emotional arousal accompanies the alarm reaction.) The hypothalamus also controls the major unconscious drives (such as thirst) and helps regulate body temperature.

Atop this reptilian brain lies the larger cerebral cortex—
two walnut-shaped lobes of convoluted gray matter, with a
white inner core. This cortex, a recent evolutionary development, is the site of conscious planning and evaluating, as
well as unconscious information storage. It also coordinates

voluntary physical movement. While the reptilian diencephalon takes care of our basic life functions, the cortex operates
the part of our nervous system in which we plan, worry,
think, love, create relationships and works of art, and respond to changes and crises in our world. With this conscious thought and planning, humanity has been able to
mold its environment almost at will.

Even so, humanity's body still retains the same automatic
pilot as its animal ancestors. Our internal conscious control
is severely limited by the independence of the cerebral cortex from the reptilian brain. Like most evolutionary develop-
ments, this disconnection has its positive and negative
consequences.

Our Two Brains and Illness

Some theorists have blamed humanity's current psychophysical ailments, and even society's political problems, on
an uneven relationship between rationality and thought on
one side and feelings and experiences of the body on the
other. Nobel Prize winner and ethologist Konrad Lorenz,
social critic Arthur Koestler, stress expert Hans Selye, British public-health physician A. T. W. Simeons, and psychotherapists from Freud to Fritz Perls to Alexander Lowen all
maintain that our current dilemmas stem from a lack of balance and integration between our two brains.[3] As we will
see, current neurological research into the psychological
links between the cortex and the diencephalon, and the mind
and the body, now support this perspective.

A. T. W. Simeons, for example, has suggested that as
humans have begun using their conscious reasoning to modify their environment, they have become increasingly separated from the instinctive physiological responses located in
the diencephalon, including the autonomic nervous system
and automatic responses to environmental changes. Relying
heavily on their cortical powers, humans have channeled

their behavior—via cultural conditioning and creation of conscience, guilt, and shame—into extremely narrow channels of acceptable behavior. In short, your behavior and responses have been molded into carefully defined "socially acceptable" actions.

In the midst of this "acceptable" behavior pattern, what happens to the diencephalon? Although now operating entirely outside of consciousness, the diencephalon is continuing as always to mobilize the body in reaction to external threats. It stimulates a pattern of physiological response, whether the threat is psychological (e.g., someone screaming at you) or physical (e.g., a fall, or a brick about to hit you). This is the alarm or fight-flight reaction, which also activates the first phase of the stress response, or GAS, and mobilizes the immune system. This series of automatic bodily events prepares the organism to fight off intruders, to lead it out of danger as quickly as possible, or to seal off and repair a break in the skin.

So our body is continually, and unconsciously, mobilizing itself in this way. But unfortunately, its response is not always helpful or appropriate for the unique social stressors that modern man faces. We must cope with far different threats from those encountered by our ancestors. To them, any movement nearby was a potential source of danger—perhaps a predator. Instant reaction was demanded for survival.

But today, we are worried and threatened less by physical danger than by psychological threats to our livelihood, our self-esteem, our feelings, and our honor. These contemporary threats are largely interpersonal or symbolic, and because of social mores or inhibitions, we are forced to react to them on a mental level, ignoring our emotional and instinctive demand for a direct, physical fight-or-flight response. After all, as much as we'd like to, we cannot hit our bosses or our lovers, or run from an insult.

So what happens? Responding to the social threats of today, the diencephalon reacts instinctively just as it did in the jungle thousands of years ago. It perceives the modern sources of arousal as physical threats, because that is all it understands, even though our rational cerebral cortex knows better. Thus we are physiologically prodded into arousal by the diencephalon, while our conscious cortex largely ignores the process, leaving the body mobilized to do battle but unable to act or discharge the tension that builds up. Stress-related illness arises out of this struggle between cortex and diencephalon. Our primitive attempts at mobilization are correctly perceived by the conscious cortex as unnecessary, but cause difficulty in the process.

That's the dilemma of modern humanity. Many aspects of the environment prepare our bodies for action, but few of our responses turn it off naturally. To some extent, playing golf, jogging, screaming, or crying may serve as a safety valve. But largely, the physiological result of our modern life-style is chronic, unremitting arousal without release. In essence, we "hold it in."

The physical consequences include strain on the heart and circulatory system, leading to hypertension, strokes, and heart disease; tension within the digestive system, causing ulcers, colitis, and other difficulties; emotional strain, leading to anxiety, worry, and neurosis; pain and muscle tension; and various other major and minor ailments.

The particular illness we contract depends primarily on which organ within us is the weakest, or on which we place the most chronic stress. However, the basic cause of the breakdown is our dual nervous system, and our excessive or inappropriate stress responses, rather than an illness or something specifically wrong with that particular organ. Scores of different diseases stem from similar environmental stress responses.

Selye's Model of the Stress Response

Much of our knowledge about stress and its impact upon our well-being is due to the pioneering research of Hans Selye.[4] Selye mapped the body's general defensive system against external changes and threats. He traced this response from the nervous system into various endocrine glands—such as the pituitary and the adrenals—through most of the internal organs and then to every other part of the body.

When Selye began his work, medicine hadn't even coined a word for the general adaptive response he described. He selected the common word "stress" to refer to "the rate of wear and tear on the body." He theorized that, over a lifetime, a person seems to have a specific amount of adaptive energy to cope with his environment. As we will see, that can create problems for the individual who uses it up too rapidly—who responds to too many life changes, who has several serious illnesses, who experiences a life of difficulty and privation, or who maintains the body in a state of chronic arousal because of real or imagined psychological threats. When this happens, the body will eventually no longer resist even mild environmental threats. At that point, with resistance depleted, organ breakdown or other illness can easily occur. Selye believed that each person must conserve adaptive energy by carefully regulating his life, especially when living in an environment in which recurrent, strong, or varied stressors are the norm.

Here's how Selye describes the GAS response, which is the mechanism by which the body responds to protect itself. At the first sign of a stressor, signals from the cerebral cortex and the diencephalon activate the sympathetic response and the alarm reaction. As the muscles become tense, the hypothalamus sends a message to the pituitary, which in turn secretes hormones that are transported throughout the body. Upon reaching their target organ, the hormones signal a particular response in that organ.

During this process, the body becomes aware of the source and nature of the threat, although as yet it is not fully understood how this occurs. Then, if the threat is to a local area—a break in the skin or a microbe—a response of inflammation seals off the area until the immune system can repel the aggressor or heal the damaged tissues. If the threat is not localized, as in a psychological or potential environmental hazard, the GAS mobilizes the body for maximum physical responsiveness—that is, for resistance to the menace.

If the stress in your life is simply a long night of study or a day of extreme physical labor, the body is placed into over-drive during this resistance period, taxing its energy reserves but providing the additional power or alertness that is needed. Even when the stress is psychological, the resistance phase is distinguished by tensed muscles, increased alertness to the environment, and inhibited digestion, as we brace ourselves for continuing action.

Selye emphasizes that when the body is mobilized to re-sist one source of stress, it expends most of its adaptive re-sources there, and is thus less able to defend us against other sources of stress. So, for instance, if you are worrying about psychological threats to your self-esteem, you actually make yourself less resistant to germs, various other threats, and diseases caused by overworking one part of your body. Re-search suggests that people may contract chronic diseases after they have worn themselves out with long-term emo-tional stress.

During the resistance stage, the way an individual reacts to stress is partly determined by heredity, and is partly a re-sponse learned from parents or other influential people. For instance, there are men and women who react to stress by tightening up the stomach muscles and breathing shallowly, as a means of inhibiting emotional reaction. Years later, they may find themselves afflicted with a lung disease such as emphysema, especially if they have irritated the lungs fur-ther by smoking. Or some people express their feelings by inflaming their stomach linings, increasing the risk of ulcers or colitis.

Certain individuals react to the emotional or psychological aspects of stress as fighters—blowing out all their emotional energy at once. This is their form of resistance, or stress re-lease. Others, called somatizers, do not allow themselves to experience the emotional effects of stress and instead localize it in a part of their bodies, where it is manifested as headaches, back pain, indigestion, or more serious illness. Still others, called psychologizers, express their resistance to stress by worry, anxiety, depression, or chronic tension. Because both somatizers and psychologizers do not respond directly to the source of stress, they leave themselves open to psychic or physical illness caused not by the particular stressor, but by their inadequate defense against it.

Diseases can result from either too much resistance on the part of the body, or too little. Rheumatism, hay fever, arthritis, hypertension, and neurosis appear to be due largely to the body's reacting too forcefully to an outside stress that is not really dangerous. Other illnesses, such as cancer, are produced by an inappropriately limited adaptive response. In cancer, the body fails to kill cells that have begun to grow without regard for their neighbors.

Finally, Selye describes the last stage of the GAS as exhaustion. During this postresistance period, the body ceases to defend itself, because it has temporarily expended all its energy. Muscles no longer function, or they become cramped. The mind fails and sleep occurs. Or the individual becomes emotionally hysterical and cries.

How can this lost energy be replenished? Selye suggests diversion—that is, resting the tired muscles; or if the mind is overtaxed, participating in physical exercise. When a person's adaptive energy is not replenished—perhaps after fighting a long-term disease, or after a lifetime of self-defense—the body dies. It has been suggested that the extraordinary longevity of certain social groups, such as inhabitants of the Soviet Caucasus, is due not so much to heredity, health habits, or leisure, but to the lack of psychological stress and change in their lives, indicating that they take longer to use up their supply of adaptive energy.

The Immune System

The immune system is another amazing, decentralized self-protective network that helps the body deal with specific invaders which break through the skin or enter the body in the air or in food. The white blood cells and lymphocytes of the immune system are some of the resources that our stress response has at its disposal to cope effectively with specific difficulties.

When activated, the immune system sends various protective cells and substances through the bloodstream, and via the internal waterways of the lymph system, to the site of the danger—an infection, puncture, cancer cell, or foreign body. The body then manufactures particular substances which can destroy the invader. If the invader is another microorganism—a virus or bacteria—the body never forgets it, and if such a germ ever strikes again, even fifty years in the future, the body unerringly defends us. Other internal forces repair the damage and scan for further injury.

The large white blood cells, which are part of the immune system, multiply and rush to the site of infection in the body. When your doctor takes a white-cell count, the presence of a large number of white cells indicates that there is an infection somewhere in the body. Other soldiers of the immune army lie in the blood plasma, the fluid that carries the blood cells. They include proteins called antigens that can place a tag on any intruding organism or protein that does not belong in the body. This allows the body to locate it and also produce another type of protein—called an antibody—which can attack and destroy it. This is how vaccines work: they give a person just enough of a disease to allow the body to tag the invader with antigens and then create its own antibodies to destroy it.

The immune system plays a role not only in combating disease, but also in encouraging it. Like the stress response, the immune system is clever but not infallible. It is responsible for many diseases, because of innate defects, malfunctions, or simply mistakes.

Sometimes, as in cancer, there is evidence that the immune system has not done its job, which is to ferret out cells when they become malignant. The surveillance theory of cancer suggests, in part, that every person develops some cancer cells each day, but the immune system successfully destroys them. Cancer may stem from a failure of the immune system.

Other diseases occur when the body develops ineffective antigens or antibodies. Still other ailments, called autoimmune diseases (such as rheumatism and allergies), result when the immune system inappropriately attacks its own cells.

As with the stress system, emotional and conscious factors affect the potency of the immune network. Psychological depression, for example, lowers the level of immune-system activity, thereby diminishing the body's self-protective abilities. If we reduce psychological depression, we may augment immune-system activity and, thus, self-healing. There is also some evidence that mental imagery and suggestion can stimulate the immune network into action.

So for every disease we develop, probably thousands of other invaders have been detected and destroyed painlessly by the immune system.

A Plan of Action

Based on this psychophysiological information, how can your own actual or potential diseases of civilization best be prevented or treated? It's essential for you to become aware of when your body is in a state of stress-related arousal, correctly label it, and understand exactly what it may do to you physiologically. Also, you must provide yourself with the means to turn off an inappropriate stress response—to activate a parasympathetic response as an antidote to an excessive sympathetic arousal.

In the following chapters, specific approaches will be offered to help you react positively to the stresses you face, and maximize your conscious control and modification of self-protective responses.

Part II

ILLNESS
and
HUMAN
RELATIONSHIPS

7 The Physical Cost of Loss and Change

The reality is that all relationships inevitably will be dissolved and broken. The ultimate price exacted for commitment to other human beings rests in the inescapable fact that loss and pain will be experienced when they are gone, even to the point of jeopardizing one's physical health. It is a toll that no one can escape, and a price that everyone will be forced to pay repeatedly. Like the rise and fall of the ocean tides, disruptions of human relationships occur at regular intervals throughout life, and include the loss of parents, death of a mate, divorce, marital separation, death of family members, children leaving home, death of close friends, change of neighborhoods, and loss of acquaintances by retirement from work. Infancy, adolescence, middle age, old age—all seasons of life involve human loss.

JAMES J. LYNCH

Charles always prided himself on his good health. At age forty-eight, he had never been seriously ill. He frequently shopped in health-food stores, always ate well-balanced meals, and played a fierce game of weekend tennis. In his forty-ninth year, he was promoted to vice-president of a medium-size company, moved to a fine neighborhood, and had been invited to join many prestige clubs.

He also had some problems that year. His father died, and his wife proclaimed that she liked their old life-style better. She felt out of place in their new social circle. And his new job carried more pressures and responsibilities, demanding more time, frequent travel, and business-related entertaining and social events (which his wife despised).

Charles' life-style was shattered one Tuesday afternoon when he suffered a heart attack. Since then, he has never been the same. Although he soon was back at work, doctors have warned him that he could experience another heart attack at any time. And so he lives with the constant fear that he is always on the brink of death, and is not sure what he can do about it.

Why did illness strike Charles when it did? Why do any of us become sick when we do? Is there any way to predict when a weak stomach or colon will ulcerate, or a frail (or even a seemingly adequate) heart or stressed lungs will finally lead to an acute crisis? During serious illness, we tend to ask not only "Why me?" but also "Why now?" Part of the answer lies in the nature of our environment, and our response to the demands it places upon us to change and adapt.

According to Alvin Toffler, in our lifetimes we endure more technological change and more environmental uprooting than were collectively experienced by several generations in past centuries. Today, only a small fraction of the population lives in a single location or keeps a particular job for very long. Almost from the moment of birth, our lives are imbued with stresses and transitions—new situations, new people, moves, job changes, and divorces and separations. By contrast, a man of a simpler era, who grew up in the town where his family had always lived, married a childhood sweetheart, and took up his father's business or profession, had far fewer adaptive demands made upon him. While there were other health threats in these earlier times that kept life spans short, it is hard not to connect the rise in stress-related illness with the pace and nature of our environment.

Our modern response to endless change often complicates our plight. Because of preference and vocational demands, the nuclear family—the married couple and their children—

typically does not live close to parents, other family members, and long-time friends. In the absence of a wider community, each family becomes a sort of pressure cooker, with its members placing greater emotional demands on one another than they otherwise might. Also, because an inner sense of stability and security is more difficult to achieve, people become emotionally attached to symbols, material goods, or a particular job or social position—all of which help them define who they are. The loss of any of these symbols, which have become an important source of meaning in life, can be a terrible blow. Just recall the many suicides of ruined paper millionaires after the 1929 stock-market crash. Or consider the abnormally high death rate of executives soon after they retire. External supports can be critically important to our health and livelihood.

In short, continual change and the loss of our most valued symbols and possessions can devastate both our psyches and our bodies. With every new situation, especially those that are sudden and unpredictable, we increase our susceptibility to illness, because we must channel so much of our adaptive energy into coping with these changes. It is as if a nation's troops were tied down to one front in a battle, leaving its perimeters, where unrelated danger might strike, less securely defended. Similarly, no matter how good our body's defenses are, the overwhelming nature of the assault will eventually wear us down. Most catastrophic illnesses, then, as well as accidents, suicides, and other expressions of psychological distress, are related to the stress of life change, crises, and particularly losses.

Life Change

The relationship between illness and life changes has been studied for years. Around the turn of this century, psychiatrist Adolf Meyer observed that illness tended to occur around significant events, transitions, and crises in people's lives. To examine this relationship more systematically, he designed a "life chart," on which each of his patients was asked to note the date of the major physical and psychological difficulties in his life, and also the important events and frustrations. The end product, in effect, was a lifeline, depicting ups and downs, changes and turning points. These charts often revealed a marked association between illness and life change.

Psychiatrist Thomas Holmes and his colleagues have continued Meyer's research.[1] Because almost everyone can pinpoint some life changes in the time preceding an illness, Holmes and his associate Richard Rahe attempted to define this relationship more precisely, by measuring the severity of the change in the pre-illness period.

Of course, two persons can respond very differently to the same change. While you may react with anguish to a divorce or loss of job, another individual may hardly be affected. Even so, Holmes and Rahe were determined to develop a ranking of the general impact of common life events, by asking people how much adaptation or accommodation each demanded. Holmes and Rahe gave marriage an arbitrary score of 50, on a scale of 0 to 100, and then invited their survey participants to assign values to the degree of adaptation demanded by other common life changes. Surprisingly, there was considerable agreement among the participants, even among people of different countries, social classes, and ages. The researchers concluded that there was some validity in assigning common life events a numerical score, corresponding to the relative degree of adaptive energy they demand from a person.

The list prepared by Holmes and Rahe contained forty-three common life changes, with their relative adaptive demands registered on a scale of 1 to 100. For example, death of a spouse was found to be the most severe, and was assigned a score of 100. A minor legal violation, like a traffic ticket, scored 11. Their original Social Readjustment Rating Scale is printed below:[2]

THE SOCIAL READJUSTMENT RATING SCALE

Life Event	*Mean Value*
1. Death of spouse	100
2. Divorce	73
3. Marital separation	65
4. Detention in jail or other institution	63
5. Death of a close family member	63
6. Major personal injury or illness	53
7. Marriage	50
8. Being fired at work	47
9. Marital reconciliation	45
10. Retirement from work	45
11. Major change in the health or behavior of a family member	44
12. Pregnancy	40
13. Sexual difficulties	39
14. Gaining a new family member (e.g., through birth, adoption, oldster moving in, etc.)	39
15. Major business readjustment (e.g., merger, reorganization, bankruptcy, etc.)	39
16. Major change in financial state (e.g., a lot worse off or a lot better off than usual)	38
17. Death of a close friend	37
18. Changing to a different line of work	36
19. Major change in the number of arguments with spouse (e.g., either a lot more or a lot less than usual regarding childrearing, personal habits, etc.)	35
20. Taking on a mortgage greater than $10,000 (e.g., purchasing a home, business, etc.)	31
21. Foreclosure on a mortgage or loan	30
22. Major change in responsibilities at work (e.g., promotion, demotion, lateral transfer)	29
23. Son or daughter leaving home (e.g., marriage, attending college, etc.)	29
24. In-law troubles	29
25. Outstanding personal achievement	28

Life Event	Mean Value
26. Wife beginning or ceasing work outside the home	26
27. Beginning or ceasing formal schooling	26
28. Major change in living conditions (e.g., building a new home, remodeling, deterioration of home or neighborhood)	25
29. Revision of personal habits (dress, manners, associations, etc.)	24
30. Troubles with the boss	23
31. Major change in working hours or conditions	20
32. Change in residence	20
33. Changing to a new school	20
34. Major change in usual type and/or amount of recreation	19
35. Major change in church activities (e.g., a lot more or a lot less than usual)	19
36. Major change in social activities (e.g., clubs, dancing, movies, visiting, etc.)	18
37. Taking on a mortgage or loan less than $10,000 (e.g., purchasing a car, TV, freezer, etc.)	17
38. Major change in sleeping habits (a lot more or a lot less sleep, or change in part of day when asleep)	16
39. Major change in number of family get-togethers (e.g., a lot more or a lot less than usual)	15
40. Major change in eating habits (a lot more or a lot less food intake, or very different meal hours or surroundings)	15
41. Vacation	13
42. Christmas	12
43. Minor violations of the law (e.g., traffic tickets, jaywalking, disturbing the peace, etc.)	11

Why not apply the Holmes–Rahe scale to yourself? Peruse the life events on the chart, and see how many have happened to you during the past year. Also, note how many changes occurred in your life during the year immediately preceding your most serious illness. If an event took place twice in that year, it should be checked twice. The number values for the changes in that year should then be added together, providing a score of a certain number of life change units (LCU's) during that time period.

Since their original work, Holmes and Rahe have suggested that people assign their own values to life transitions. So, go back over your list of changes and estimate for yourself, on their scale of 1 to 100, how much adjustment each transition demanded of you. For example, if you have moved and estimate that the move entailed a major life adjustment for you, you might give yourself a life change score of 30 or 35 instead of the suggested 20. Now recalculate your LCU's, using your own estimates. This will give you a much more accurate score of your own adjustment demands.

Since 1945, Holmes, Rahe, and others have used this scale on over five thousand subjects. They found that patients who suffered many disorders (including tuberculosis, skin disease, problem pregnancy, heart disease, accidents, multiple sclerosis, cancer, and mental illness) experienced significant elevations of life change units in the year preceding the onset of sickness. For example, 37 percent of those who scored from 150 to 200 LCU's in a twelve-month period contracted a serious ailment during that year. Those with scores of from 200 to 300 had a better than even chance of becoming sick. Eighty percent of the people with over 300 LCU's in a year experienced illness within that period. Furthermore, the severity of the disorder was correlated with the LCU score, especially in relation to chronic, stress-related illnesses.[3]

These findings have subsequently been supported by other studies. For example, Rahe examined the illnesses of twenty-five hundred Navy men on shipboard duty and correlated them with their LCU scores for the previous year. Sailors with scores in the highest one-third suffered twice as many illnesses in their six months aboard ship as those in the lowest one-third.[4]

Still another study indicated that accidents, as well as illnesses, are related to life change. In a survey of college football players, half of those who ranked in the top third in terms of LCU's were disabled during the season, compared to only 25 percent of the middle third, and 9 percent of the bottom third.[5]

It really doesn't take much to bring a person above 150 or 200 LCU's for a year. For example, let us explore the life changes that took place in the twelve months preceding Charles' unexpected heart attack, mentioned at the beginning of the chapter. His promotion (No. 22 on the chart) would give him 29 LCU's, and his change in working hours (No. 31) would add another 20. His new house (No. 32) would contribute an additional 20 LCU's, with the heavy mortgage (No. 20) meaning 31 more. The death of his father (No. 5) would add 63 LCU's, and his new social activities (No. 36) another 18. This gave Charles a total of 181 LCU's for that year, placing him at some risk for illness. The additional stress caused by the friction between him and his wife was another contributing change, although it is not measurable on the general life change scale.

On the Holmes–Rahe rankings, ten of the fifteen most demanding life events are associated with the family, demonstrating the importance of family relationships to one's health. Other researchers have substantiated this conclusion. C. Murray Parkes has reported that it may literally be true that individuals die of a broken heart. Parkes found that within six months after their wives died, men over fifty-five had a 40 percent higher death rate than the normal population. The greatest cause of these deaths was heart failure.[6]

R. W. Bartrop studied twenty-six widows and widowers (ages twenty to sixty-five) within a few weeks of the loss of their spouses, and compared them with twenty-six hospital employees. The bereaved group suffered from a depressed lymphocyte function, indicating a deficient immune system. Bartrop concluded that the stress of loss not only affects the hormonal system, but also, independently, the immune system which protects the body from danger.[7]

Of course, as the Holmes–Rahe scale indicates, change

need not be negative to increase a person's susceptibility to illness. As probably happened to Charles, too many promotions, sudden increases in wealth, moves to better houses, and long vacations can contribute to a person's LCU's. The unfamiliar responsibilities of a new job and the problems of meeting new friends or entering a higher social class all entail adaptation, and, potentially, illness.

In a study of company employees, Lawrence Hinkle reported that people whose social class, backgrounds, aspirations, or interests coincided with their jobs were the most healthy. By contrast, individuals frustrated by their jobs, as well as those promoted beyond their expectation, education, or social class, had more illness. Workers who did not alter their social class, or life or job status, had less illness. But those who experienced blocked mobility and upward mobility—one entailing disappointment and the other stressful adaptation—had more illness.[8]

I suggest that you use the Holmes–Rahe scale primarily as a guide, enabling you to understand and predict potential sources of difficulty. For example, let's assume that next month you're offered your third promotion and relocation in five years. Based upon your knowledge of the stress that would be involved, you might consider refusing or deferring the offer. Or even if you decide to accept it, you will be equipped with information that will allow you to anticipate and prepare for the effects of severe change. So if you're aware that a series of minor events or a major transition involves severe stress, you can counteract it by, for instance, beginning a deep relaxation program, or by being extrasensitive to the demands of your body.

Holmes has devised some suggestions for helping people use his scale to maintain their health effectively and help prevent illness:

1. Become familiar with the life events and the amount of change they require.
2. Put the scale where you and the family can see it easily several times a day.

3. With practice you can recognize when a life event happens.
4. Think about the meaning of the event for you and try to identify some of the feelings you experience.
5. Think about the different ways you might best adjust to the event.
6. Take your time in arriving at decisions.
7. If possible, anticipate life changes and plan for them well in advance.
8. Pace yourself. It can be done even if you are in a hurry.
9. Look at the accomplishment of a task as a part of daily living and avoid looking at such an achievement as a "stopping point" or a "time for letting down."
10. *Remember*, the more change you have, the more likely you are to get sick. So, the higher your life change score, the harder you should work to stay well.[9]

Mourning a Loss

At his physician's suggestion, a man sought treatment from me for his chronic asthma and chest pains. A timid and nervous person, he was just entering a new marriage five years after the suicide of his first wife, whom he had divorced shortly before her death. While he had suffered from asthma and occasional chest pains for many years, these conditions became disabling after his ex-wife's suicide. Believing that the divorce had contributed severely to his first wife's distress, he felt some responsibility for her death.

In counseling, this man explored his guilt, and he started profoundly experiencing the pain of her death. He eventually came in contact with many other sources of pain from both his present and his past. He learned to eliminate most of these attacks by allowing free expression of his feelings, so that when they did occasionally occur, they were far less disabling.

Another case study concerns the wife of a businessman. After twenty years of living in a small community, she and her husband moved to a large city. Apparently, she made a healthy adjustment to the move, overcoming the dislocation and loss of friends, and she created a new life for herself. But then her husband received another promotion, entailing a transfer to still another city. A few days later, she suffered a heart attack, interrupting their preparations for the move.

When I began counseling this woman, she was not making a good recovery. I asked her what would happen when she finally got well, and she became distraught and weakly replied, "Well, I guess we would have to move." She doubted that she could survive another loss, especially with the recent departure of their youngest son to college, and the increasing time her husband spent on the road. The only way she felt capable of responding to the impending loss of her new community, and the loss of her family, was by becoming ill. Her husband, when made aware of his wife's problems, turned down the new promotion and made a conscious effort to reattach himself to his family. Almost immediately, his wife's health improved dramatically. Instead of experiencing yet another loss, she regained both her health and an intimate relationship with her husband.

Losses can be reflected and responded to in many ways, some of which may surprise you. I once counseled a woman who developed severe angina (chest pains) upon reaching the same age at which her mother had died. An anniversary, a related loss, or a new life transition can reactivate old feelings, opening an individual up to illness. Effectively coping with loss and mourning is critical to avoiding and overcoming many illnesses.

George Engel, a leading psychosomatic researcher at the University of Rochester, gathered newspaper accounts of sudden deaths (excluding suicides or accidents) and pieced together the events preceding them. He found that in 59 percent of the hundred and seventy cases, death was preceded by some type of loss. For example, thirty-six people died after the collapse or death of a close relative; thirty-five people died within sixteen days of a period of acute grief; sixteen died after the threat of the loss of a close person; nine died after loss of status or self-esteem; and five during mourning or the anniversary of a loss.[10]

In another study, William Greene interviewed the wives of twenty-six men who had died suddenly. Half of these men had experienced an increased workload and depression, with the latter often associated with the departure of the youngest child from the home.[11] Another researcher, Arthur Schmale, studied forty-two consecutive patients admitted to his hospital, with a range of medical problems. Twenty-nine of the illnesses were associated with the recent loss or departure of a loved one, coupled with feelings of helplessness or hopelessness about their new life situation. This emotional reaction often triggered recollections of an earlier separation or loss of a parent.[12]

Public life and politics are brimming with examples of the impact of loss. Patricia Hearst's lung collapsed when she was found guilty of bank robbery. Richard Nixon suffered an attack of phlebitis when he was under pressure to resign the presidency. After Robert Taft was defeated in his quest for the presidential nomination in 1952, and after Hubert Humphrey lost the presidential election in 1968, each was soon stricken with cancer.

Cancer, in particular, has been linked to such loss. LeShan and Worthington, studying hundreds of cancer patients, reported that 72 percent of these patients had experienced the loss of an important relationship within two years prior to the tumor diagnosis. Many (47 percent) of these patients had difficulty expressing hostile feelings toward people, and 37 percent still experienced tension over the death of a parent which often had occurred many years earlier. Over and over again, the recent lives of cancer patients are linked to loss and life change.[13]

Despite the growing evidence of the influence of emotions upon cancer, this is still a controversial hypothesis. In essence, the notion that cancer is partly of psychosomatic origin contradicts the generally accepted medical opinion. Interestingly, the National Cancer Institute has not funded any studies in this area, and does not consider the research to date important enough to do so.

Still, in a 1959 review of psychological research for the *National Cancer Institute Journal,* Lawrence LeShan presented scores of studies suggesting that recent loss, plus a personality pattern that has been characterized as "helpless and hopeless," may predate the onset of cancer.[14] Some psychologists have actually been able to predict the presence of cancer from psychological testing. For example, LeShan differentiated twenty-four of twenty-eight histories of cancer patients from those of a control group suffering other illnesses. Bruno Klopfer, a noted authority on psychological testing, could almost unerringly single out which cancer patients had slow- or fast-growing tumors, only on the basis of their Rorschach test results.[15]

LeShan described the typical terminal cancer patient as an individual who has suffered a recent loss and reacts in a particular way to it. Cancer patients, he said, are often people who, from early in life, distrust emotional relationships. For a time, they are able to develop a satisfying relationship, career, or interest, which absorbs their emotional energy. But, prior to their cancer, for a variety of reasons, it is lost.

Their reaction to loss, according to LeShan, is one of terrible despair rather than mild or moderate depression. They somehow continue going through the motions of life, as they always had, but inwardly the loss only confirms to them that it was futile to commit their emotional energy to anything. Their cancer in turn further confirms their negative outlook on life. But LeShan believes that intensive psychotherapy can help these cancer patients assume a more hopeful, forceful approach to their future, and suggests that this therapy can have a positive effect on their disease.[16]

Psychiatrists Engel and Schmale relate this despondent attitude to a number of other illnesses:

> . . . The onset and exacerbation of many types of illnesses were noted commonly to be preceded by affective states variously

described as "despair," "depression," "giving up," "grief," and others, all in some way indicating a sense of irresolvable loss or feelings of deprivation. Intrigued by the wide variety of conditions—literally the whole range of organic disease—for which this seemed to be the case, we have attempted to delineate more precisely the characteristics of this predisease state. . . .[17]

These people, say Engel and Schmale, relate their feelings of helplessness and hopelessness to their own failures. As a consequence, their remaining relationships are ungratifying. They sense a disconnection between their past and present, and an inability to develop confidence in their future.

Meyerowitz has linked rheumatoid arthritis, a chronic condition which tends to strike middle-aged women, to their feelings of frustration at not having fulfilled their ambitions, and to their doubts that they would have been good enough if they had tried. Often this disease strikes soon after the last child has left home and affects a mother who is already depressed and uncertain about what she will do in the last half of her life.[18]

Actually, according to Engel and Schmale, such feelings, when combined with a biological predisposition and a suitable life crisis, can trigger any type of disease. In these situations, medical treatment will often be frustrated, unless the inner condition is treated as well. As we will see in later chapters, a process of counseling and reconnection, along with medical treatment, has considerable therapeutic potential for someone in this state, who has seemingly lost the will to live.

When I ask individuals to explore their past life changes and losses and their general attitude toward life in relationship to their illnesses, there are several common reactions. Some say these factors simply don't apply to them. Such a reaction may be justified. While clearly loss and change can be factors in illness, we would expect that many ailments bear no relation to life events.

Other patients react with an immediate recognition of the connection. They then begin the difficult emotional process of coming to terms with their loss, and learning to view the future differently than they have before. A third, and probably the largest, group is initially suspicious and surprised at my description of this connection. But after some reflection, they begin to understand it and see how this awareness can be applied.

You can conduct your own personal exploration of loss, life change, and illness, in two ways:

1. Reflect back over your life, pinpointing the most difficult or devastating changes or losses. Next, examine the toll that these events have taken on your life, and how you reacted and coped with it. Some people find that this reflection comes easiest during a relaxation exercise (to be described in chapter 13). You should then ask yourself if there is any unfinished psychic business connected with these changes or losses. Often, writing a letter to someone who has died, or a short note about the consequences of a change in job, can alert you to the way the change continues to affect you.

2. Study the significance of each of your major illnesses (which you may have already done in the previous chapters). For every illness, write down the reasons for it—perhaps the contributing causes in terms of life changes or losses. Look for two kinds of causes: the original factors at work at the time of the onset, and those which, if you still suffer from the disease, continue to affect your ability to overcome it. Can you find symbolic or actual connections between your illnesses and the losses or life changes you've experienced?

We must realize that the diseases of civilization can largely be blamed upon our modern life-style, and our inappropriate physiological responses to changes or losses. Environmental carcinogens (also a by-product of modern life) and diet do contribute to cardiovascular, lung, and liver cancer epidemics. But in essence, I think that people who become ill are more susceptible to the stresses that we all encounter. An awareness of this situation can alert us to take remedial action before serious illness results. Most illnesses are far from inevitable.

8 Coping and Control: Protecting Ourselves from Stress

> *We experience stress, I suggest, when we lose confidence in our ability to handle relationships, either with the physical world or with each other. This loss of confidence arises from failing to control, from the breakdown of expectations, from a sense of being at the mercy of unpredictable and indomitable forces, from complexities and contradictions we cannot master.*
>
> PETER MARRIS

At the coaxing of his wife, a middle-aged man with serious hypertension came to see me. During our initial session, he revealed that he had been depressed for as long as he could remember. Few things in his life—neither his work nor his family—gave him pleasure. He was a partner in a family business and was afraid to take even short breaks because his cousin might complain. He knew what would make him happier and healthier—losing weight, stopping smoking, taking vacations—but for some indefinable reason, he chose not to do them. He felt he could not change or escape the stressful situations in his life. In a sense, he felt beyond help.

After working with this man for a while, I believed there was a connection between his negative feeling toward life and his hypertension. Imagine, for instance, the strain of spending a lifetime doing things because of a fear of others, not for personal pleasure. The turmoil within him must have been terribly destructive.

My patients often mention their difficulty in coping with life's demands and relate this problem to their chronic but minor psychological and physiological symptoms. Their worries, aches, and discomforts seem to be the fallout of their incomplete, displaced, or overdone reactions. Their bodies and their feelings say to them that their style of living is harmful and in need of modification. They come to behavioral or psychological health programs, usually after a long period of taking painkillers or tranquilizers, finally convinced that the best medicine is to change the life pattern in which their particular symptom originated.

The life changes (especially losses) discussed in chapter 7 are only one link in a chain of reactions and events, the final outcome of which may be a chronic or degenerative physical illness. I'm sure you know some individuals who react disastrously to minor stresses, such as hearing that a daughter has taken a lover, or having to compete with a colleague for a promotion. And there are others who thrive on challenge and difficulty or are seemingly unaffected by struggle and change. In essence, we can think of life changes and environmental stress as forces entering the physical boundaries of the person, then to be processed and transformed into internal psychophysiological reactions and a personal response to them. Every person is always reacting to the change and stress in his world in his own unique way.

Mobilizing Ourselves for Danger or Threat

As I discussed in chapter 6, many of the diseases of modern life result from misguided attempts to protect ourselves. Psychological illnesses are often caused by an exaggerated or inappropriate reaction to psychic pain, anxiety, or imagined harm. Similarly, physical stress symptoms result from the body's overreaction to threats that do not demand such severe responses.

George Engel and other stress researchers have defined

the kinds of environmental threats that typically lead to psychophysical stress responses:

1. Perceived or actual *loss* of a person, object, or activity in which we are psychologically invested
2. Actual or threatened *injury* or damage to the integrity of our body (e.g., injury), or to our self or self-esteem
3. Actual or potential *frustration* of what we perceive to be our basic needs and drives
4. *Ambiguous* or incomplete perception or information, leading to the belief that something might be a threat or danger[1]

Stress symptoms may thus be activated not only by actual environmental changes and threats, but also by psychological factors. Worry, or anticipated pain, are sufficient to trigger the stress response. For example, what happens to you before a dental appointment? The mere thought of possible discomfort gives many of us a headache or jaw pain. The tension, and your physical response to it, becomes even more extreme when the dentist picks up his drill or administers a shot of novocaine. Sure enough, the shot really hurts. But how much of that pain was caused by the injection itself, and how much by the anticipation of it? How much damage has this mental picture of possible pain inflicted upon your body?

This same pattern of mobilization occurs in hundreds of common experiences. Some people react anxiously about relationships with the opposite sex. Others respond this way to encounters with an employer. After a few such negative experiences, an individual may become tense at the mere sight of the person he fears, and eventually, even at the thought of that person. Entire days may be ruined by this anxiety or rage, provoked only by the thought of possible interactions. Even though no actual confrontation may ever occur, headaches, stomachaches, or even ulcers may develop.

By now you may be thinking, "Why can't I just tell myself to stop worrying, becoming upset, or responding negatively to stress?" Well, go ahead and try. It simply won't work. The mind doesn't respond to such verbal commands. It errs on the side of caution, and when in doubt, it automatically sends us into a state of arousal. In fact, trying to convince yourself to relax can often make you more upset, as you become aware of how helpless you are in this situation.

But even though the stress response is mobilized automatically, conscious processes do play some role in its activation. In a sense, they act as a mediator. After all, we couldn't very well become angry or upset over a conversation if we didn't know what it meant and couldn't interpret it as threatening to our self-interest. Or we couldn't fear another individual without the thought processes that define his menacing role.

For an environmental stressor to do any damage, it must first pass through an individual's cognitive and perceptual filters. In short, the stress must be *perceived* as a threat or danger. Some may interpret an insult as a joke; to others, it may represent a menace. The way we perceive the remark will determine our reaction. To complicate matters further, some of our responses (say, to loud noises and sudden movements) are relatively automatic, without conscious thought, while others need considerable conscious thought (like the real meaning of a spouse's tardiness).

Thus, our stress level is determined by what we expect from our environment and how we interpret the events that occur in our lives. These interpretations are typically made in the ongoing inner dialogue within our minds. For as long as you can remember, you've probably been aware of the almost nonstop internal conversation that your mind has with itself. Biochemist Robert DeRopp has labeled this phenomenon "roof-brain chatter."[2] This dialogue may be a replay of a conversation, a fantasy, daydreams, a song fragment, plans, worries, or anticipations. It occurs simultaneously with many of our daily activities, as we chatter to ourselves at work, around the house, driving the car, and even while talking with others.

The dialogue is in no sense just a mental phenomenon.

Rather, it is connected to other aspects of our nervous system—most important, our autonomic nervous system. When it concentrates almost exclusively upon past and future anxiety-producing events or thoughts, it will set the sympathetic nervous system into action, if only slightly. The stomach tightens and acidifies, the muscles tense, perspiration is produced, and respiration becomes shallower. With each mental replay of anxiety-related events, these stress responses will again be activated.

The mind, then, is the major factor in determining how much stress we are under. But, as we will see in later chapters, it is also the key to the opposite state of being—relaxation.

Your Personal Stress Responses and Habits

There are many adaptive and nonadaptive ways that you can respond to the world around you. Awareness of these patterns is the first step toward any meaningful, positive alteration in this process.

Take a moment to think back to several events or situations where you felt very stressed or pressured. Try to recapture the feelings and responses you had to them then:

What kind of situations were they?

Did the situations have anything in common?

What did you feel, and how did you respond?

How did you feel afterward? What kind of physical and emotional fallout did the event leave behind with you?

You will probably find it useful to write down your responses to several stress situations, as a way of focusing your memory on the patterns that underlie your responses. However, as you proceed through this exercise, you'll probably realize how imperfect your memory is. Consequently, you should carry a piece of paper with you for the next few weeks to record your ongoing daily stresses and responses.

Here's the best way to proceed. On a sheet of paper, make four columns. The first should contain the time, place, and situation of any event during the day that you perceive as stressful. Write down what you were doing and what happened to you.

In the second column, estimate—on a scale of 1 to 100—how stressful the event was. A frustrating work situation might rate 30 (a relatively low stress), while a fight with your spouse could require a higher score of about 70 or 80.

In the next column, describe how your body responded to the stress, and how you felt during the episode.

Finally, in the last column, write down your own response to the stress and its effects on your body. That is, what did you do about it? Did you take an aspirin or a Valium, go to sleep, leave the scene, scream at your spouse, play tennis, or simply get depressed or anxious? How did you try to overcome the stress of the event? This will tell you something about your approach to coping. How, for example, do you handle frustration? Tension? Pressure? Disappointment? Misfortune? Challenges? The unexpected? Events beyond your control? Whether or not you get the job after an interview?

You will learn quickly the kinds of things that cause the anxiety and physical symptoms that indicate stress. You'll also define the kind of pace you maintain—whether you're a turtle or a racehorse, or something in between.

As you recall and observe your responses, not only will habitual patterns become evident, but you will probably begin to sense a style in which you perceive the world. Your particular response to stress is determined by an amalgam of influences, as personalized and unique as a fingerprint. Perhaps some of your organs are hereditarily weak or sensitive, and therefore respond poorly to excess stress. This weakness can be further amplified by an injury to a particular organ earlier in life. Also, learned health habits—ranging from diet and smoking to chronic tension caused by the emotional nature of childhood experiences—can contribute to a particular pattern of response.

Think back over the past week to the times you were under the most tension. What was your response? Do you

	TIME, PLACE, SITUATION	LEVEL OF STRESS	BODILY RESPONSE	YOUR PERSONAL REACTIONS
*Stress #*1				
*Stress #*2				
*Stress #*3				
*Stress #*4				

have nervous habits such as tics, headaches, nailbiting, stomachaches, diarrhea, or screaming—all of which are means of discharge? Or do you hold it in and not openly release the internal agitation?

One of my patients noted that as he drove to work in the morning, he could feel himself becoming tense. He would drive erratically and get angry at other motorists. The demands of his work—with its pressures from deadlines and superiors—were overwhelming. I asked him to concentrate on where the stress was localized in his body. He pointed to his stomach. Indeed, he had digestive problems.

This man was unable to find a constructive outlet to discharge his tension. He would come home, read or watch TV, ignore his wife, and wait for his body somehow to calm down miraculously and recover its energy. The miracle never happened. Until he learned to relax, he had no outlet, and therefore the information he had acquired about his chronic tension was of no benefit to him.

At the times you were under severe stress, can you remember what particular bodily organs or areas were the most vulnerable? If it is hard to recall where you localize stress, this exercise will probably refresh your memory:

Sit quietly, making yourself as comfortable as possible. Next, become aware of the sensations coming from each part of your body, asking yourself at each point if that particular muscle or organ is tense or relaxed. Do you feel any tension in your face or jaw? In your stomach? In your thighs, legs, arms, back, neck, head, or lungs? If you can concentrate intensely on each part of your body, you will probably be able to identify where you habitually carry your tension.

Now, focus your awareness only on that particular part of your body with the most tension. In your mind's eye, try to imagine what that spot looks like when it is tense. Make a mental picture of how the tension feels to you. Is it all knotted up? Is it being strangled by an outside force? Is it being crushed by heavy weights?

Imagine how you could change that mental picture to relax that part of your body. For example, if you pictured your stomach as a huge, solid knot, tight and wet, you might visualize the knot slowly and gently untying itself, and finally lying limp and loose on a sunny beach to dry. As we will see in later chapters, mental images like this can stimulate positive bodily changes.

Caroline B. Thomas, a psychosomatic researcher at Johns Hopkins medical school, compiled a list of some of the common signs of nervous tension. In her research, these habits correlated with many types of ailments. She asked patients to check their common reactions in situations of undue pressure or stress.[3]

___Exhaustion or excessive fatigue

___Exhilaration

___Depressed feelings

___Uneasy or anxious feelings (sighing, tight feelings in throat or chest, dry mouth, clammy hands, etc.)

___General tension ("keyed-up" feelings; difficulty in becoming relaxed)

___Increased activity

___Decreased activity

___Increased urge to sleep

___Increased difficulty in sleeping

___Increased urge to eat

___Loss of appetite

___Nausea

___Vomiting

___Diarrhea

___Constipation

___Urinary frequency

___Tremulousness or shakiness

___Anger (expressed or concealed)

___Gripe sessions

___Concern about physical health

___A tendency to check and recheck your work to assure yourself of accuracy

—An urge to confide and
seek advice or reassurance
—Irritability with concern
as to who is to blame
—Philosophic effort with no
reactions out of the
ordinary

—An urge to be by your-
self and get away from
it all

To give yourself a rough indication of your degree of chronic or unrelieved stress, note the number of these responses that you have.

Many of these habits can be divided neatly into pairs of opposites, suggesting that stress can tip the balance of the body too far in either direction. Each person, according to Thomas' research, has a particular pattern of frequency, type, and severity of such habits. Most of them are unpleasant in themselves, and more important, they can lead to severe medical complications if they continue for many years. Tense people must learn to balance their responses.

One of my patients suffered from an assortment of ailments, including hypertension. In charting her stress responses, she began to see that she reacted not only to her own dilemmas with worry and anxiety, but also to those of her children, husband, and parents. When family members had a problem, she experienced stress, aggravated by her feelings of helplessness. Her response was to become obsessed with their quandaries, which were beyond her control, and she suffered constant worry and apprehension.

Another patient who diligently kept a stress log discovered that her back pain flared up only when she thought of leaving her husband and becoming sexually involved with other men. The pain kept her home, and was an expression of her fear of ruining the marriage as well as of her sexual frustration. In another case, a young man concluded that his epileptic seizures occurred whenever he did something that made him more independent of his parents.

After a week or two of keeping your own stress log, and a few evenings recalling common responses to stressful events in your past, you should write a profile of the most frequent ways you experience stress, the feelings it provokes, the ways it affects your body, and your habitual responses. Then analyze how adaptive or maladaptive your responses are, and determine what changes you might make, or what new responses you could adopt, that would be more flexible and would resolve the aftereffects more completely. If you have trouble with this last part, later chapters will provide you with a variety of techniques for creating these new habits and responses.

Type A—Achievement, Anger, Repression and Control

Analysis of the stress profiles of many individuals indicates that particular responses and behavior sometimes can be linked to particular illnesses. The greatest body of evidence relates to how a style of stress response is connected with heart and coronary-artery disease.

The research in this area was begun by cardiologists Meyer Friedman and Ray Rosenman. Peculiarly, their interest was piqued by the puzzled observation of an upholsterer who was fixing the furniture in their waiting room. The upholsterer wondered why only the front edges of the chairs and sofas were worn. Until then, the researchers had been concentrating on the traditional physical risk factors for heart disease (smoking, lack of exercise, diets high in saturated fats and cholesterol). But subsequently, they began to investigate why a majority of their patients exhibited an aggressive, achievement-oriented, time-dominated approach to their lives.

Type A is the name Rosenman and Friedman gave to the highly competitive life-style associated with coronary-artery disease. Perhaps you know people (usually men) with this Type A personality: the driven, work-obsessed executive who is always under time pressure, does not know how to relax, and is usually difficult to be around. He strives to be in constant control, can't delegate authority, and is very demanding. Their symbol for these Type A individuals is a forearm with a clenched fist, and a stopwatch around the wrist.[4]

Rosenman and Friedman, along with psychologist David Glass, believe that the driven quality of nervous energy and continually impending deadlines keep Type A individuals in a continual state of psychophysiological arousal. They try to do many things at a time, living by their clocks and calendars. This causes muscle tautness, especially around the face, nervous jiggling and tapping of fingers, and rapid speech. They eat and walk rapidly and find it hard to sit and do nothing. Their minds are never in the present, but always on the next task. Obviously, this pattern tends to drive the body to its physiological limit.

Whether or not these people admit it, there is evidence that considerable anger and hostility lie behind Type A behavior. Type A people are easily irritated and frustrated by waiting, by the unexpected, and by the inadequate work of others. They always play to win, and they distrust the motives of those around them. They expect the worst from people, which suggests how they feel about themselves. Glass found that Type A people pushed themselves nearly to exhaustion on a treadmill exercise, yet admitted less fatigue than their Type B counterparts, who quit earlier.

Glass has evolved a theory about how the Type A personality deals with perceived environmental threats. The Type A person, he explains, tries to be fully in control of his world, so that he can live in orderly, predictable surroundings where he is king. He dislikes the unexpected in personal relationships and in work. To him, the world seems hostile and threatening, and his answer is to exert as much control as he can.[5]

In many research studies, this behavior pattern is a stronger predictor of heart attacks and other forms of heart and artery disease than the more commonly accepted risk factors. Rosenman and Friedman say that as many as three-fourths of the men they have studied exhibit this response pattern. Many men have been trained to behave this way from childhood and see it as a requirement for success in our culture.

The contrasting behavioral pattern, Type B, is less hostile and aggressive, better able to relax and enjoy life and other people. While it would seem that the law of the jungle would favor the A's over the B's, in fact, not only is the B pattern healthier, but more B's than A's rise to top leadership positions and high executive posts. The A's cluster at middle levels, because they lack adaptability, flexibility, and the capacity to work well with others. While most people fit somewhere midway between the A and B types, you might take some time to assess roughly which qualities of each you possess.

Perhaps you're thinking that the Type A orientation is totally opposite from the helpless-hopeless response, outlined in the previous chapter, which may help trigger cancer and other diseases. However, Glass' research suggests that, when faced with situations that are unique or that frustrate his desire to control them, the Type A person actually lapses into this same helpless-hopeless attitude.

Glass placed Type A and Type B men in a room where they were subjected to very loud noises that they couldn't control. Then they were given a frustrating task to master. After hearing the noises, the ordinarily fast and efficient A's did poorly on the subsequent learning situation, in comparison with B's. Glass concludes that Type A's are more seriously affected by losses in their lives over which they have no control. Type A's, he says, have more helpless and difficult reactions to losses than the more easygoing Type B person. It may be that the angry, driven Type A life-style is an attempt to avoid the helpless-hopeless reaction to events. When that fails, illness may result.

These studies once again link sickness not only with external sources of stress, such as losses and frustrations, but with a person's emotional response to them. The degree to which a person feels he has lost control of events and the fear he has of this loss of control apparently affect the adaptability and vigilance of the body against illness.

While Type A behavior has been directly linked to heart disease, its consequences may be more general than that. Just as the helpless-hopeless response was linked not only to cancer, but then to other illnesses as well, Type A may be connected to many stress-related symptoms. Of course, too many other factors—from the quality of our food and environment to hereditary influences—may be involved to permit simplistic generalizations about the potential impact of Type A behavior. Ongoing studies should further illuminate the full role that Type A behavior plays in our health.

When I describe the Type A characteristics to people, they typically want to know, "Am I one, or am I not?" Their assumption is that if they are, their health is in peril, while if they are Type B, they are free from danger. However, to some degree everyone has these Type A qualities, because the characteristics are the most common adaptations to life in our culture. All of us feel driven to some extent, and experience frustration and anger at our inability to control the complex, ambiguous, and confusing events around us.

How can you modify your responses, learning to be more adaptive and direct in facing and overcoming stressful events? Altering Type A behavior is a long process, demanding careful, patient changes in all aspects of your lifestyle. You must become aware of your own particular qualities and then create a plan to vary them.

Coping Effectively with Stress

Research can tell us not only the variables that make us ill, but also the methods of responding to our environment that may keep us healthy. As executives and other harried people frantically attend stress-management seminars and seek methods of relaxation, medical researchers have tried to determine just what types of attitudes and responses help keep us well.

Pioneering research by psychologist John Lacey demonstrates that each person has certain tendencies in his physiological response to a variety of stressors. Lacey subjected individuals to the mental stress of difficult arithmetic problems and word association tests, and the physiological stress of hyperventilation and dipping a foot in water. He found that each person had a certain pattern by which his body responded to all four stressors. Some people responded and recovered quickly, while others peaked more slowly and recovered over a longer time. Thus, according to Lacey, a person has certain particular patterns of response which are, to a degree, independent of the stress involved. People have a physiological signature, he says, which may predispose them to particular stress-related diseases, regardless of the kind of stress they are under.[6]

Selye, noting an individuality of response, divided people into "racehorses" and "turtles." The racehorses thrive on pressure, demands, stimulation, challenge, and competition. Removed from such situations, they will experience stress. Some of them have difficulty vacationing or escaping from their work, although others vigorously thrust themselves into leisure in the same way they approach other activities. The turtles, said Selye, are quite the opposite—slow-paced, and needing measured stimulation, expectations, and pressure. Otherwise, they experience anxiety, worry, and severe stress.[7]

The various by-products of modern society's stresses—pain, tension, discomfort, or depression—can devastate us unless we learn to turn stress off. However, not all stress symptoms are bad. Psychologist Irving Janis has examined the relationship between preoperative anxiety and postoperative recovery rate. He found that the two extremes—people who worried too much, and those who worried too little or not at all—both experienced greater discomfort than patients who worried a moderate amount. He suggests that there is a "work of worrying," which prepares the body for the impending shock and protects it. However, too much or too little is inappropriate; too little denies the stress and hence does not prepare for it, while too much involves an overresponse.

Janis also believes that each stress symptom has a particular functional range and usefulness. So like the moderate worrier, we must learn to stop our response when the symptom has done its work. Of course, there are reasons for worry, tension, and depression. But just as resistance to stress eventually leads to exhaustion, the adaptive usefulness of a symptom ultimately gives way to harm.[8]

From these observations we learn that correct pacing, withdrawing from certain challenges and difficulties and taking others in stride, is a critical aspect of stress control. We each have a proper rhythm of life, and we can expect danger when environment, work, or family imposes a different pace upon us. Many job and household conflicts arise because two people simply live by different biological rhythms. Attending to yourself and placing yourself in positions which suit your turtle or racehorse nature (your particular stress tolerance) is probably the most effective way to modulate your negative stress response.

Another important aspect of stress control is the nature and degree of our preparation for difficult events. Barrell and Price found that the way a person faced a stressful event determined its physiological effect upon him. In their research, individuals reacted very differently to the news that they would receive a painful electric shock some time during the experiment. Some became confronters, focusing their attention on the coming shock, trying to prepare for it. Others— the avoiders—remained passive, trying to keep their mind off the impending shock while waiting for it to strike. Physiologically, the confronters had greater muscle tension, while the avoiders experienced faster heart rates. The confronters, who believed they could do something about the stress, prepared their bodies and minds for it. The avoiders, who felt impotent in confronting the crisis, coped by denial, with accompanying anxiety.[9]

The implication of the Barrell and Price study is that the most adaptive approach to stress is one in which you exert the maximum control and preparation. By responding directly to potential stress, you will experience a minimum of frustration, anger, and associated physiological changes.

Other psychophysiological studies offer additional suggestions on handling stress. A study of the coping strategies and physical responses—blood pressure and cholesterol, triglyceride, and uric-acid levels—of three hundred managers provides some useful suggestions on dealing with job stress.[10] The most effective strategy is to keep physically strong through good eating habits, adequate sleep, and exercise (the latter is a particularly good antidote to stressful experiences at work). Also, you should physically withdraw when you feel yourself under stress, taking a few minutes to unwind or relax before reentering the scene. Another strategy is to separate your work life from your homelife. Try to leave job problems at the office, not discussing frustrations and problems with your spouse, which will maintain your level of stress arousal. Instead, talk over your work problems only with your colleagues and co-workers, as close to the time when they occur as possible.

Who's in Charge?

You have much greater control over your own destiny than you probably realize. After working with hundreds of ill patients, I believe that an individual's attitudes about life and his expectations about coping with the world often influence his future. Some people think they are impotent, and they anticipate collapsing when the demands upon them become too intense. By contrast, others approach life with the attitude that they'll do the best they can and will only be minimally affected by events they cannot control. On balance, the more you are comfortable with your own effectiveness and are able to accept both your achievements and your limitations, the more you will be free to adapt to the changes and obstacles that life presents.

Under stress, the Type A person reacts like the individual plagued by helplessness and hopelessness. Both feel their worlds slipping out of their grasps. To them, their futures seem bleak, and they give up efforts to maintain their integrity against a world that does not fulfill their needs and expectations. Intuitively, it seems logical that these people are at risk to develop illness. It is as if they have lost the interest or the desire to protect themselves, or have futilely exhausted their resources fighting a nonexistent enemy.

Can these people be helped? Presumably, if you could modify their pattern of response, the negative physiological effects and distress would decrease. But you cannot order a person to change instantly, because he will probably become anxious or angry, feel unprotected, or argue that he is incapable of exercising any more control over his life events and situations.

The process of change, then, must be made in small increments. The first step should include a self-definition of the problem and the creation of a plan to modify not the symptoms, but rather the attitudes toward the world that seem to underlie the stress response. If you're a helpless person, you should attempt to experience more personal power; if you're a Type A individual, you should try leaving things as they are, and delegate authority. You need to learn to relax (see chapter 13) and to trust the world to support your best efforts.

Once you begin to perceive your potency and needs differently, and start appraising your environment in another way, your attitude toward stressful events and worldly threats will become less rigid, and you can begin to change and adapt.

9 Repressed Emotions and Self-Care

*Back home, the healing has continued. I am learning
to release my anger. I don't hold back anymore. My
children and I yell at each other openly when we feel
like it, and we have never been so close. When I go on
walks, often I yell to the roar of the ocean—yell out my
strength, rage, laughter, joy, whatever comes. I feel a
part of the whole world, at home in it. When something doesn't go my way, I let go of my idea of how it
should be, trusting that my mind doesn't know the
larger picture. . . .*

*I am learning more and more deeply what a pre-
cious gift this cancer has been, teaching me how to
live.*

ELIZABETH RIVERS

For most of us, acne was as much a part of adolescence as
physical awkwardness and emotional turmoil. Because of its
universal nature, we hesitate to label it a disease. After all,
isn't it a normal and expected part of growing up?

Intrigued by how common acne is, Wallace Ellerbroek, a
surgeon turned psychiatrist, decided to investigate the role
that emotions might play in provoking it. He selected
thirty-eight patients of various ages, all of whom had acne so
severe that it clearly interfered with their lives. None of
them had sought treatment by a dermatologist. However, all
but six were receptive to Ellerbroek's psychological approach, which led to a remarkable improvement within two
months for thirty of the thirty-two cooperative subjects.

Ellerbroek began by observing the acne patients as they
discussed their lives:

When I was discussing unpleasant matters with a patient, often his hand would go to his face, chest, leg or opposite arm, and one or more fingernails would scratch for a moment while he was searching for words. I began to watch for this response while deliberately stressing patients, and was amazed with the consistency with which this bit of behavior was produced. In addition, I became aware that, as far as I could tell, every time I felt picked on, I itched! . . . I also subjectively and introspectively noted that if the 'picked on' feeling metamorphosed promptly into a mild depressed feeling, the itching did not occur, and instead a typical depressive sigh was the reaction. It appeared to me that this itching behavior occurred in greater intensity and higher frequency in individuals with either active acne or acne scars.[1]

Ellerbroek concluded that acne may be a reaction to an emotional attitude of being picked on, nagged at, and wanting to be left alone. These suppressed and perhaps unconscious emotions are expressed through an itching sensation, which in turn leads to habitual scratching. The facial lesions, then, are the result of an infection of already sensitive skin. In patient after patient, Ellerbroek identified a feeling of being chronically picked on; almost all of life's setbacks were interpreted by these individuals as abuse personally directed at them. Treatment, Ellerbroek reasoned, should be aimed at changing the patient's outlook on life, rather than simply curing each new infection.

Through psychotherapy, Ellerbroek tried to help his patients resolve the unhappiness in their lives. He guided them toward expressing the negative emotions that had built up for months or years. In effect, he also taught them "positive thinking" and positive behavior, and how to improve their posture and facial expression. Miraculously, the acne cleared up as Ellerbroek's program was put into effect.

Although most dermatologists agree that emotional factors play a significant role in the development of acne, few have ever attempted to treat the physical symptom by trying to change emotional attitudes and behavior. Ellerbroek placed the illness in its context, which more physicians must begin to do with all illnesses if an enduring change in the disease process is ever to occur.

Illness as a Sign of Emotional Repression

Not long ago, I began treating a woman in her late twenties who was unable to hold food down. She was recently divorced and was struggling to make it on her own without support from her parents. She felt isolated and had little sense of her capabilities and long-term goals.

For one of her therapy sessions, I asked her to bring a meal to eat with me. Shortly after we began eating, she gagged and vomited. I then told her to focus totally on the feeling in her stomach. As she did, the gag reflex evolved into an unbearable pain near her heart. Whenever she turned her attention away from the terrible discomfort, she started to gag again, so I asked her to keep concentrating on the pain.

As the minutes passed and as she continued exploring the pain, feelings and memories about her parents began to surface. She was obsessed with negative thoughts of herself, which she said were related to an absence of love and nurturing from her mother. Her way of escaping from her rejecting mother was, in essence, by throwing her up. She cried uncontrollably for several minutes, but after the session was over, she was able to eat a meal without vomiting. We had pinpointed a clear connection between her throwing up and the repressing of painful and threatening feelings.

Another patient, a victim of an ulcer, experienced her stomach pain as a lid that restrained and inhibited her. After I asked the woman to imagine herself removing the lid, she began to dance freely, she became very happy, and the intensity of her pain decreased sharply.

Still another ulcer patient told me he had reluctantly taken over the family business to please his parents, and he resented them for the pressure they placed on him to do so.

He expressed his anger only inwardly, finding it difficult to confront his parents, or face the consequences of making his own decisions.

Such examples suggest the direct link between physical symptoms and suppressed emotions. The symptom is actually a veiled expression of the feeling, or perhaps a message that the emotion within needs to find a more outward expression. Very often, an exploration of hidden feelings leads to discoveries that significantly alleviate symptoms.

To some extent, I believe that a physical symptom masks an emotional attitude. Once this feeling is uncovered and expressed, the body is freed to heal the symptom, or cease reinfecting or reinjuring the affected part of the body.

Emotions and the body are deeply intertwined. Emotions, apparently produced at the intersection of the visceral brain and the endocrine system, seem to be part of the body's primitive alarm network. Most of them particularly rage, fear, joy, and happiness—are positive or negative expressions of physiological arousal.

Even the finer shades of emotion are connected to physiological activation and our conscious perception of what is happening to us. Anxiety, for example, seems to be a state of expectation that something is going to happen, combined with an inability to pinpoint what it is or to react appropriately. The body is aroused for action, but we don't know where, how, or what to do about it. Emotions, then, might be defined as an attitude and the associated bodily changes.[2]

When an emotion is directly experienced in both the body and the mind, it is accompanied by a discharge of psychophysiological tension and arousal. For instance, don't you feel relieved after an emotional cry or an angry exchange? Isn't your body calm and relaxed? Even so, you probably grew up with some degree of distrust or dislike of your emotions. Many families, as well as most school and work environments, encourage the control and inhibition of one's feelings. In fact, penalties are often placed on people who react emotionally. Almost everyone has at some time been punished for becoming angry, or cautioned not to cry when he or she is upset. Even love, joy, and affection are often discouraged, because they are considered unseemly, or we fear that such feelings will be rejected . No wonder so many of us quickly learn to fear and even distrust our emotions.

Some people eventually lose all awareness of their emotions. Freud and other psychoanalysts detailed the process by which individuals repress, or learn not to experience, their feelings. By adulthood, a person may be aware of few, if any, emotions, although these restrained feelings still manifest themselves through behavior and physical symptoms.

P. D. MacLean, a leading researcher into the connections between brain structure and emotion, has suggested that many illnesses may result when an emotional response is blocked in the conscious brain:

> One of the striking observations regarding the patient with psychosomatic illness is his apparent intellectual inability to verbalize his emotional feelings. . . .
>
> It would almost seem there was little direct exchange between the visceral brain and the word brain [cortex], and that emotional feelings built up in the hippocampal formation [part of the limbic system], instead of being relayed to the intellect for evaluation, found immediate expression through autonomic centers. In other words, emotional feelings, instead of finding expression and discharge in the symbolic use of words and appropriate behavior, might be conceived as being translated into a kind of "organ language."[3]

MacLean suggests that symptoms can be relieved by helping the patient understand and experience his feelings and reactions to life.

I have heard from a seriously ill woman who used her sickness as a motivation to intensively examine her feelings and relationships. She wrote the following about her life situation at the time of her illness:

> I felt trapped from all sides in my marriage. I married for some kind of security, and I suffered from one obscure ailment after another. I couldn't separate depressions from chronic fa-

tigue, and I wanted to look everywhere but at my marriage for reasons. I saw doctors continuously with pains, headaches, etc. I finally went into therapy but continued to skirt my trapped feelings. I couldn't move in any direction and I was screaming inside, ready to explode.

My face broke out in big boils and deep acne six months after I had a baby. A year later I had a malignant growth taken from my leg. I took the surgery like a soldier, brave and stoic, feeling nothing. My life continued on that repressed plane, and another growth formed. I began to think I was a surefire candidate for cancer, and I began exploding. Nothing was more important than breaking out of an unbearable steel trap. I hate to hurt others, but everything had to change for me to free myself from the destructive patterns. I quit smoking, my job, my marriage, and toxic relationships. Finally, I was overtly angry, but I couldn't understand it. I seemed to be hurting myself as I attempted to free my emotions.

Anger is still most frightening to me as it now comes easily at inappropriate times. But my health has returned, for the first time in years. I seem to have exchanged deep and confusing feelings, that I still struggle to understand, for deep and destructive physical illness.

Many types of illness have been linked to inhibited frustration and anger. Studies by Herbert Weiner indicate that ulcer patients have more in common than simply hypersecreting stomachs. Typically, they also have intense psychological needs to be loved and cared for, which have been chronically frustrated. However, these people repress their anger, fearing that it will alienate others. Instead, they are withdrawn and inhibited, and they develop a sense that their world is largely out of their control. When Weiner's study observed these individuals under the stress of an army induction process, their stomachs all ulcerated, as Weiner had predicted.[4] Such studies are only suggestive, but they add to the growing body of evidence linking unmet needs to subsequent helplessness and disease.

Those with other types of chronic symptoms are also often frustrated. They are afraid to ask for what they need, fearing that they won't get it. The Type A person, for example, rather than requesting help, tries to do things for himself. In the process, his blocked emotional needs find expression in the body as illness. In these situations, a stress symptom or pain may simply be an indirect cry for help, or an expression of a half-hidden need or desire.

Consider the case of a middle-aged businessman who developed early signs of multiple sclerosis soon after a setback in his otherwise successful career. His disappointment had left him with lingering fears of losing his job, accompanied by feelings of frustration and helplessness. He eventually expressed his feelings in the organ language of neural decay and stiffening.

A woman developed the same disease during a stressful time in her marriage. Her daughter had suffered several serious childhood illnesses that necessitated hospitalization, and she did not feel the support from her husband that she desperately needed during this difficult period. Like the businessman described above, her feelings were eventually mirrored in her body.

What about less serious diseases? Are even colds or flu connected to emotional stress? Thomas Holmes and his colleagues looked at the emotional life situations of several patients with colds. They found that in most cases, repressed feelings such as anger preceded the onset of minor illness. During interviews with these patients, when their emotionally upsetting circumstances were discussed, their nasal congestion levels immediately rose.[5]

So next time you sneeze, itch, cough, choke, or develop a twinge or slight pain, ask yourself if there might be a feeling within you struggling for expression. In a sense, this is a form of preventive medicine, keeping your feelings from accumulating to a level where they could cause more serious problems.

Unfortunately, it is not always easy to detect an inhibited or repressed emotion. That was the case with a twenty-two-year-old overweight woman with an ulcer. She was a loving, giving person and held a responsible social-service position.

Her boyfriend was a drug addict who, with her help, was forever trying to reform. Yet she never expressed anger or frustration or asked for anything for herself. All she did was give to others. After several therapy sessions, I learned of her resentment, and of her own needs for nurturing and care. I encouraged her to seek fulfillment of her own needs, which she did. Eventually, the condition of her ulcer improved.

A caveat that has already been stated is worthy of being repeated here. My suggestion that each patient explore his hidden emotions or repressed needs does not assume that these feelings necessarily caused an illness or symptoms. However, research studies such as those I've cited indicate that emotional repression can exacerbate or complicate the treatment of simple difficulties. When psychological pressures are removed, the body is freed to work full time on healing. So although emotional expression may help healing, I am not proclaiming that feelings cause illness—a belief that some skeptical physicians mistakenly attribute to holistic practitioners.

Definitive research is still many years away. But because your own needs are current, experiment with some of these connections. There are no dangers or negative side effects in doing so.

Emotions, Attitudes and Specific Illnesses

Are specific diseases related to particular life crises, personality types, or emotions? Perhaps, although there are too many other disease-related factors, including physical influences and various intervening events, to make such an association clear-cut. But even though I have studiously avoided proclaiming this connection as a reflection of reality, physicians have detected a link between emotions, personality, and specific illness for centuries. A growing number of recent studies have added support to this hypothesis.

Psychosomatic experts W. J. Grace and D. T. Graham

conducted in-depth interviews with one hundred twenty-eight patients, each of whom had the symptoms of one of twelve different diseases. The researchers were trying to determine what life situations were associated with attacks of the patients' symptoms. Certain emotional attitudes, they found, were related to the onset of symptoms of each specific disease. They speculated that, in effect, the patients were expressing physiologically what they felt was being done to them in their everyday lives.

For example, twenty-seven patients reported attacks of diarrhea when they wanted to end a particular situation, or to get rid of something or somebody. One man developed this symptom after purchasing a defective automobile, telling the researchers, "If only I could get rid of it!" Defecation, of course, is ridding oneself of substances after the body is done with them.

Another seventeen patients had constipation when they were grimly determined to persevere through a seemingly insurmountable problem. They used statements such as "This marriage is never going to be any better, but I won't quit." And what is constipation but a bodily process of holding on to substances without change, despite discomfort?

Twelve patients with hay fever and seven with asthma articulated another set of attitudes. They faced a situation that they would rather not have had to confront, or that they wished would disappear. They wanted to hide from it, avoid it, and divest themselves from all responsibility for it. Grace and Graham noted that these two syndromes—asthma and hay fever—often occurred together. They are both reactions to an external irritant in which the membranes of the nose and lungs swell up and narrow, in their attempt to dilute the irritant or wash it away. The body, just like the person, wants to get rid of something.

Thirty-one patients suffered from urticaria, a skin reaction to trauma, leading to blistering and inflammation. The patients with this ailment felt they were being interfered with or prevented from doing something they wanted to do. And they could not find a way to deal effectively with their frustration. They were so preoccupied with the way that others interfered with them that it was as if they were being physically beaten by their adversaries—hence the skin blisters. This parallels the "picked-on" feeling of Ellerbroek's acne patients, who, ironically, literally picked on themselves as well.

Nausea and vomiting (in eleven patients) occurred when a person wished something had never occurred. Ulcers (nine patients) were characterized by desires for revenge and getting even. Migraine headaches (fourteen patients) were provoked after a person had made an intense effort to complete a task. Hypertension was common among those who continually worried about meeting all possible threats (Type A behavior). Low-back pain (eleven patients) was found among people who wanted to do something involving the whole body, usually running away.[6]

I find this study particularly useful, not for the purpose of compiling an atlas of feelings embedded within disease symptoms, but because Grace and Graham demonstrated the pathways by which emotions can be translated into body language, particularly when the individual does not think it safe to admit or act on these feelings. My experience suggests that such patients do not initially want their attitudes to become conscious, and look instead for alternate solutions to them. So the feelings simply simmer in hidden anger, frustration, helplessness, anxiety, or pain.

Look back over the list of these attitudes again. We might generalize that many of the most common and chronic diseases occur when a person is unable to deal effectively and adequately with something he dislikes. Disease seems to result when a person inhibits an effective response to the events of his life.

So if you suffer from repeated hay fever, hypertension, diarrhea, constipation, skin disease, pain, or ulcers, your illness may be a negative side effect of your maladaptive response to the stresses and demands you face. In such a situation you should explore your own feelings of inadequacy and ineffectiveness. Do you turn your frustration and negative emotions inward? After exploring your feelings and discovering more effective ways to cope, do your symptoms diminish?

Unfortunately, many of us go through life denying or evading the experience of our feelings. But chronic illness should teach us that although these feelings may be consciously ignored, they continue to act underground on our bodies.

Take an inventory of your common beliefs and attitudes about life events. What do you expect from people? Do you hold others in high or low repute? Do you often feel exploited, or do you experience others as having basic integrity? How do you value your relationships and your work? Do you find yourself optimistic in most situations, or do you expect to be frustrated? On the whole, do you feel that you have received more than you have given to others?

With awareness of your basic attitude, you can begin to challenge it, and discover alternatives to how you perceive and approach life. By making positive changes, you can influence the way you experience your body, and the way it reacts to you.

Healing and Self-Care

I have noted a striking similarity among nearly all the people whom I have helped to examine the psychological dimension of their illnesses. Almost none of them felt good about themselves, nor did they spend much time taking care of their personal needs, either physically or emotionally.

At one of my health-promotion groups, the patients were all presenting similar themes. One woman, for example, felt incapable of expressing her desires or needs to her husband, for fear of angering him. She also believed that he would consider her demands silly. Another woman was burdened by having to care for everything around the house—including the illnesses of her daughter—with little support from her businessman husband, who preferred to ignore emotional problems.

Several other group members had spouses who failed to meet their emotional needs. Even so, not one of them expressed a desire or an ability to seek gratification elsewhere—whether from other people or from a job. One man showed us lists he made each day of what he had to do, but never included anything for his own pleasure or well-being. Another had toiled for years in a profession he was uninterested in, within a family in which he felt ignored and ineffectual. Yet he felt impotent to change his unhappy life situation.

These stories could go on and on. So many of my patients have experienced a neglect of their most basic, deepest human needs—for touching and for companionship, for sharing inner feelings, for expressing creative energy, for sexual fulfillment, for personal validation, and for the giving and receiving of love. Instead, their lives were characterized by duty and obligation to the very people who gave them little or nothing in return.

I often find these people unaware of their needs and unable to talk about them. "Sex!" one woman said. "I guess I have just learned not to want it." Others have similar attitudes about other basic needs. They have accepted a reality of being unsatisfied and believe that life holds no gratification. Hence they simply go through the motions of living, without inner feelings of energy or vitality. They are numb, often sad, depressed, deeply frustrated, or somewhat angry. Yet do they demand redress, or look for change in their world? No; they are like condemned prisoners.

Lawrence Hinkle studied a group of over a thousand telephone company employees. He compared the ten healthiest people in that group with the ten who had the most episodes of illness. He found that the frequently ill had developed a despondency about their role in life:

The members of the high-episode group were more predictably oriented toward an identification with goals in which their own self-interest was not of paramount importance, and with duties, responsibilities, and ideologies; and they showed more concern about, and reaction to, the events and situations which they encountered than did the members of the "low-frequency" group.[7]

In a sense, healthier people are more "selfish." Or perhaps they are simply more aware of their emotional and psychological needs, and thus take more care to satisfy themselves.

By contrast, less healthy people are unable to articulate their personal needs. They are more accustomed to living for others, and they often do too little for themselves, even at the levels of basic hygiene and adequate rest. In treatment, they are, as MacLean suggests, initially unable to pinpoint their feelings, frustrations, anger, or depression.

Fortunately, I find that most of us eventually begin to discover our own needs and our feelings about the people around us. In groups, as well as in individual and family therapy, people with chronic symptoms plan ways to meet their needs and to experience themselves as less helpless. They create a health strategy that includes basic hygiene and physical self-care, and they also look at what they want in emotional, vocational, and family relationships.

Invariably, these men and women become less depressed by their illnesses, and they experience their symptoms as less limiting, painful, and oppressive. Patients who had once told me such things as "I can't do things because of my back" stop using their illness as an excuse for not getting or doing what they want. When this happens, they find more energy within themselves.

Of course, some of us have difficulty deciding exactly what our desires are. For example, one woman consistently said, "I want my daughter"—or son, or husband, or mother—"to be happy; that would make me happy." I find that this pattern reflects more self-denial than self-care, even though it obviously does feel good to help one's family.

My own conclusions are that negative feelings and lack of self-love and self-respect may be mirrored in our bodies. It is a persuasive hypothesis, and it bears exploration in your own life. Individuals who take care of themselves, feel optimistic, receive as well as give, and are aware of and use their negative and positive feelings as guides for action are likely to be healthier people.

10 *The Family: Crucible of Illness*

*It is necessary to realize that every individual born
into a society is from birth—and in all probability
from before birth—subjected to progressive moulding
by the culture, mediated through all those with whom
he comes into contact, so that the cultural pattern is
built into his whole personality in one process in
which no dualism exists, so that the temper tantrums,
the tightened muscles, the change in the manufacture
of blood sugar, and the verbal insults hurled at an of-
fending parent, all become patterned and integrated.
Then we see that every individual, and not merely
every patient, may be viewed from the psychosomatic
point of view, within which individuals who show definite organ neuroses are merely extreme and special de-
velopments of one potentiality of the total personality.
And we further see that there is no basic human personality but that every individual must be seen against
the cultural base line, that he is a special idiosyncratic
variant of one of many culturally unique ways in
which human personality is developed.*

MARGARET MEAD

The patient enters his physician's office alone. In this setting
there is rarely an exploration of the possible relationship of
the family to the particular illness. Although a physician
would never examine an organ system out of the context of
the whole body and try to understand its dysfunction, he
probably won't investigate how the family environment has
affected the physiology of the patient.

Tina, a victim of multiple sclerosis, had been treated by
some of the nation's best specialists. In the two years imme-

diately before I saw her, she had rapidly degenerated. MS is a disease that may have years of comparatively minor pains, but it can lead to serious nerve damage and crippling and severe incapacitation. I was determined to find out whether family and psychological factors might have affected Tina, particularly during her recent degeneration.

In our first meeting, Tina did not seem to care about helping herself. She was carried into the interview by her son, who was visiting on his college vacation. Her daughter had just graduated from college. We talked about her family and personal history. She had grown up as the responsible, oldest daughter in a close-knit family. When she was twenty, she met her husband and decided to leave college to marry him. At the same time, her younger brother developed a severe case of MS, which soon confined him to a wheelchair.

Tina felt guilty about not staying to nurse her brother. But she did marry and move to a distant city—her first separation from her parents. Each year, when she visited her brother, she left with a stiffness in her legs, an early sign of MS. Also, she believed from the moment her brother was diagnosed that she too was destined to develop the disease.

The growth of Tina's family followed the standard American dream. She became a housewife and raised her children, while her husband worked. He was an assertive businessman who had earned prominence in local affairs and was a pillar of the community. She described her marriage as both "happy and fulfilling" and said that her spouse made the decisions in the household. Sometimes she wished he would work less and take more vacations with the family. Two years before, when her son had left home, her symptoms had dramatically worsened. Never having worked, she said she had nothing to do or look forward to.

A few days after my initial session with Tina, she returned for her next meeting accompanied by her husband. He was an engaging and earnest man, and he was very concerned about her. As we talked, I noticed that he almost totally dominated the conversation, speaking directly to me and almost ignoring her. I asked her if she ever felt angry at being cut off or not listened to, and she responded, "A little." As our conversation continued, I discovered that the only time that she had ever influenced his decisions (regarding what to do, when and where to take vacations, or when to spend time with her) was when her legs hurt.

Tina seemed angry and disappointed with some aspects of her life and her relationship with her husband, although she had been taught never to express feelings. Instead, her unhappiness and depression seemed to be manifested against herself. She refused to participate in a physical-therapy program, and while she could have learned to walk with a cane, she used a cumbersome walker, or was carried. She rarely left the house, and she had turned down an offer from a friend to work in her boutique. She seemed de-energized and hopeless—a psychic state which has negative implications for healing.

My work with Tina took several directions. The first step was to involve her in a treatment program and to find a fulfilling activity for her. With the encouragement of her children and husband, she began to work in her friend's boutique. She developed her own physical-therapy program and adhered to the regimen regularly. She also started practicing the relaxation and visualization exercises that will be described later in this book. Using biofeedback equipment, she was able to see that her efforts were giving her more control over her muscles than she had had in years. Tina found this encouraging, because it proved that she had some power over her illness.

I worked extensively on her marriage and her feelings of low self-worth and powerlessness. She became more sensitive to her anger, and learned to talk about it with her husband. She openly discussed her guilt at having "abandoned" her parents and brother, and how she had perceived herself as only a servant—not only to the family she grew up with, but to her husband and children as well. As Tina began to think of life's potential, and as she pursued a family-oriented psychological and physical treatment program, she improved dramatically.

As Tina's story demonstrates, sickness is definitely a family affair, which both affects and is affected by family bonds. Rarely is illness suffered in solitude and silence. Instead, as I pointed out earlier in the book, the patient often enters a state of childlike dependence, expecting his family members to help him make doctors' appointments, comply with his medical treatment, and, most important, offer solace, sympathy, and care. Because of the strong emotional bonds in a family, the patient's periods of gloom and depression are often reflected in everyone around him.

We cannot understand health or illness if we look at mind and body alone. Rather than existing as isolated units, we are part of a larger set of systems, including a family, an extended family, a community, a work group, and a society. To understand the roots of your particular illness, you have to look not only at yourself, but at your external life context as well.

I often think of the family as a protective envelope, forming a first line of defense and protection against the environment. The home is like a social skin. The people within that skin, like the organs of the body itself, can function as a harmonious whole, or as a series of conflicting elements. A person's most basic needs—for food, clothing, and shelter—can be met within the family unit, as can his or her sexual and emotional requirements. The family nurtures and protects a young child, and over the years helps him create his own identity so that eventually he can establish a more independent life.

An individual's state of health can be influenced by the way his family raises him and meets his emotional needs and by the degree of harmony or conflict within the household. When family relationships are secure, comfortable, nurturing, meaningful, pleasant, and supportive of his well-being, they contribute to his health. When he experiences a conflict, loss, breakdown, or other difficulty within the family, he will mobilize his adaptive energy resources (via the stress response) to protect himself—but not always successfully.

Family Conflict and Homeostasis

"You make me sick!"

Those words are often shouted in anger between spouses or between a parent and a child. And although the phrase is rarely meant literally, it is frequently an accurate reflection of how emotional turmoil can indeed drive a person to physical illness. Conflict within a family can cause symptoms to surface almost instantly. A therapist I know described a couple visited by the wife's mother, who had a poor and unpleasant relationship with her son-in-law. Within a day, the mother developed insomnia, the son-in-law eczema, and the daughter depression. When the mother left, so did all the symptoms.

Or perhaps you can identify with "vacation fever." It is common among students returning home for the holidays, and among families unaccustomed to spending much time together. These situations can be a source of anxiety, often expressed by becoming sick.

Even the most minor symptoms—colds, headaches, flu—can be related to family feelings. If you suffer them with regularity, you might minimize their frequency by examining your circumstances and emotions when the symptoms arise. Often if one simply recognizes and acknowledges the existence and validity of a particular emotion, the cold or headache will not occur. Some discover they must openly express their conflict, anger, or feeling to the relevant people to avoid physical symptoms.

But not surprisingly, many find it difficult to express anger or respond directly to conflict with other family members. Instead, they are content to treat their symptoms by consuming bottle after bottle of aspirin, antihistamine, or more potent drugs, without ever exploring why the symptoms surface so often. So a despondent wife, infuriated at her husband, takes pills and retires to bed. Or the father, defied by his son, suffers an angina attack. That is his way of saying, "Look how painful your defiance is to me," without ever having to speak openly about his feelings. Also, by becoming ill, he makes it difficult for his son or his wife to respond to his feelings. Instead, the wife may think, "How can I be angry at him? After all, he's sick." Or the son may say, "I feel terrible about this. I've got to start being nicer to Dad."

The connection between emotional stress, family conflict, physiological reactions, and physical illness has been demonstrated in an ingenious research program by family psychiatrist Salvador Minuchin. He was working with a family in which the daughter had a highly variable form of diabetes, which seemed to be activated by certain kinds of family conflicts. Minuchin conducted a family psychotherapy session. Each member was connected to a blood catheter, which took samples of blood at five-minute intervals. He then measured the level of free fatty acid in each sample, which is considered to be a physiological indicator of emotional arousal.

Minuchin discovered that each person's acid level, and hence emotional arousal, increased during discussion of topics personally relevant to him or her. For example, the arousal level of the parents was lowest when their attention was focused on the problems of their diabetic daughter, while during those same times, their daughter's arousal was high. It rose even higher when the therapist placed the young girl in a situation in which her parents were in conflict and she felt she had to choose sides. Subsequently, the daughter was taken out of the room and allowed to watch the family through a one-way mirror, while the parents talked between themselves about difficulties in their marriage. Her level of arousal dropped significantly, while that of her parents soared.[1]

Of course, family conflicts are hardly the sole or even the primary cause of disease. Other factors—including hereditary predisposition, weak organs and physical systems, personality makeup, stress management, beliefs, and expectations—can also play a role. But Minuchin clearly demonstrated that family conflicts affect the status and perhaps even the origin of many physical ailments.

I have worked with many families plagued by physical illness and have found that in almost every instance, some connection existed between illness and family relations. In most of these cases, a relatively brief period of psychological exploration uncovered ways that the family complicated the illness, and successful approaches to decrease stress were developed.

Lethal Dyads

According to folk wisdom, a married couple may begin to look alike after years together. Although it's doubtful whether the physical appearances of spouses really do start to coincide, many or most other aspects of their lives eventually overlap. By sharing a house, children, sex, housework, economics, and experiences, they become interdependent, and their inner and outer rhythms harmonize.

Working with this premise, it's not surprising that couples can escalate each other's potentiality for illness by their way of responding to conflict in their relationship. It is not simply a particular personality makeup that triggers illness, but a pair of personalities, each responding to the other in a certain way. Unless the pattern can be changed, they drive each other to chronic illness, a fate which perhaps neither would have faced if they had never met.

I have come upon many examples of these "lethal dyads," as have other researchers. Psychosomatic researcher Sidney Cobb and his associates noted such a pattern in their article "Why Do Wives with Rheumatoid Arthritis Have Husbands with Peptic Ulcers?"[2] The ulcer personality is typically hard-driving and anxious, with a need to please and receive praise. He may be attracted to a woman with the rheumatoid-arthritis personality, who has always wanted status and esteem, but has been frustrated. They each initially see the other as meeting their needs and desires. As the marriage unfolds, the wife finds that her needs are unmet, and she becomes angry. Meanwhile, her husband worries, and is frustrated because he does not receive the emotional support he wants.

This growing and mutual hostility finally leads them both to develop, or exacerbate, their potential illnesses. Their patterns of avoidance and anger provoke their physiologies, swelling the wife's joints and ulcerating the husband's stomach. If either had married into a more benign environment, their physiological and personality predispositions might never have been triggered.

One middle aged couple I worked with were lethal dyads. The husband described himself as a "workaholic," an engineer whose personality could clearly be labeled Type A (aggressive, driven, competitive, obsessive). He had experienced a serious coronary and had subsequently reduced his workload. Soon thereafter, his wife contracted cancer.

Before their illnesses, the husband had always willingly shouldered responsibility in the household, while his wife became more and more helpless and dependent on his initiative. His heart attack forced her, in essence, to switch roles. At this point, she developed cancer, which in turn concerned him so that he began assuming responsibility again, paying the bills and taking care of her.

Thus, a lethal cycle was set in motion. His illness seemingly resulted, at least in part, from his taking on too many obligations and driving himself too hard. When the roles with his wife were reversed, she reacted with a physiological breakdown herself, as if trying to return him to his accustomed role. After I had helped them balance their lives and they began assisting each other as well as doing things for themselves, each began to recover.

Another researcher, F. C. Hoebel, noted that some male

coronary patients ignored advice to improve their diet, smoking, exercise, and relaxation programs. He decided that their wives could decisively affect their behavior, helping them give up their dangerous activities. Thus, he asked the spouses to participate in a therapy program on their own. Over several sessions, he helped them recognize how, despite good intentions, they may not have been helpful to their husbands' medical recovery. He guided them to develop strategies to encourage positive change within their spouses. Even without the husbands' cooperation, he was able to influence the men to change simply by helping the wives to alter their own behavior.[3]

Hoebel showed that even when the husbands were not cooperative, family treatment might still be successful. The behavior of all family members is important to the ill member's recovery or eventual relapse. If a couple can lead each other to illness or do things that hinder the spouse's recovery, I believe they can also learn to help each other regain health.

The Child as Family Scapegoat

As I emphasized earlier, childhood health is indeed susceptible to the same forces as that of any adult. Both research and clinical practice demonstrate that in many families, the ill child is merely a pawn—a short circuit—for a conflict in the parental relationship, or a reflection of mistaken beliefs on the part of a parent. The child may, in fact, become an innocent victim of a lethal dyad between spouses.

Minuchin divides a psychosomatic crisis in a child into two phases. Here's typically what happens. In the first or "turn-on" phase, a family conflict or interaction during a particularly stressful family event creates a physiological response which triggers the child's illness—perhaps asthma, diabetes, or abdominal pain. The second, or "turn-off," phase may occur after the crisis, when the physiological response decreases and returns to normal levels. However, in some families, the turn-off doesn't occur, because the family maintains its high stress level. And so the child remains ill, and his symptoms become difficult to control via medical treatment.[4]

Often, the ill family member, particularly if a child, becomes the scapegoat for conflict in the home. The illness indirectly helps the other family members feel better, for they can focus their energy and attention on the child and avoid each other and their own troubles. To protect the family, the child in effect has to stay sick! To overcome this dilemma, therapy is aimed at helping the family discontinue the processes which provoke the physical symptoms in one person, and instead look at their own conflicts.

Minuchin has defined certain interaction patterns that are inherent in families with psychosomatically ill children. The first quality is enmeshment—that is, parents and children seem to be excessively involved in each other's affairs, such as regularly intruding on each other's privacy. These families take togetherness to an extreme and have almost no private life. Children are dragged into their parents' struggles and are part of every aspect of their lives.

The family members are so concerned for one another that the slightest indication of an illness or problem arouses a flurry of nurturing responses. A sneeze, a fever, or any sign of discomfort worries the others into action. The family is always concerned about the child's health, often being so overprotective that the child is kept from doing anything independently.

Still another family quality is a very rigid system of interaction, with an intense need to maintain the status quo and avoid change. Thus, a physical difficulty is not turned off, gotten over, or forgotten, but rather becomes a chronic part of the family. It is difficult to adapt to new situations (such as developing independence in their youngsters), which can be perceived as threatening and fearsome. Parents often "infantilize" their children, using their supposed weakness and vulnerability to keep them from leaving the house. Finally, these families have problems discussing their conflicts and

differences of opinion, tending to deny that such differences
even exist.

Imagine growing up in such an environment. A youngster
may feel pressure to side with one parent or the other, and
fear saying anything that one or the other parent will interpret as against him. Or he may become allied with one parent against the other.

Not long ago, I treated a woman who, whenever she was
angry at her husband, would confide in her asthmatic ten-
year-old son, telling him that he was the "only one who understood her." The father was indifferent and seemingly uninvolved in the family. The parents had no sexual relations.
The mother seemed to put all her energy into her son, taking
care of him and in a sense asking him never to leave her
emotionally the way his father had.

As the boy felt the conflict and the responsibility of his
role, he became weak and developed a serious case of
asthma, aggravating a hereditary predisposition. Ill children,
whether as a consequence or a cause of their malady (probably a little of both), tend to be protected by parents, and
they develop few relationships with friends and achieve little independence from the family. They are enmeshed, unable to separate from each other.

In this case, I helped the boy become more independent
from the family and persuaded his parents to be less concerned, intrusive, and involved with their child's physical
state. I tried to cut any secondary gain the son might be receiving by encouraging him to play more often with friends.
I asked the physician to reassure the family that the child
was not seriously ill and could be active without medical
risk. This eased their anxiety to some degree. I also tried to
motivate the father to do more with his son. Both were interested in sports, but the father had avoided them because
he felt his son was not interested or strong enough. But my
suggestion allowed the boy to make contact with his father.
And the youngster's attacks became less severe.

At this stage of the treatment, the distance between the

parents became obvious, as their child moved away from them and more toward his friends. This parental conflict was not so obvious until the child's illness was no longer the family's central focus. So it was addressed in the final stage of therapy. I began to see the couple separately, and they recognized that they had very little to say to one another and had spent very little time together. They also faced the fact that their lack of sexual contact was damaging their relationship and keeping them distant from each other. They entered therapy together to work on these issues, and their son's asthma ceased to be their main object of attention.

Too often, then, the sick child becomes a defense mechanism, a stress response, on a family level. The therapist needs to help the parents reverse the negative side effects of this process by removing the child from the major focus.

From the parental point of view, the entire situation may sound rather evil, but it is not one of conscious duplicity. It usually starts with an unavoidable episode of illness. But gradually, other expectations or needs come into play. Psychiatrist Warren Brodey relates the story of a family he calls the Targets, who focus all their concern, anger, and energy on a person they have selected as the family "target":

> The Target family tracks targets against which all the family forces can be directed. One child, one parent, one cause, one illness, are seemingly specific, but whatever is convenient is actually converted into focus. This focus takes all the attention. They lose track of one another except in target practice. They may each destroy the other.
>
> "He is a little nervous." This off-hand comment by the teacher may set him as the target. A diagnosis may call forth its symptom, and the child behaves to fit the role expected.
>
> Target: "Dot was premature," said Mother. "She's been sickly since. Bad chests run in the family. My sister had TB. We always look after her health. She won't play because she doesn't have any muscle coordination. No. She rarely goes out. The children say she doesn't play; it gets so raw outside, and she looks so pale and sickly. She tries to be brave and wants to

go out, but we know she just doesn't want us to worry because she isn't well."

The family focuses down on one single event as on a spot. They do not see the spiral, the reinforcement, over time.[5]

In this way, a child can have a congenital weakness which over time evolves into a chronic condition. The youngster "cooperates" because of the attention he may be receiving, unknowingly creating a situation in which he gets worse ⁻ather than better. The physician can become an accomplice as he cautiously tries to discover what is wrong—but only with the child, not with the family. In a family-oriented treatment program, the physician must be active. The child is slowly weaned from his symptom, eventually to the point where he is not rewarded by attention and love when he is ill.

Not surprisingly, a child is susceptible to much more than a direct conflict between his parents, but also perhaps to something more subtle—conflict from preceding generations. In one family, the son had a severe, uncomfortable, and intractable skin illness. After a period of unsuccessful treatment, a family therapy session revealed that the illness had developed soon after the father's parents died suddenly, within months of each other. Evidently, the father's stress was communicated to the boy. Psychological tension, then, can be passed from one family member to another.

Psychiatrist Norman Paul has traced some family conflicts, and their subsequent physical symptoms in individual members, to the death of a relative who was not fully mourned. In his therapy, he helps the family to mourn and remember the dead relative. In turn, this relieves the burden upon the person suffering from the symptom.[6]

For example, a child born soon after a relative dies may be pushed into playing that person's role in the family, or being like that individual if he resembles the deceased. That role may include taking on some of that person's physical illnesses.

We also know that the beliefs of other family members can easily become transferred to ourselves. If we expect to die at a certain age just as our father or mother did, as many people do, we might find our dire prediction coming true. Or a young girl who is told she will end up like her mother may begin to believe this.

The methods of inducing illness in other family members are an area which health professionals have only begun to examine. As of now, aside from a few researchers such as Minuchin, it is explored mainly by certain family-oriented psychotherapists.

But even at this early stage of research, I believe that illness does not simply occur within an individual but is a process that is affected by, and alters, family relationships. Physician Richard Arbogast is developing ways that doctors can assess these factors in illness—and in essence, see the "family as patient."

I always ask an individual who comes for help with an illness to bring his or her spouse. A child is accompanied by parents. When I assign a patient an exercise, I include the other family members in this therapeutic process. Their perspective is invaluable, and with a little encouragement, they can help uncover the role of a symptom. While family relationships may help trigger ailments, it is rarely a conscious, dishonest, or intentionally harmful act. Most often, when the connection between habitual behavior, inhibition of feelings, and hidden conflict is recognized, a family spontaneously begins to work together to alter these patterns, and its members become positive influences on each other.

11 *The Lost Connections: Individuality,*

Meaning and Community

The Cure comes from the medicine
and the art of medicine
originates in charity.
Hence,
to be cured is not a work of Faith
but one of sympathy.
The true ground of medicine is love.
PARACELSUS

In the early 1960s, medical researchers marveled at the residents of Roseto, Pennsylvania. A comprehensive study of the people of this closely knit Italian-American village revealed a startlingly low incidence of the most common diseases of civilization. Only one in 1,000 Rosetan men died of heart attacks (compared to the national average of 3.5 per 1,-000), while the female rate was even less—0.6 per 1,000 (far below the national average of 2.09 per 1,000 women). Rosetans also experienced lower levels of other ailments—including peptic ulcers and senility—than the rest of the country.

Doctors were initially puzzled by the good physical health of these people, particularly because they exhibited various "risk factors" typically linked to heart disease. Both the men and women of Roseto were comparatively overweight, with levels of animal fat in their diet at least equal to neighboring towns. They had serum cholesterol, hypertension, and diabetes levels comparable to the nearby communities, and their exercise and smoking patterns were about the same—but nevertheless, their overall physical health was better.

After ruling out genetic and ethnic factors, researchers ultimately concluded that the supportive cultural structure of Roseto deserved the credit for its people's physical well-being. Stewart Wolf, vice-president for medical affairs at St. Luke's Hospital in Bethlehem, Pennsylvania, said that Roseto's culture "reflected tenaciously held old-world values and customs. We found that family relationships were extremely close and mutually supportive. This cohesive quality extended to neighbors and to the community as a whole."

The researchers noted that the elderly were loved and respected, and cared for in the homes of their families when illness struck. When a particular individual or family experienced financial problems, relatives and even the community in general offered assistance.

However, as the 1960s proceeded, changes occurred in Roseto. Many of its residents in their thirties and younger showed some dissatisfaction with the tradition and social isolation of their community. They began striving for certain common American middle-class goals, including job advancement, larger houses, and other material possessions. And the town gradually changed.

By 1965, Wolf noted that the young adults in Roseto "joined country clubs in the nearby Poconos; they bought Cadillacs; they replaced old, tradition-rich wooden houses with sprawling suburban ranch-style structures; they began attending outside churches, or no church at all. . . . It seemed like a capsulized, accelerated fulfillment of the American dream."

Amid this transition, one other major change occurred in Roseto. The heart-attack death rate rose dramatically, particularly among men younger than age fifty-five. Researchers concluded that the breakdown of families, community purpose, and camaraderie was to blame for the increased number of heart attacks.[1]

Roseto is not a rare phenomenon. Although many factors

can provoke illness, some research now indicates that the loss of cultural connection and human interdependence is often a critical influence. When a person loses intimate, meaningful contact with his or her community, with the love and care of others, and with a sense of inner coherence, unity, and purpose in life, the seeds of disease are created. This illness is an outgrowth of a social/spiritual/existential crisis.

Before aspirins, tranquilizers, and high-risk operations, an ill person had no choice but to begin the process of self-reflection and explore the possibility of his own responsibility in the development of the illness. Today, all that many patients want—and receive—from their physicians is some relief so that they can return to their lives exactly as they had been leading them, even though their lives may have been contributing to their illness. Too often, patients simply tell their doctors, "Please give me a pill so I can get back to work."

Ancient healers recognized the importance of community influences in the manifestation of disease. To them, illness was a message from the gods that the afflicted person's soul was in disarray. He had ignored the natural order, perhaps by excessive striving. Today, that wisdom is strikingly applicable, particularly in towns like Roseto where various ailments are prevalent because of a community undergoing change.

Long ago, healing involved discovering the reasons for suffering, and making changes which brought an individual back into balance with himself and his community. The cure often involved a journey to a healing shrine or temple, where a person first purified himself. Then he proceeded on to a healer or oracle, who sometimes appeared in a vision or a dream and offered information that the patient acted upon to change his life. This healing "miracle" was not something given from the outside, but was instead an experience from within.

With our modern, scientific orientation, we generally perceive such spiritual perspectives of disease, healing, and life as contradictory and unable to coexist with contemporary medical teachings. The typical physician believes that he has made the spiritual approach obsolete and that until the present century, there was really no medicine, and hence no healing. However, in these complex times, when we have lost touch with so much that is important, I believe that a re-examination of the spiritual aspects of illness and healing is needed, not to supersede science, but to expand upon it.

The Individual and the Collective

Many observers of contemporary society, writing in popular magazines and specialized journals, have labeled this era both the Age of Anxiety and the Age of the Self. At first glance, the two might not seem related. But as in cases such as Roseto, evidence is mounting that overinvolvement with oneself, at the expense of the community, leads to psychological dislocation that results not only in anxiety, but in various physical ailments as well.

Often an individual will become preoccupied with himself amid a search for personal enlightenment or self-actualization, perhaps during psychotherapy. Or this self-indulgence may be a consequence of the individualism and capitalistic ethic which are the foundations of our culture.

You may have been raised believing that if everyone concentrated primarily on his or her own self-interest, the community as a whole would prosper. It's one of the basic dogmas on which this society was founded. Yet take a look at the world around you. Has commitment to the self created the paradise we've sought? The communities in which we live show signs of decay, marriage and other forms of personal commitment are dispensable, and few individuals are concerned about the environment as a whole. In general, our sense of collective purpose and meaning is languishing.

Were any of the ancient shamans here to advise us, they

would recognize these signs as important social omens. Collective pain, suffering, and disaster are difficult symptoms to ignore. The ancient prophets believed that no one could meaningfully be considered apart from the community. The modern concept of individuality or personality, of one's own fate as separate from that of one's fellows, had not been developed. Therefore, individual illness conveyed a message about the whole community.

When a person becomes ill, he is lost as a productive member of the community. Ideally, the role of his physician or healer is to help the patient reestablish contact with the rest of society.

The research at Roseto is not the only support for the view that loss of an individual's place in the community is related to illness. One study by Pflanz discovered that "voluntary exclusion or forced expulsion from a community or group coincided, with astonishing frequency, with the onset or the relapse of a peptic ulcer."[2] Research by Thomas Holmes showed that tuberculosis occurred more frequently in "marginal" people who had been deprived of meaningful social contact. Men and women who lived alone, who were single or divorced, who were members of minority groups, or who moved frequently and consequently felt displaced were more likely to get TB.[3] This same finding applied to schizophrenia.[4]

At the turn of the century, the French sociologist Emile Durkheim, in his monumental work *Suicide*, demonstrated that suicides (the best measure of social distress at that time) occurred more frequently among those who lived isolated lives or were part of cultures that offered fewer guidelines for living and sense of community. Suicides were more prevalent among urban, Protestant, widowed, and divorced people, and during periods of economic uncertainty. By contrast, those who were married, Catholic, or lived in rural communities had correspondingly lower rates. Suicide levels were also lower during times of prosperity.[5]

The implications of Durkheim's study for modern society are grim. His research suggests that the current trends toward divorce, constant job and status changes, frequent moves, abandonment of one's extended family, and declining sense of community all increase the tendency toward illness. It is as if we need more life energy to adapt and cope in such environments than we would in a predictable, static, and interconnected community in which we were sure of our place.

I was amazed when I first compared the health statistics of Utah and Nevada. In Utah, the population is 72 percent Mormon. Mormonism is a religious sect with strong family ties and community obligations. Nevada's chief industry is gambling, and its population includes many rootless, isolated, mobile people. Of all the fifty states, Utah has the lowest incidence of tuberculosis, major cardiovascular and renal diseases, psychological illnesses, hypertension, infectious diseases, and infant mortality. It ranks forty-ninth in flu, pneumonia, and arteriosclerosis. But in neighboring Nevada, the health patterns are dramatically different. It is at or near the top of the list in most of these same ailments. While Utah's nonurbanized life-style may partially account for the population's health, the social cohesion and community stability of the Mormons surely support their well-being.

People's inner reactions, including their tangle of emotional responses, provide clues to explain illnesses. It has often been noted that survivors of such trauma as military combat, air crashes, hijackings, and natural disasters develop a variety of serious physical and emotional symptoms. Survivors and also those connected to them clearly perceive how fragile human life is, the terrible irrationality of fate, and the lack of justice or meaning in a traumatic disaster. The senselessness, and the feeling that life may be quite meaningless, can precipitate both physical and emotional symptoms. "Why bother, nothing seems to matter," the body seems to say. Until survivors receive emotional counseling to help them make sense out of their confused feelings of anger, responsibility, guilt, and confusion, they remain at risk for all types of ailments and problems.

Why should there be such an intimate connection be-

tween dislocation and the health of the individual? Philosopher David Bakan envisions health as a state in which the organism is guided by a harmonious sense of purpose. When
this purpose is ignored or distorted, he asserts, disease results. Cancer, for example, results from damage by maverick
cells that have lost touch with an organizing center which
tells them their place in the whole person.

In disease, says Bakan, the harmonious integration of the
body breaks down into two opposing forces. The result is a
civil war, of the body or the mind against itself. Freud's theory of neurosis and Selye's theory of diseases of adaptation
are both premised on this internal-conflict principle. The
goal of healing is to restore harmony, unity, balance, and
integration.[6]

Sociologist Philip Slater relates a vivid example of how
love and acceptance—even from himself—led to his own
healing. For years he had had an ugly, disfiguring wart on
his thumb. After seeking medical treatment, he decided to
try an experiment. He began to love and accept his thumb.
He bathed it, kissed it, talked to it, and looked at it constantly. Within a few days, the wart went away and has
never returned.[7]

But what about the more startling "miracle" healings we
hear and read about, where some force beyond the individual seemingly intervenes to restore health after all medical
measures have failed? Most physicians discredit such stories,
refusing to inquire into what might have actually taken
place. One explanation for these "healings" is that perhaps
the patient rediscovered some transcendental or spiritual
purpose in life, and the love and feelings of connection with
a spiritual power or community. Could this have provided
the needed resources to restore him to health?

A study by cardiologists White and Liddon of heart-attack
victims who recovered found that five out of ten of them experienced what they called a "transcendental redirection"—
a spiritual experience of rebirth and transformation—which
they felt benefited their healing.[8] People who decisively

overcome a life-threatening illness very often undergo such an experience as part of the recovery process.

This is certainly an area that needs further research. As I observe many cases of so-called spiritual healings, I find my curiosity aroused, not my assumptions threatened. How, I wonder, can I increase the frequency of these experiences for my patients, since they so clearly facilitate healing?

Healing Relationships, Rituals and Communities

What is the worst possible punishment for a crime? Life imprisonment? Death by execution? In many "primitive" cultures, the supreme punishment was neither death nor long-term imprisonment, but banishment forever from the community, and from contact or connection with its people. This was considered worse than death, because the community was viewed as a single body from which each person gained life. As research is now verifying, disconnection from the community or from loved ones—via death, divorce, loss of job, or loss of faith and meaning in one's life and future—can lead to many types of psychological or physical illness.

I believe that such events, when they lie behind an illness, are very important because they often point us in the direction of a possible cure. A sensitive and caring physician or therapist can be an extremely important partner in this healing ritual, guiding the patient in the reunion, reconnection, and unification with his family or community. When psychologist Carl Rogers tried to isolate the qualities that made prominent psychotherapists effective, he found that theory and technique were insignificant compared to human qualities of warmth, acceptance, and empathy. The more of these qualities a therapist demonstrated, no matter what his theoretical orientation, the more effective was his work. Rogers learned that healing relationships are not much different from any other caring, intimate partnership. In such a relationship intimacy forges a connection that seems to help create good health.[9]

If you're in pain, whether psychological or physical, you may feel lonely and afraid, isolated from your community. In such a situation, you can really benefit from a healer who can restore wholeness to your body and help you reconnect with your environment. By being cared for by the healer, and intimately connected to him, you may once again sense yourself able, or worthy, to rejoin the community. He can help you understand your pain and discover ways to overcome it. The more you feel cared for, the more faith and hope you will have in your healing and your future.

If you've been fortunate enough to locate a sensitive physician, you know how valuable he can be to the healing process. Bakan suggests that when two people (patient and healer) establish a shared therapeutic goal of healing, this bond in itself begins to soothe the discord in the body.

Thus, the essential element in all healing relationships may not be knowledge or technique, but rather care, love, and concern for the patient. When you approach a doctor, suffering from an ailment you do not understand, you should be concerned with finding its meaning and then overcoming it. You also want to be loved and touched as a human being. For centuries, the caring respect of the healer for the patient was a cornerstone of healing, but it is frequently ignored in the modern doctor-patient relationship. Too often, physicians view their patients as merely diagnostic puzzles. Interestingly, most of the public's complaints about medicine today stem from anger at not being respected and listened to, as if patients know how central this is to healing.

Almost all caring and healing encounters will be most effective when they assume a ritualistic quality. Whether a patient journeys to Lourdes or to the office of a noted medical specialist, he arrives full of hope and expectancy, to be in a unique presence. It's difficult to pinpoint how potent the spiritual aspects of these rituals are, but perhaps we aren't tapping them nearly enough.

Consider, for instance, Rolling Thunder, the Shoshone medicine man, who performed a healing ritual at the Menninger Clinic on a patient with an infected leg who knew nothing of his practices. As participants in the scientific convention looked on, Rolling Thunder proceeded through the ritual, which concluded after he sucked the "poison" from the leg, vomiting it out in the corner of the room.[10]

The healing was effective, but why? Was it because of the sensitivity and the concern that Rolling Thunder felt for the man he healed, which he communicated to that patient? Or was it the intense focus and concern of the entire convention, contributing to the healing magic? Collective community rituals have always played a part in healing practices.

Just as we have rituals to mark occasions such as births, weddings, and deaths, we might begin to create, or recapture, healing rituals for people who are ill. Psychiatrist Ross Speck, for example, has created a method for treating psychotic patients that he calls "network intervention." He gathers a healing network composed of every individual the patient knows or has contact with, including family, cousins, friends, neighbors, and teachers. During several communal meetings, these people focus all their attention and energy on the sick individual and very often succeed in mobilizing change in illnesses that had previously seemed hopeless. Speck calls this effect "retribalization."

Such rituals can be adapted to the specific belief systems or inclinations of the ill person. The ritual might include symbolic acts which evoke the illness and request the strength to change, or ask for a sign of how a person needs to change. As in the ceremony of the wedding ring, the ill person might make a pact with the community and then be embraced back into its bosom. As with ancient rituals, Speck notes that positive changes result not only for the ill person, but for all who participate.[11]

Are successful rituals simply examples of the placebo effect operating in a positive healing environment? We can't yet say for certain, but they may have more potency than mere positive expectations. Recently, Lawrence LeShan has

proposed a provocative explanation to account for the effectiveness of love, care, prayer, ritual, and intimacy in healing.

LeShan has always been intrigued with the phenomena of
psychic healing. In every culture, there have been religious
and medical healers whose touch or presence had a positive
effect on illness. A renowned healer will have hundreds of
documented miracle cures, from Olga Worrall (who has
conducted free weekly healing services in New York for decades) to Edgar Cayce (who gave health readings and whose
work continues in several clinics today). LeShan was interested not so much in proving that these cures actually
happened but in speculating on *how* they might occur.

LeShan began his research by asking noted psychics to
explain their state of mind during their healings. With great
uniformity, they reported that when they healed, they entered a level of consciousness quite different from the ordinary state of mind. Rather than seeing the world as fluid and
ever-changing, they viewed it as unified, and they felt
closely connected and at one with the people they were
healing.

If that was their state of consciousness, LeShan decided
that the next step was to teach himself to attain that state.
He practiced various forms of meditation and contemplation
and soon found that he, too, could perform healings. He then
began to teach other people and discovered that the gift of
healing potentially lies in everyone and could be developed
through training. He has educated many psychic healers,
who are not charging for their services and are carefully doc-
umenting the success or failure of each attempt at healing.

LeShan also suggests that the healer's state of consciousness is not just a state of mind, but a totally different, yet
valid, way of experiencing reality, with its own strengths
and weaknesses. He finds that with practice, a person can
shift from one level of consciousness to the other. In the
psychic reality of the healer/meditator, all individuals are
experienced as connected. Therefore, one can be in that state
and affect another's illness. This mechanism may, along with

the placebo effect, explain meditation's power for healing, as well as the combined effects of group meditation and other collective rituals, in which a large assemblage enters an alternate reality in which different things are possible.[12]

Other research suggests the measurable effect that psychic healers can have on the body. Dolores Krieger, a nursing professor, has trained herself and many student nurses in what she calls "healing touch," which she believes is an old tradition in nursing. She describes several experiments in which the touch of healers has affected the ionic composition of water in test tubes. In Krieger's own research, a psychic healer touched a sample of blood plasma. The touched and untouched plasma samples were analyzed for the oxygen content of their hemoglobin. In every one of the experiments, the samples touched were richer in oxygen.[13]

In this chaper, I have traveled a long distance from what many people consider the boundaries of medicine—even psychosomatic medicine. In the inquiry into the roots of illness and the possibilities for healing, almost every aspect of life has been shown to relate to a person's health and sickness. As a whole, research is now suggesting that illness and health cannot be circumscribed as purely physical phenomena. In fact, such limits have themselves become health hazards, because they prevent people from taking important steps to further their own health and healing. I urge you to explore every possible avenue of the causes and potential cures of your own illnesses, and to proceed with an open mind. Regaining your health often involves attitudes, approaches, and life changes you may never have considered.

Part III

WORKING
for
YOUR HEALTH:
A SELF-HELP
PROGRAM

12 *The Body Is the Temple*

The body is flexible, a fluid energy field that is in a process of change from the moment of conception until the moment of death. The flesh is not a solid, dense mass; it is filled with life, consciousness, and energy. Although you probably would readily acknowledge this quality of the flesh, is it a conscious, operative reality for you? Are you aware of the forms of life in the hands holding this book and in your rear end touching the surface of your chair, of the movement deep in your skull and your lungs?

. . . most people experience their bodies as opaque, solid masses that, except for deterioration due to age and accident, are by and large fixed. . . . "I'm easily hurt. That's the way I am. My dad was like that too." "I get angry any time anyone criticizes me. That's the way I am." "I have a scoliosis (curvature of the spine). It's genetic. My father and grandfather have one too." The destruction of that notion of the real liberates one into an exciting world where one can find out for oneself what is really so. This world is filled with the unexpected, with surprises. The surprise packages to be uncovered . . . are within your skin.

DON JOHNSON

How do you relate to your body?

If you're like most people, you probably regard it somewhat as you do your car, your TV, and your household appliances. They are all instruments used to accomplish certain goals—that is, they are means to an end.

As with your machines, you learn to operate your body by turning on or off the external controls (muscles and senses). However, rarely do you consider or understand what lies beneath your skin—the inner machinery that is just as critical to your well-being as the more visible bodily parts. Nevertheless, your body usually operates smoothly and remains largely unnoticed until there is trouble—pain, disease, damage, or loss of energy. If the problem doesn't disappear, you may rush to an expert for a checkup, medication, or drastic repairs such as surgery.

This common approach to the body is woefully inadequate and shortsighted. Because chronic disease is typically the ultimate consequence of years of small, incremental misuses and stresses of the body, you must learn to be sensitive to your body's total functioning, and recognize problems in their earliest and most curable stages.

Well, you may be asking, how does one get in touch with the inner workings of the body? After all, the five primary senses focus solely on the external world. But fortunately, we have other senses as well. Each of us possesses a kinesthetic sensory capacity, which we often neglect or discount, that can make awareness of our own inner body possible. This sensing system allows us to turn our personal searchlight inward, discovering a wealth of information about our inner status. Intuitions, subtle internal cues, and even dreams can make us aware of early signs of illness or imbalance, long before physical dysfunctions are large enough to be measured and tested by physicians. Similarly, by learning to control our physiological stress response and alter such functions as gastric secretion and blood pressure, many potential problems can be avoided.

In essence, when you learn to communicate and control your body to this extent, you can make an evolutionary leap backward of a million years, by making contact with your reptilian brain, which regulates the visceral nervous system, the stress response, and primitive emotions. While each of us is born with the capacity to interact with this "old" brain, it is a skill we must constantly cultivate, or it will become dormant, as it has with most of us. Today, the cost of neglecting that skill is reflected in the epidemic of self-degenerative diseases related to our life stress.

Jungian analyst Russell Lockhart notes that the Greeks referred to the body as a "temple," and treated it with appropriate reverence.[1] Hindu and Chinese civilizations did not distinguish mind from body; their spiritual exercises contained a physical component, and often led to incredible mental control over the body.

With my own patients, I often find that healing begins with the initiation of a dialogue with their bodies and the nonconscious aspects of themselves. In the process, they reclaim the biological wisdom that they have neglected for so long. To help us in this quest we have few cultural rituals or institutions, like the healing shrines and oracles of the Greeks and the meditation and spiritual disciplines of the ancient oriental cultures. Yet this dialogue with the body can still be—and is being—reactivated today by many people.

It's time to observe and reevaluate the functioning of your body. It is not simply an instrument to get things done; it can also be an intimate friend and a wise counselor. If this potential is stifled or ignored, the body can become your mortal enemy. The choice is yours.

Kinesthetic Awareness

Try this simple exercise. For a few moments, observe the room you are sitting in now. Look at it as if you had never seen it before. Do you notice things that you haven't been aware of for months or years—if ever? We all tend to gloss over details, and ignore the obvious things around us.

The most familiar—and most overlooked—object is, of course, yourself. How often are you cognizant of your breathing, or your stomach when it is neither extremely full nor empty? How frequently are you aware of the feel of particular muscles when they are pain-free, or of normal movement? The reticular activating system (RAS) of the brain censors the information, since there is no need for us to be informed of the everyday activities of the body.

This limitation of our bodily awareness may not seem especially threatening or dangerous, particularly if the RAS automatically lets through the messages from the body that urgently need our attention. But that is not always the case. The rule of entry is not danger, but uniqueness, suddenness, and even grossness. Unfortunately, a repeated sensation, even if warning of peril, will rarely filter up to consciousness.

Let's assume that you constantly hold your neck in a stressful position, or tighten your back muscles. After a few initial messages communicating the novel situation of tense muscles, the RAS will give up trying to educate you. Therefore, the muscle tension in your back is registered as normal—and ignored. That situation will change only if a particular pain threshold or level of deterioration is reached. At that time, the accumulated damage will finally cause a breakthrough into awareness, with such suddenness that you will probably ask, "What hit me?"

Seymour Fisher, a psychologist, has carefully and systematically studied body awareness and its effects on our lives. He agrees that we neglect, even reject, our physiological body messages. Fisher warns that although we may train ourselves to become conscious of these kinesthetic messages, we are apt to read even the positive ones as signs of malfunction or abnormality. With the exception of physiological pleasures, such as sexual arousal, we regard most kinesthetic feelings as pathological.

But it is also possible, adds Fisher, for our attitudes and awareness to be reoriented toward the body, reversing this trend:

> Perhaps we will someday realize how much important information is cut out of the life of the average person by our present socialization practices that are so blind to, and basically suspicious of, the messages that come from the body. It would make good sense, in terms of what we already know about body perception, to provide the growing child with formal training that would help him to interpret his body more sensibly as a psy-

chological object. We need to do so not only to affirm that it is neither irrational nor bad to tune in on the body world, but also to provide a rich vocabulary for capturing the events of that world. Aside from routine words like "anger," "fear," "tension," "headache," and "stomachache," we need to offer terms that will capture finer shades of distinction. To illustrate, why would it not be possible for each child to learn to differentiate among the sensations in his stomach area so that he could clearly state whether he was experiencing indigestion due to eating too fast, indigestion due to eating too much, nausea expressive of a "fed up" attitude toward the world, unpleasant stomach movements indicative of a sense of deprivation and aloneness, stomach tightness reflecting a wish to eject (vomit out) unpleasant wishes or thoughts, and so forth? Why could similar fine judgments not be learned about head sensations, heart feelings, pelvic experiences, etc.? Such body-experience education would probably have more long-term general value in dealing well with life than so-called sex education or training in specific athletic or motor skills.[2]

Scanning Your Body

You must try to open up the communication channels of awareness with your body. If you regularly pay attention to your body, scanning it for signs of strain or tension, and practice feeling subtle degrees of change and difference, you can achieve this ability. Try the following exercise:

Sit in a comfortable chair, where you'll be screened from most external stimulation. To avoid distractions and interruptions, choose a place removed from the nearest street, take the phone off the hook, and ask a family member to keep the children away. The room you select should be dimly lit, and perhaps smell sweet or neutral.

Sit quietly, and gently close your eyes. Take a few moments to become aware of how your eyes feel with the lids shut. What are the sensations around your eyesockets? Is there tension? Fatigue? A relaxed feeling?

Now turn your entire awareness inside your body. As you begin to observe your body, your mind will probably be crowded with sensations. What are you aware of? Do you feel your buttocks where they touch the chair, or your feet being caressed by your socks or constricted by your shoes? Are some of your clothes too tight? If so, how different do you feel when you unbuckle a belt or remove a shoe?

While performing this exercise, some people become aware of a particular part of their body—a cramped leg, a tight shoulder, a full stomach. If this happens to you, explore that area as much as you can. Ask yourself what this portion of the body is trying to tell you. Perhaps it is saying, "I'm tired," "I've worked too hard," or even emotional messages such as "I'm lonely." This message frequently reflects a neglected psychological or physical need.

Next, conduct a head-to-toe body scan—an inventory of your internal geography. Start at the top of your head, focusing upon your scalp, hair, and then forehead. Place your awareness inside each area, and discover how it feels. What sensations are there? What do you perceive when you flex or move the voluntary muscles in that part of your body? Are there nearby areas that move or respond in unison?

Gradually proceed down to your eyes, mouth, neck, arms, torso, abdomen, waist, legs, and feet, focusing your awareness on each part, taking a few moments to explore sensations you may have never consciously observed before.

Many people discover through this exercise that their internal environment is just as accessible as their external one. By tensing, flexing, relaxing, and moving each bodily part, they recognize—often for the first time—the many shades of experience that lie within them.

Like any new skill, this exercise will become more valuable with practice. Eventually, you will probably find yourself becoming aware of your body at random times throughout the day.

This drill is a forerunner for many of the self-healing and relaxation exercises in later chapters. So be willing to spend some time perfecting it. Since the eyes must be closed, some of my patients record the instructions onto a cassette tape, reading them slowly and allowing time to carry out every instruction. Then they play the tape each time they do the exercise.

I also suggest that you keep a notebook or journal of your experiences. After scanning your body, take a few minutes to write down your impressions, feelings, and discoveries. What information did you acquire about your body and your health? This journal will allow you to review your self-discoveries periodically. Over time, it will help you recognize patterns and progress.

Body Awareness and Emotional Blockage

When I ask people to become aware of their bodies, some visualize their tension as a knot separating the head from the body, or the torso from the abdomen. This kind of person may live consciously only in his intellect. There is essentially no communication link between the upper and lower portions of the body, until ultimately, physical illness forces attention to particular areas.

This unfortunate disconnection between body and mind can almost be expected in our culture. As a society, we extol intellect over the physical body. We try to divorce sexuality from the rest of life. For many people, the unexplored, hidden parts of the body become like a black box, void of experience and open to many potential difficulties.

No wonder that many psychotherapists are studying both the body and the mind, exploring the dark closets of muscle tensions and other physical symptoms which can be reflected on a psychological level. By working directly with the body, either through touch or structured movement, tension is released. When this happens, a memory or emotion also emerges.

Wilhelm Reich parted company with his mentor, Freud,

largely because he believed he had to work toward the physiological release of tension as a means to liberate emotional blocks. He touched his patients, while Freud only listened. Reich, in fact, was the most notable founder of a physical mode of psychotherapy. Since then, it has been adapted and refined by clinician-researchers such as F. M. Alexander, Ida Rolf, Alexander Lowen, and Moshe Feldenkrais, all of whom contend that physical release is accompanied by psychological discharge and transformation.[3] These styles of therapy begin with the assumption that mental and physical events are clearly linked, and therefore change can begin at either level.

Reich recognized that certain psychological characteristics and defense mechanisms are accompanied by muscular rigidity. He labeled this rigidity "character armor" and believed that people can hide disturbing memories of traumatic events in their bodies. For example, a child who is repeatedly told to suppress his natural curiosity will not only fear new experiences, but will physically restrain himself, developing a stiff physical posture. This muscular rigidity reflects the emotional fear of punishment; it also can lead to breathing, digestive, or muscle dysfunction.

By loosening various rigid or armored body parts, an individual typically relives the experiences, or feels the emotions, that the body has repressed. It is almost as if the memories or feelings were stored and hidden within the body's tension. We might therefore expect that the exploration and release of this tension can lead to psychological and emotional healing as well as physical recuperation.

The body-oriented therapists preach that the physical being has much to tell the psyche about itself. Feelings resting within the physical structure can become part of the total healing process. A truly healthy person must have a flexible, responsive body that is not blocked or restricted by muscle tension. While most psychotherapy appears to have neglected this dimension of distress, medicine has erred in the other direction, usually neglecting the role that emotions can play in illness.

Loving Your Body

A woman I was treating had lost her leg to cancer. One day she informed me that before the cancer had ever developed, she had prayed for an accident so that she wouldn't have to work around the house. Another woman, who had begun to gain weight after her father's death, told me she had wanted to be as ugly as possible so that no man would like her.

These examples are typical of the ways that individuals assault, reject, and annihilate their bodies. You must know people who push and punish their bodies relentlessly. They work long hours, neglect nutrition and proper exercise, and simply take their bodies for granted.

Tragically, many individuals treat material goods better than their own bodies. Think of an object that you treasure very much—perhaps a work of art, a house, a garden, a car. Imagine how you feel about it, how you care for it, how you value it, the pleasure you get from it. Now, concentrate on your body, and picture giving yourself the same love, attention, and care. If you're like most people, you'll realize that you regard and treat your body less lovingly.

To regulate and heal your body, you must first accept it as belonging to you. The rejection of your body is often reflected when you refer to "it." If you had love and respect for your body, you would feel an integrated relationship between mind and body and probably use terms like "us" or "me."

The goal is to rid yourself of all alienation and unfamiliarity and create an intimate relationship with the body, based on trust, friendship, acceptance, dependability, awareness, mutual support, and interdependence. It sounds like the formula for a good marriage—which it is.

When you take time to reflect upon it, it's really no surprise that many people learn to repudiate the body. Try the following exercise:

Write down everything you were taught about the body throughout your life, and about your body in particular. If you're like most others, you ought to be able to come up with scores of negative messages, and almost no positive ones. For example, do you remember your parents telling you to stand up straight or risk permanently bad posture? Or were you warned that you'd get sick by doing certain things, such as leaving the house without a coat? Or perhaps you learned that it was wrong to touch yourself, especially around the genitals. Or that you'd get fat if you ate certain foods. Maybe you even heard others make fun of some part of your body, and accepted and internalized their rejection.

Many people grow up thinking of illness as God's punishment for not following their parents' advice. Or they believe that the body is simply undependable, falling prey to illness at the slightest wrong move or negative thought. Parents in our culture seldom teach children to take pleasure in their bodies, so many of us grow up with inhibitions against feeling good things from our bodies and against touching or being touched.

In your list, note the specific attitudes and sayings about the body that you remember. Reviewing them may convince you of the need to think and feel positively about your body. For example, how many of these old feelings and attitudes do you think are still buried within you, affecting your life today? If you have not worked consciously and explicitly to change them, they may remain part of you, at least to some extent. If you eventually come down with a chronic illness, these well-established attitudes may intrude, as if to say, "You see, your actions made you sick. It serves you right!"

Each individual grows up with an image—conscious or unconscious—of his or her body. What might happen to a girl who is teased by her father for having small breasts? Very likely she will accept the remark inwardly at face value for her entire life, always feeling self-conscious about her breasts. Or a large-breasted woman whose parents openly compare her to the glamorous (but not particularly healthy) models on TV and in magazines may become embarrassed and uncomfortable with herself. We can only speculate how such a negative evaluation of the body becomes translated into physical symptoms and illnesses, but this may be an important contributing factor to sickness.

I try to tap a patient's conception and feelings about his body by asking him to draw a picture of himself. The drawings are likely to reveal some central aspect of how he experiences himself. Try it, and examine the person you have drawn. What does this caricature look like, and how does it make you feel? The picture usually is more a reflection of your self-image than the actual reality of your body.

The size of the figure you draw is important, as is its relative sharpness or vagueness, and how static or mobile it is. Also, what parts of the body are missing, or are larger or smaller in relation to the whole? Look at the hands, and see how they interact with the environment. How large and important is the head in relation to the rest of the body? All features of the drawing are indicative of your inner feeling about yourself and your body. With some reflection, you should be able to interpret the meaning of your picture with considerable insight.

I recall the picture drawn by a woman who wanted to discover why she couldn't lose weight. She described the sketch of herself as very strange and ugly. Then she drew a second person inside the skin of the first body, and that became a symbol of her real self, which she had covered with a thick shell. She believed her obesity was protecting the inner self from hurt.

Touch, Pleasure and Sexuality

Loving, accepting, and nurturing your body and living fully within it can have a positive effect on your health. You can explore this important dimension of your existence by doing the following exercise:

Take off all your clothes and look at each part of yourself in the mirror. Touch yourself while you look. Take stock of how you actually are, and compare that with how you feel from both inside and outside.

Compliment those bodily parts you most like. Discover as many positive aspects about sections of the body you haven't liked before. Apologize to the stomach, the genitals, or the face you have hated, and then forgive yourself while changing your attitude consciously. Then let yourself move and jump with abandon, and discover how flexible and changeable your body actually is. Rather than being self-indulgent or narcissistic, this experience should be natural, lovely, and pleasurable.

This exercise will often uncover certain feelings, fears, and guilts which we once labeled sexual. Even in this era of so-called permissiveness, sexuality and bodily pleasure are among the most rejected and repressed aspects of our lives. In our culture, both men and women deprive themselves of uninhibited sexual enjoyment, a deprivation that could lead to impairment of health.

I counsel many couples in which one of the partners has a serious chronic illness. Typically, they report minimal or no sexual activity. Most physicians might assume that the lack of sex is a result of the illness, even though there may be no physical reason for abstention. I examine closely which seemed to come first—the serious illness or the sexual distance. In most situations, the sexual problems preceded the illness.

Touching is as basic a need as sexuality. Freud and his successors suggested that a deficiency of touching, and perhaps sexual expression, is the root of neurotic and psychosomatic disorders. In many marriages, touching and sexual vitality have all but disappeared. Might there be a connection between the deprivation of touching and sexual pleasure, and illness symptoms?

Do you and your spouse, children, relatives, and friends hug and touch a lot? For my patients who don't, I recommend a program of regular massage and hugging. A disabled or ill person is certainly in need of touching, and often can reciprocate as well. Yet both preceding and in response to illness, there is typically an absence of bodily contact. It is as if one mate feared contamination from touch, or as if pleasure would interfere with the healing process. An ill person is often touched more by a nurse than a spouse.

Some of us are actually "pleasure-phobic," seemingly fearing the results of receiving pleasure from the body. That was the case with a woman who came to see me with advanced cancer. She was warm and charming, a perfect wife, mother, and part-time secretary. Were it not for her cancer, she might qualify as the ideal American woman. Whenever I asked her how she took care of herself, she always responded in terms of others—how good she felt helping her children, husband, friends, or boss. Her entire concept of pleasure was based on serving others.

One day I asked this woman how she could possibly help others if she died of cancer. That seemed to change her entire way of thinking, and she began doing things for herself, without feeling that she was denying others. She started enjoying her body, regularly getting exercise and massages. She learned to touch herself and give herself pleasure, by adhering to a program developed by Lonnie Barbach which helps women who are non-orgasmic and generally neglectful of physical joys.[4] She felt more energy and strength and experienced many new positive feelings about herself.

The Conscious Body

A positive health program does not solely involve establishing external goals for the body and then attaining them. To reestablish health, we need to *become* our body, not simply have it do our bidding. In short, we have to develop a "conscious body."

The exercises in this chapter were designed to make you

aware of how deep feelings and attitudes toward your body may have contributed to your physical and psychological illnesses. The screen which has been erected between your consciousness and your visceral, automatic, emotional, and physical functioning must be eroded, so that you become sensitive to the subtle, but critically important, messages that the body sends you about how to take care of it.

As you develop awareness of your body and heed its messages, you will certainly be better able to take care of it. Its smooth operation is a source of infinite pleasure and creativity and can restore the important balance between body and mind. Once tensions are released and physical feelings are restored, you can develop the ability to play with your body, to take pleasure and joy in its movement, and to feel that it is a healthy, dependable component of yourself.

13 *Pathways to Relaxation*

> *The overfatigued as well as the neurotic individual has partly lost the natural habit or ability to relax. Usually he does not know what muscles are tense, cannot judge accurately whether he is relaxed, does not clearly realize that he should relax and does not know how. These capacities must be cultivated or acquired anew.*
>
> EDMUND JACOBSON

Anxiety, worry, insomnia, stomachaches, heartburn, indigestion, headaches, high blood pressure.

These or other ailments are part of many everyday lives. They are the symptomatic fallout of a chronically stressful existence, in which the individual is unable to counteract its self-destructive effects. While the external stressors themselves do not inflict the damage, the nature of the response, or nonresponse, to them does.

Most visits to the physician end with the familiar refrain "You have to try to relax, Mr. Jones." And how we wish we could! But like attempting to sleep, "trying" to relax—in the sense of consciously willing our muscles and body to release their tension—is impossible. As we have seen, you can't will it to happen, largely because much of our tension stems from muscular contraction and arousal of the visceral, nonconscious part of the nervous system.

The psychophysiological state that cardiologist Herbert Benson has called the "relaxation response" can be an antidote to stress.[1] The parasympathetic response in the autonomic nervous system is dominant during relaxation. The individual feels calm, peaceful, and alert, and because the nerves are not sending messages to his muscles, the muscles are almost limp. Benson and others have found that this response is very similar to the psychophysiological state attained by the practice of one of the ancient methods of meditation.

Just as the aroused state is linked to emotions such as anxiety, fear, and rage, the relaxed state is connected to the opposite feelings. Indeed, studies have shown that it is impossible to feel anxious when your body is relaxed, because anxiety is a direct by-product of the physiological arousal for stress.

What is the most common way to relax? Sleep is our most frequent approach to relaxation. While we dream, in some incompletely understood way, the body releases much of the day's tensions, allowing us to awaken somewhat renewed. Interestingly, people deprived of dreaming time experience psychological distress during their waking hours, even if they've had a full night's sleep. Insomnia, or disturbed sleep, interferes with our nightly relaxation, and can cause great distress as well. (Sleeping medication, along with its other undesirable physical side effects, actually interferes with necessary dreaming time, and thus should not be relied upon to safeguard sleep—and daytime well-being.)

Despite sleep's benefits, it does not offer relief from life stress. Even during sleep itself, some degree of physiological tension exists, and thus it can't protect us entirely from stress-related ailments. We need instead a method of relaxation that can augment sleep and other forms of daily rest and offer more complete stress relief.

Physical exercise can provide some relief from stress. However, research suggests that a conscious, wakeful relaxation procedure—progressive relaxation, meditation, autogenic training, self-hypnosis, and psychic visualization, to name a few—can be even more stress-relieving than physical exercise or a good night's sleep (although such a procedure is not a sleep substitute). These alternative methods have one common denominator. They utilize our natural ability to obtain greater control over the visceral nervous system. They thus mobilize potentialities already within us, rather than relying on external chemical treatments.

Like most people, you probably need a daily program to relax tight muscles, as well as decrease worry and anxiety, in order to avoid the physiological damage they can cause. I suggest a wakeful relaxation procedure to enable you to deal actively with the stress response. Rather than consciously willing yourself to relax, you can reach this state by essentially letting it happen. Once you achieve this self-control over autonomic reflexes and chronic muscle tensions, you will have an alternative response to stress that may be as medically potent as the so-called wonder drugs.

The Pitfalls of Pills

Unfortunately, if you were to ask the typical physician for relief from stress, he'd probably prescribe tranquilizers, which are not a means to relaxation at all. They only mask the properties of stress. Many nonmedical routes to stress relief, such as alcohol and tobacco, do the same, covering up stress rather than reversing or curing it.

Below is a typical exchange from a Sunday-magazine medical advice column, entitled "Your Prescriptions":

Q. I am in my early forties. My husband said I was snapping at him and the kids all of the time and suggested I go to the doctor to get something for my nerves. The doctor said I was very healthy but gave me a prescription for Valium. I now find that all my friends are taking Valium. One woman tells me she's taking it to relax the muscles in her back. What's with this Valium, and will I get hooked if I take it?

A. Valium is a tranquilizing drug that also has muscle-relaxing effects. Sometimes muscles become tight or go into spasm due to tension. Because Valium relaxes tension or muscles, it is frequently prescribed for both. Valium can be habit-forming and if you find you are taking more than your doctor has prescribed, it is time to see your doctor again and tell him what you are doing. Valium is an excellent drug but it should not be abused. Abuse of Valium is not just restricted to "street people." Many who receive prescriptions from their doctors are also abusers. Valium should never be taken when you are going to have alcoholic drinks. When your prescribed Valium is nearing the end, visit your doctor again to see if you still need it. He may reduce the dosage or tell you not to take it at all.

Valium is the nation's number-one prescription drug, accounting for over $130 million in sales in 1979. Along with its cousin, Librium, it is also the nation's most abused drug. These minor tranquilizers are prescribed primarily by family physicians in response to emotional or behavioral complaints such as stress, pain, agitation, anger, anxiety, and negative feelings. They are used less frequently by psychiatrists, for the reasons advanced by psychiatrist Gerald Klerman, director of the National Alcohol, Drug and Mental Health Administration:

> Anti-anxiety drugs are of value in the treatment of anxiety and tension associated with situational states and stress. They seem to be of most value for short-lived episodes of neurotic symptoms, and experienced clinicians discourage their use beyond a number of weeks. They are widely prescribed and their high rate of prescription generates important questions about the boundaries between psychopathological forms of anxiety and tension and the emotional changes associated with the stresses of everyday life. Lively controversy exists about the moral implications of the use of these compounds in American society, and the concern about whether or not we are becoming a "medicated society" with an excessive tendency to rely upon drugs as modes of coping.[2]

Here is a typical scenario involving tranquilizers. A housewife like the letter-writing woman above experiences distress. Defining this anguish as an illness, she seeks a physician to change her state of mind and internal feelings. The physician, finding nothing in her physical condition that he can change or that needs altering, prescribes tranquilizers.

These pills decrease a person's awareness of his stress, producing the "tranquilizing" effect that gives them their name. But, as Klerman explains, they have no effect on the autonomic nervous system, the arousal state, or the stress response by which the body reacts to tension. Instead, they only mask symptoms. Thus, it is not surprising that when people resort to such drugs as their exclusive treatment, the improvement is only temporary unless the stress- or anxiety-producing situation in the environment is changed. When the added factors of drug dependency and side effects are also considered, the advisability of using these pills is very much in doubt.

Even so, most physicians continue to prescribe them for millions of their patients. Experiencing vague discomfort and tension, these patients trust their physicians to give them a chemical potion to make them feel better. They rarely ask for help in overcoming the stress-provoking events themselves. Likewise, their physicians seldom inquire into the environmental sources of stress, relying instead on a masking drug.

As a society, we are probably not ready for the proposal of Ivan Illich, who suggested that we increase our capacity for suffering rather than turn to doctors for magical and misguided attempts to cover our feelings and stresses.[3] However, I agree with Klerman that if tranquilizers are to be prescribed at all, they should be used only for short-term stress reactions to specific difficulties. The use of these drugs is as severe a medical problem as the stressful conditions that draw people to them.

Mental Approaches to Relaxation and Stress Relief

While the antidote for excessive life stress is not available in a pill, it is accessible in a variety of forms, including physiological self-control through mental exercises. The recent flowering of mental approaches to relaxation occurred almost simultaneously in several clinics. While the superficial trappings of each method appear to vary, they all involve the same essential elements. Still, different approaches appeal to different people, and are prevalent in different parts of the world.

In Germany in the 1930s, psychiatrist J. H. Schultz and his student W. Luthe created "autogenic training," a medical treatment emphasizing self-control over autonomic functions.[4] Used by thousands of trained European physicians, autogenic training has been researched more thoroughly than any comparable technique. Yet only recently has interest in autogenics surfaced in the United States.

Chicago psychiatrist Edmund Jacobson was one of the earliest researchers to study the role that muscle tension and anxiety play in illness. He hypothesized that if people could be taught to release the residual tension in their muscles, they would eliminate psychological tensions and anxiety as well as physical stress. He developed a program of "progressive relaxation," which many behavioral therapists began adopting as treatment for a wide variety of psychological and physical ills.[5]

Still another contemporary approach to relaxation is self-hypnosis. Using this technique, a person talks directly to his unconscious mind, suggesting a state of relaxation. All forms of relaxation—including autogenic training and even meditation—are technically forms of self-hypnosis. But hypnosis deserves separate mention, because it has been an organized medical specialty for the past hundred years and is presently part of the mainstream of medical practice. We now know that all forms of hypnosis are voluntary, incorporating neither coercion or the overpowering of an individual's will. Instead, they consist of suggestions made directly to the deepest levels of consciousness.

Most of the relaxation methods I teach are derived directly or indirectly from the long tradition of medical hypnosis and meditation. Consequently, the side effects associated with chemicals are avoided, as well as the drug's illusory feeling of tranquillity. The loss of bodily awareness associated with drugs is also absent, since relaxation tends to heighten sensitivity to the body at a very deep level. Also, rather than relying on an external agent to relax him, the individual depends on himself, and therefore can feel a real sense of satisfaction when he succeeds.

Because of its clear advantages, I hope the day will eventually come when physicians will regularly prescribe relaxation classes, rather than Valium, for patients with chronic stress. Learning a relaxation technique is easy; more difficult is making the commitment to practice it daily. Only then can it become an effective inoculation against stress. Your own relaxation program must include a determination to perform the exercises once or twice each day, for a period ranging from five to twenty minutes. After several weeks or months, you can evaluate its effectiveness. While some people experience an immediate positive impact, others do not feel any initial benefits. But even for the latter, change will usually come with time.

To help form the habit, I suggest that you attend a relaxation training class, where you will receive support and encouragement to practice the exercise regularly. You should also keep a daily chart of your progress. The chart here is the one I recommend to keep people aware of their commitment to their relaxation program and its effects on them. It is divided into two blocks—one for your morning, and the other for your afternoon or evening relaxation periods. The far-left vertical column provides space for the date, and a notation of the major stressful events preceding the exercise that day. The next column asks you to gauge your level of stress just prior to relaxing, and then your level of relaxation after the exercise. Make your judgment on a 1 to 10 scale, where perfect relaxation is 1 and extreme stress or anxiety is 10.

Your relaxation goal should be to reduce your level of stress as much as possible, and eventually approach or even reach a rating of 1. The chart also provides space to enter any significant experiences, feelings, thoughts, or difficulties during each exercise. These latter remarks will be a reminder to yourself of important inner experiences, plus a guide to possible issues to discuss with your instructor. Complete the chart before and after each relaxation period for at least the first month of your practice.

WEEKLY RELAXATION LOG

A.M. EXERCISE PERIOD

	1. stressful events of the morning	*2. S/R levels*	*3. experiences during relaxation*
MONDAY		*before__*	
		after__	
TUESDAY		*before__*	
		after__	
WEDNESDAY		*before__*	
		after__	
THURSDAY		*before__*	
		after__	
FRIDAY		*before__*	
		after__	
SATURDAY		*before__*	
		after__	
SUNDAY		*before__*	
		after__	

Before you start your relaxation, note in column 1 the stressful events in your day preceding your exercise. In column 2, write down your pre-exercise S/R (stressor/relaxation) level, using a subjective scale of 1–10. 1 reflects total relaxation, while 10 indicates being very highly stressed or tense. Write in the space following

Simple Relaxation Exercises

Because this book is designed to be a practical guide, it is essential for you to validate my assertions with your own experiences. Thus you should take the time now to begin

WEEKLY RELAXATION LOG

P.M. EXERCISE PERIOD

	1. stressful events of the evening	*2. S/R levels*	*3. experiences during relaxation*
MONDAY		*before__*	
		after__	
TUESDAY		*before__*	
		after__	
WEDNESDAY		*before__*	
		after__	
THURSDAY		*before__*	
		after__	
FRIDAY		*before__*	
		after__	
SATURDAY		*before__*	
		after__	
SUNDAY		*before__*	
		after__	

"before." Then do your relaxation exercise. After the exercise, note your stress or relaxation level again in the appropriate "after" location, using the 1–10 scale. Then fill in some of the thoughts, feelings, body experiences, and/or other distinguishing occurrences during your exercise period in column 3.

practicing relaxation, before proceeding on with the rest of the book. If you don't begin immediately, you will find it hard to perform the imagery and dialogue exercises in the following chapters, which require you to reach a state of deep relaxation quickly and effortlessly. Learning relaxation is the first step not only to relief from stress, but also to most forms of deep inner self-communication.

The best way to practice a relaxation technique is to take a cassette recorder and read the instructions slowly into a tape. (Some prerecorded relaxation exercises prepared by therapists and practitioners are now available.) I suggest that you practice the exercise once each day with the tape, and then once without it while remembering the exercise as best you can. Soon you will no longer need to use the tape.

Relaxation exercises can be effective only if you approach them with what is termed "passive attention" or "volition." In other words, you will relax not by forcing yourself to, but by simply allowing it to happen. Psychiatrist Kenneth Greenspan explains, "In teaching relaxation you're teaching people to win races by taking their foot off the pedal, to win by not fighting, the ultimate paradox."[6]

Passive attention is difficult to describe; it must really be experienced to be fully understood. If you give yourself a command, or concentrate or try too hard, you will achieve a result opposite to the one you desire. A few people initially experience the relaxation exercise as causing more tension rather than less. Despite what you may encounter, it is important to continue practicing the exercise, since such feelings are simply reflections of the stress you are under. As the muscles or the mind releases tensions, these negative experiences may enter your consciousness. When something like this occurs, try to stay relaxed and not fight the experience.

Instead, while remaining as relaxed as possible, turn your attention to the area of your discomfort, or to your distressing thoughts. Let your awareness rest there. Tell yourself that it will eventually pass, and simply wait for it to do so. In almost all cases, it will disappear after a few moments. If you're learning the relaxation technique in a class or training program, your instructor can help you through any negative experiences.

Let's now begin your first relaxation period. You can choose one of the following exercises, or combine them, or try the progressive-relaxation, autogenic, or meditation exercises presented later. If you eventually attempt them all, one will probably seem most comfortable for you personally, and that is the one you should regularly use.

1. Body Relaxation

Get into a comfortable position. You may want to lie down on a bed or a rug, or sit on a chair. If you tend to fall asleep, sitting up is best.

When you are comfortable, transfer your awareness from the outside world to inside your body. To do this, close your eyes, and become aware of your breathing. Breathing is the source of life energy, and the connection between your inner world and the outer world. . . . You may even imagine your breath as a vapor, moving into your mouth, down your windpipe, and into your lungs, and perhaps even down into your stomach and solar plexus, and then out again, into the world. Spend a few minutes focusing your attention on your breathing. . . . Let your breathing be effortless and spontaneous. Let it happen by itself without consciously forcing it. . . . Whenever your mind begins to wander, simply return your awareness to your breathing.

(Pause for a few minutes)

Now become sensitive to your entire body. Beginning at the top of your head, place your awareness in each part of your body. How does it feel and look for your mind's eye to be in the top of your head? Are you aware of any tension or discomfort there? If so, simply breathe into that area. Imagine your breath going there and cleansing and bathing it with energy. As you exhale, imagine passing all the tension or discomfort out of that part of your body.

Now let your consciousness descend to your face. How does it feel? Is there any tension or discomfort? If so, let your breath bathe that area, and as you exhale, release the tension in your face. Experience how pleasurable and relaxed your face now feels.

Then do the same with each part of your body . . . first your neck . . . then your shoulders . . . your arms (one by one) . . . your hands . . . chest . . . stomach . . . waist . . . genitals . . . hips . . . legs . . . feet. . . . When you focus your attention on each part, let the air flow in and bathe that area, soothing it, and releasing any tension. Then experience the pleasure of that part of your body being relaxed.

Spend a few minutes enjoying your relaxed body, and the calm feelings that are now part of it. Become aware of your breathing once more, and with each exhalation, feel even more tension—the last little bit—leaving your body. . . . Continue for a few more minutes. . . . Then, slowly return to the room.

Try to prolong the sensation of well-being, relaxation, and peacefulness as you return to your activities for the day. Whenever you are under stress, you can simply sit down and recall this state of relaxation, and from memory, you will be able to recreate it at will.

This is basically a simplification of Edmund Jacobson's progressive relaxation program. The first few times you perform this exercise, spend a full half hour scanning your body and releasing tension. Eventually, with practice, you will learn to move through your body in just a few minutes, releasing or letting go of tensions wherever they exist.

Now let's move on to the second relaxation exercise.

2. Mental Relaxation/Self-Hypnosis

Get into a comfortable position, either sitting or lying down. Focus your eyes intently on a spot directly ahead of you, until your eyes feel tired and your vision begins to blur. Then roll your eyeballs to the top of your head and shut your eyelids. Imagine you feel a warm cloud bathing the center of your body. As the cloud touches you, it will warm and relax that part of your body.

Next, imagine that the cloud is slowly expanding from your center, growing larger, and touching each part of your body in turn with its warmth, energy, and peace. You are being totally bathed in the revitalizing cloud, which releases any tension within you. . . .

(*Pause*)

When you are entirely engulfed in the cloud, feel your body become lighter, warmer, and calmer. Imagine yourself beginning to float upward, completely weightless, soaring into the sky. The cloud, with you at the center, takes you to a special place, where you can be completely calm, relaxed, and at peace. Visualize how beautiful that place is. Imagine how it looks, smells, sounds, and tastes. Also recognize how pleasant you feel in there, how vital, warm, alert, relaxed, healthy, and calm you are. Experience the pleasure of total well-being.

(*Pause*)

When you decide to return to the room, simply imagine yourself ascending once again on the cloud and being settled gently back in your room. Before you open your eyes and complete your return, however, spend a moment recalling how you felt, and remind yourself that you can reexperience that sensation anytime you wish. Take some of that feeling of peace and well-being with you for the rest of your day. When you are ready, open your eyes, and sit quietly for a few moments.

3. Combined Relaxation

Sit down in a comfortable place. You may find it most comfortable to put your feet flat on the ground and leave your hands in your lap or on the arms of your chair. Look at a point directly ahead of you on the wall. If you are lying down, look at a point on the ceiling. As you focus on that point, you will begin to experience a fuzzing of your peripheral vision. As things get fuzzier and fuzzier, your eyelids will grow heavier. Don't resist the impulse to close them. Let them gently close. As your eyes close, you will feel a wave of relaxation begin to pass through your entire body starting from your eyes, going through your face and head, down across your shoulders and arms, all the way down your body, making you feel very, very warm, very, very peaceful and relaxed.

Turn your attention to the feelings that you are getting from your body: feel the chair or the place that you are lying; feel the

messages that come from the different parts of your body; and
then, eventually, begin to pass your attention to your breathing—breathe in and breathe out. As you breathe in, say to
yourself the words "I am," and as you breathe out say the
words to yourself "at peace." As you get into the rhythm of
your breathing and in your mind you hear the chant "I am at
peace," you will feel yourself letting go of tension and of outside things, and you will begin to feel a deep contentment, a
deep soothing sense of relaxation passing through your entire
body.

Begin to feel the relaxation radiating from your eyes (which
are already relaxed), across your face, across your scalp, and as
the relaxation passes across your body, feel yourself relaxing.
Say to yourself "let go" if you encounter any tension, and you
will feel the tension in each muscle letting go; you will feel the
tension in your jaw, you will feel the tension in your mouth and
in your face just beginning to melt away. You might imagine
that as you breathe in, your breath is a million little fingers
massaging the tired muscles of your body, and as you breathe
out, you breathe out tension that has accumulated in each muscle, each area of your body, leaving yourself with each breath
more and more deeply relaxed.

Now turn your attention to your neck, your shoulders, and
feel yourself relaxing and letting go of the tension that may
exist in your neck and in your shoulders. Move your head
around a little bit and then let your head fall comfortably down
to your chin—relaxing your neck and relaxing your shoulders
even more—letting go. Feel the waves of relaxation passing
across your shoulders and down your arms into your hands;
feel the relaxation pulling at each of your fingers in turn, relaxing that finger, relaxing your hands, and just feel your hands
and arms fall heavily in your lap or on the seat of your chair,
and feel the great relief of letting go of the tension in your arms.
Feel the relaxation flowing down your chest and down your
back, massaging out the tensions in your breathing, and in each
breath you will find yourself breathing more deeply. As you let
go, with each breath, you let go of some more tension and you
will feel a very pleasant sensation—a sensation of lightness or of
heaviness, a sensation of peace, a sensation of well-being, of
warmth, a sensation of letting go. Let the weight of the day, let

the cares of the day move out of your body with your breath. As you breathe out, with each breath breathe out some tension, breathe out some frustration, let the cares of the day just flow out of your body, leaving you deeply relaxed. Feel the relaxation moving through your stomach, your abdomen, feel the relaxation warming and soothing your stomach, the muscles in your lower back; feel the relaxation going around your seat, across your genitals and down your legs, relaxing the muscles there, leaving you with a sense of deep relaxation. Take a deep breath and as you breathe in, imagine that the breath is going down, down, into your stomach and deep into your abdomen, deeper than you ever thought you could breathe. As you feel the breath going deep within you, let it relax your stomach, relax your whole abdominal area. Breathe out and let go. Feel the relaxation moving across your legs and down across your knees, down your calves, across your ankles, your feet, and your toes, and just imagine the tension flowing out through your shoes and into the floor. As the tension moves out, a sense of deep peace and well-being takes its place.

Now, imagine that there is a source of light, a source of energy and peace, emanating from deep within your heart. Feel the light moving out in every direction, bathing you in a soothing, warming, relaxing aura, radiating relaxation like a stone that you drop into the water—the waves, ripples, move out in all directions, gently in all directions, nothing stops them and you feel a sense of peace, a sense of relaxation. As you become deeply relaxed, I want you to be aware that *you* are the cause of your relaxation, that I gave you some suggestions but *you* transferred them to your body, and that you can attain this state simply by attending to your body and attending to yourself for a few minutes anytime during the day, anyplace. You can create a state of deep relaxation simply by closing your eyes and letting the relaxation wash through you.

Now very, very slowly begin to return your awareness to the room, to the people around you, to your environment. Count to three, begin to blink your eyes and come awake: one (keeping the relaxation with you but increasing your alertness to the outside world), two (blink your eyes a few times, sit quietly), three (just rest for a moment and very, very slowly make the transition back to activity).

Meditation

As with many of the techniques presented in this book, the ultimate goal of meditation is to make contact with the unconscious and allow its wisdom to guide you in the healing process. Spend a few moments now listening to your stream of consciousness. Sit quietly, with your eyes open or shut, and watch and listen to the many sensory impressions, thoughts, and feelings which enter your mind. It resembles the switching on of a fountain with a never-ending spray. Your thoughts and impressions are random and seemingly without focus, as the searchlight beam of your consciousness moves from the inner to the external world and back. Even if you were to shut yourself off from the outer world by sitting in an isolated area, you would still be visited by countless inner forms, thoughts, feelings, memories, and ideas.

The Bhagavad Gita, an Indian guide to life and meditation predating Christ by centuries, suggests that enlightenment consists of turning off this flow of outer stimuli and turning in to one's inner self:

> The wind turns a ship
> From its course upon the waters:
> The wandering winds of the senses
> Cast man's mind adrift
> And turn his better judgment from its courses.
> When a man can still his senses
> I call him illumined.

I'm certain you've experienced moments when your mind was still. Watching a sunset, climbing a mountain, focusing on a lovely piece of music or performance, making love, working in the garden, potting or sewing, playing an intense game of tennis, or pursuing a creative idea—they are all moments when we are totally centering on one thing, to the exclusion of the drift and flow of extraneous thoughts. Can you recall the beauty and completeness of those times? Did you feel whole and uniquely alive? Humanistic psychologist Abraham Maslow has named such moments "peak experiences." In his research, he has correlated them with personality integration, creativity, and personal satisfaction. The more peak experiences one has, suggests Maslow, the better and more complete life will become.[7]

Lawrence LeShan defines meditation as the process of learning to do one thing at a time.[8] By concentrating on a single thing—whether it be your breath, your garden, or your jogging—you will enter not only an altered state of consciousness, but also an altered (and more positive) state of physiology.

Let me introduce you to a simple exercise adapted from a form of Zen Buddhist meditation. It is particularly effective as a healing meditation because of its emphasis on breathing, which is a physiological process. It deepens the breathing, exerting a harmonizing and balancing effect directly on the body, as well as the mind.

To begin, find a quiet place free of distractions. Because you want your mind to get into the habit of regularly attaining a state of meditation, you need to create a regular time and location for your daily meditation. For best results, it should not take place immediately after a meal. A meditation site becomes so special for many people that they decorate it with personal or symbolic objects to affirm its significance. Such gestures indicate the seriousness of commitment to the process:

> Sit quietly in a position where your back is straight, supported, if need be, by the back of the chair. Close your eyes.
>
> Make a quick inventory of your body, checking for any special tensions or discomforts. As you learned in the previous exercise, become aware of any tightness, tension, or strain in your muscles. If you find some tension, breathe in and then, on exhalation, gently but firmly relax your muscles as much as possible.
>
> When your physical evaluation is completed, you should perform a mental and emotional inventory. If you find any spe-

cial anxiety or uncomfortable thought, experience it for a few moments, but then ease it out of your mind. Rather than trying to force it away, simply allow the thought to flow out of your awareness by turning your attention away from it. You may not be able to remove yourself entirely from your concerns, but at least this method provides a start.

You should now be relaxed both physically and mentally. Begin breathing, without forcing your attention to it. That is, utilize passive volition rather than active concentration. Instead of attempting to coerce away thoughts that distract you from your breathing, let them come. When you become aware of them, consciously return all your attention to your breathing. Do not expect your mind to remain easily focused on your breathing. During a ten-to-twenty-minute meditation, you can anticipate that your mind will wander away many times. But be patient. You are still meditating well, even if your mind does wander. The meditation process consists of bringing your mind back, time after time, to your breathing, until focused attention becomes a habit.

Rather than just centering on your breathing, you may find it easier to use variations of this approach. For instance, as an aid to visualizing your breathing, try imagining your breath as a vapor. See it flow into your nose or mouth and down your throat, into your lungs and then through your body. You might envision the vapor flowing deep into the abdomen, swirling around, and then going up and out as you exhale. Observe the vapor mingle with the air, and then begin the process once again.

Another variation is to count breaths. As you inhale, silently count "one." In the exhalation, say, "and." The next breath is "two," and so on, until you get to "four," when you begin again. If you lose count, start again at "one."

As you concentrate on your breathing—whether by visualizing, counting, or any other method—do not try to alter or control it in any way. Instead, let your breathing regulate itself, spontaneously and effortlessly.

About ten to twenty minutes after beginning this exercise, you should be ready to conclude it. Stop concentrating on your breathing. This will return you to your normal stream of awareness. Blink your eyes several times, then open them and sit quietly for a minute or two. When you get up, you will feel refreshed and energized.

There is a great range of initial responses to this meditation exercise. Some people feel peaceful and relaxed immediately. Others, like myself, sense very little change at first and have almost had to restrain themselves from stopping the exercise by jumping from their seats. Still others, although determined to make the exercise work, discover themselves replaying worries or problems they have, finding it impossible to still these thoughts.

In teaching men and women to meditate and relax, one of my major objectives is to reassure them that these problems are common and to support their continued practice. People usually begin relaxation or meditation with many positive preconceptions and expectations, and when they don't materialize—when the mind isn't instantly still, or it continues to think the same thoughts it did at other times of the day they see themselves as failures. But skill at relaxation cannot be bought ready-made; it must be gradually developed. Even when it seems you are not making any progress, the exercise is probably having some beneficial effects. Using biofeedback machinery, I have often shown doubters that while they may think they're doing nothing more than just sitting quietly, their muscles are relaxed, their respiration is deeper, their hands are warming, and their brain waves move into the alpha and theta range. And, as one skeptical researcher observed, even without such physiological advantages, it is probably healthy just to get an overactive, overstressed individual to take time to sit and reflect twice a day.

Autogenic Training

Autogenic training is actually a series of messages, called orientations. During the training, a person suggests or imagines these orientations to himself while sitting in a comfortable, relaxed state. These messages activate a visceral response, which deepens relaxation and even increases the effectiveness of the body's self-healing ability. The state achieved is one of parasympathetic dominance and regenerative rest, as the following description suggests:

> The skeletal muscles, the "antagonistic pairs" as they are called, are relaxed. We speak of a loss of "tone," and by this we mean the reduction of the permanent muscular tension that is essential for an active organism. The blood vessels, particularly in the extremities, are dilated and carry more blood. The blood is more evenly distributed throughout the body; this is subjectively perceived as a pleasant feeling of warmth. The rhythmic biological activities—respiration and heartbeat—find their own unforced pace and work at a reduced intensity but with optimum efficiency. This is experienced subjectively as pleasantly restful and harmonious. The whole abdominal cavity, as a result of this physical relaxation, functions smoothly and spontaneously. Subjectively, this has the surprising effect of drawing our attention to areas of the body of which we are generally unaware, and gives rise to a feeling of pleasant well-being.[9]

To begin a modified form of autogenic exercise, lie comfortably on your back, or on a recliner chair, and repeat the phrase "I am at peace." Say it slowly, again and again, for about a minute. Do not *force* yourself to concentrate on it, and if you find your mind drifting, gently bring yourself back to it. After a minute of practice, rest and then repeat the same process again. Continue alternating between rest and focusing several more times.

After you have practiced this initial phrase, you should be ready to add, one at a time, the six basic orientations. These are a series of commands, or suggestions, to the body. They will induce a deep, calm, restful state of activation of the parasympathetic nervous system. They are listed in order below, and are to be practiced one at a time, each for a week or more. For best results, perform the exercise several times a day. You must be satisfied that your body has accepted each suggestion before going on to the next.

The six orientations are:

1. My right arm [for right-handed people] is very heavy.
2. My right hand is warm.
3. My pulse is calm and strong.
4. My breath is calm and regular.
5. My solar plexus is growing warm.
6. My forehead is pleasantly cool.

Begin with the first orientation. Spend a minute gently suggesting heaviness to your arm (you might imagine something tugging at your hand). Then alternate with a minute of rest, perhaps accompanied with the suggestion "I am at peace." For a few days to a week, practice only this exercise.

Next, start working with the second orientation. After about a week of practicing this hand-warming message, then combine the first two orientations. When you have mastered them on the dominant arm, begin the process over again with the other hand and arm.

Then, one at a time, practice each succeeding phrase. In about two months, you will be able to combine all the orientations, and induce the entire set of changes in your body within a few minutes.

Here are instructions for an exercise that is related to autogenic training:

Sit down, or lie down, in a comfortable place, loosen your clothing, maybe take off your shoes and just take some breaths and as you breathe become aware of how the simple act of taking a deep breath, holding it for a second, and then letting it go, is one very, very quick and easy way to begin the process of relaxation. Take a few more breaths and feel your body already beginning to respond to its own internal desire to enter a state of relaxation. When you feel ready, let your eyes close gently and become aware of your breathing. As you breathe in, begin to imagine, or think, or repeat to yourself, the phrase "I am," and as you breathe out, repeat to yourself the phrase "at peace." This is your personal meditation mantra that you can use to begin to suggest the feeling of peace, warmth, and well-being throughout your body. Just pay attention to your breathing:

inhaling "I am," exhaling "at peace." Feel your body respond,
"I am" "at peace."

Now I want you to repeat to yourself the phrase "my arms
are heavy," and as you say this phrase over and over again, I
want you to see if you can experience a heaviness growing in
your arms. See if the power of your mind, your imagination,
can induce a change in your body. Now I would like you to say
to yourself, over and over again, the phrase "my hands are
warm." As you say "my hands are warm" you might imagine
something happening—you might imagine being in a warm
place, dipping your hands in warm water: begin to imagine and
experience your hands becoming warm. "My hands are
warm"—repeat this over and over again to yourself. Now,
combine the two phrases by saying to yourself "my arms are
heavy" and "my hands are warm," and you will begin to feel
your body responding. As your arms become heavy and your
handᶜ become warm, you will feel yourself relaxing. Now repeat to yourself the phrase "my breath is calm and regular" and
as you say this to yourself, over and over again, you will begin
to feel the calming effect, the deepening effect, on your
breathing.

Now I would like you to repeat to yourself, over and over
again, the phrase "my pulse is strong and regular." Imagine, if
you will, that your circulation, your blood flow, is moving effortlessly through your body, reaching every corner of your
body, and the life blood is making you strong and healthy. "My
pulse is strong and regular," sending a direct suggestion to your
entire body to work more effectively, to safeguard your health.
Repeat to yourself, "my breath is calm and regular" and "my
pulse is strong and regular." Just let those two phrases echo in
your mind over and over again so they can begin to have an effect on your body, relaxing and transforming your body in the
direction of health.

Now return again to the original phrase "I am at peace." Feel
how your body has responded to the suggestions "I am" (inhale) "at peace" (exhale). Feel the great sense of well-being
and relaxation that you have been able to attain simply by repeating to yourself the five phrases—"I am at peace," "my arms
are heavy," "my hands are warm," "my breath is calm and regular," "my pulse is strong and regular." Repeat each phrase to

yourself and see how it has begun to affect your body, see the effect the phrase has had on your physiological functioning. Now, very slowly, begin to return your awareness to the room, taking with you, for the rest of the day, a sense of well-being, a sense of peace that you have attained in this exercise. Again, very slowly, blink your eyes and return to this room.

Progressive Relaxation/Desensitization

Progressive relaxation should be performed while lying flat on your back. Whereas autogenics uses mental commands and images to affect the body, Edmund Jacobson's relaxation technique employs physical reeducation to affect the mind and the visceral nervous system. Mental images are used to desensitize oneself to stressful or fearful stimuli or situations.

To begin the exercise, take a single muscle group—say, the hand and arm—and explore how it feels to tense and relax each muscle alternately. While clenching the fist or bending the hand, note the sensation of tension. With practice, you can learn to become aware of the tension and then to relax yourself.

Jacobson believes that people carry chronic muscle tension, and the accompanying anxiety, within them because they have lost contact with the actual extent of tension in their muscles. His "progressive relaxation" technique is designed to create awareness of how muscles feel when they are tense and when they are relaxed. Then slowly and painstakingly, a person learns, muscle group by muscle group, to relax each muscle. When relaxation of the voluntary skeletal muscles is achieved, the mind and the visceral muscles will be relaxed as well.

The desensitization phase of training involves attaining relaxation in situations that are stressful or anxiety-provoking. You can try to practice reading, which demands hand and arm tension, while maintaining relaxation in the rest of the body. You can learn to tense only the muscles you are using. Ultimately, you will be able to relax in everyday stressful situations. When faced with a fear, or a negative emotion, you will merely need to tell yourself to relax. Once you're relaxed, it's impossible to feel anxious or tense. This training has been used successfully to help remove stage fright, tics, examination anxiety, phobias, and tension headaches.

If you practice letting your muscles relax, one by one, or allowing your physiological functions to change, you can eventually make it happen. A trained person will be able to relax every muscle within a minute or two.

When a person is able to regulate some aspects of his internal physiology, the stage is set for further exploration of other types of internal self-control. Eventually you will use the knowledge gained in relaxation training to gather information from your unconscious concerning the nature and causes of illness. The relaxation technique can also be an important step toward encouraging your body to heal a specific illness.

14 Biofeedback: Learning Internal Self-Control

Training programs are feasible for the establishment and maintenance of psychosomatic health. If every young student knew by the time he finished his first biology class, in grade school, that the body responds to self-generated psychological inputs, that blood flow and heart behavior, as well as a host of other body processes, can be influenced at will, it would change prevailing ideas about both physical and mental health. It would then be quite clear and understandable that we are individually responsible to a large extent for our state of health or disease.

Perhaps then people would begin to realize that it is not life that kills us, but rather it is our reaction to it, and this reaction can be to a significant extent self-chosen.

GREEN, GREEN, AND WALTERS

Ellen, a forty-five-year-old woman with many vague pains and bodily stress symptoms, was overweight and walked clumsily, demonstrating that her body was largely alien to her. Although she was skeptical about attaining control over her problems, her distress had become severe, and she was afraid of what might happen to her.

My first step was to initiate communication between Ellen and her body and to help her learn something about her pain and how she could control it. Because she was resistant and unmotivated, I needed to convince her of her own potential power. I decided that biofeedback would be the most effective method. For many people, whether highly educated or untutored, science and technology provoke a trust and credibility that are accepted the way religious truth and God's will were a century ago. With biofeedback apparatus, sophisticated medical technology allows the patient to observe and control the inner workings of his body.

Ellen agreed to biofeedback training, primarily because of her confidence in technology. Also, her insurance company would pay for biofeedback, while it would not reimburse her for the costs of meditation training or health classes. That suggested to her that biofeedback had validity as a treatment.

As Ellen soon learned, biofeedback equipment is compact; it looks like a trio of portable cassette tape players, with a few additional meters and dials. But the wires from the machine lead not to speakers or other devices, but to the body, monitoring and measuring muscle tension, skin resistance, brain waves, blood pressure, and temperature. On a small screen or via a modulating sound, the subject can perceive the tiniest fluctuations in internal functioning.

The technician placed a tiny temperature detector, or thermistor, on Ellen's middle finger. Another sensor, to measure the skin's resistance to a minute electrical current, was attached to the back of her hand, and still others were placed on the frontalis muscle of her forehead to detect muscle tension.

When the session began, Ellen's hand temperature was 76 degrees, not uncommon for the extremities. I explained that if she relaxed herself, the blood vessels would dilate and her feet and hands would warm up. With this understood, I asked her to warm her hands, to demonstrate the control she did possess. She tried, and very quickly one of the sensors registered an increase in muscle tension and a sudden drop in skin resistance, signaling a rise in anxiety. The reading of her hand temperature, displayed on the screen in front of her, dropped nearly a degree.

Why had Ellen's first attempts at biofeedback failed? Her

conscious efforts, which included bracing herself for a difficult ordeal, had inadvertently thrust her body into the alarm
reaction. In the process, her blood vessels contracted and
blood withdrew from the extremities, as a way of preserving
the life fluid in case the skin was punctured. Her response,
then, was inappropriate, which was probably a reflection of
how she reacted to other situations in life. She prepared for
any challenge or responsibility by mobilizing for fight or
flight.

After a few minutes, I gently suggested that she not try so
hard. I hinted instead that if she could think of something
relaxing and pleasant—perhaps a lovely day at the beach—
she might have more success. She followed my advice, and
within moments, her hand temperature increased slightly,
her skin resistance rose (a sign of relaxation), and the muscle tension in her forehead decreased. She was on the road to
relaxation. As she visualized the pleasant scene, which included memories of her pain-free, idyllic past, her thoughts
drifted away from changing her hand temperature. And in-
exorably, the temperature climbed, until fifteen minutes
later it registered nearly 90. Not bad for a first attempt.

Ellen was delighted. "How did it happen?" she exclaimed.
How could she be so successful by simply visualizing situations in which she felt relaxed? Actually, her experience is
quite common. Others warm their hands by imagining them
being dipped into a bowl of hot water, or baking in the sun.
Ellen succeeded by adhering to the law of "passive volition":
Don't try, just let it happen. As biofeedback researcher Barbara Brown proposes, there doesn't seem to be any internal
process, from the functioning of organs to the workings of
single cells, that a person can't learn to control consciously,
provided he has the tools and can properly cultivate the
skills.[1]

The act of trying, which involves intense concentration, is
the method of altering our voluntary nervous system, our
external muscles and skeletal system. But it is not the way to
attain internal self-control. Here is a simple demonstration,

with which almost everyone can identify. Do you remember a time, perhaps during an intermission of a concert or a movie, when it was necessary for you to urinate very quickly? Could you do it? Very likely, the more you tried to speed up the process, the harder it became to do. If you want to urinate, you have to relax, not *try*. You must allow your bladder to take control, and just let things happen. If a situation ever arises again when you want to urinate in a hurry, just think of a relaxing scene and forget what you are doing on a conscious level. You will find your speed improving considerably.

Using the same principle, Ellen had learned two crucial experiential skills. She could control the workings of her body, and the way to do so was by letting it happen passively, using imagery and an absence of conscious effort. Her success lifted her out of her rut, and on the road to change.

In the rest of that first session, Ellen worked swiftly and confidently. With her mind focused on pleasant scenes, I guided her toward relaxing the various muscle groups in her body. Once the frontalis muscle was relaxed, we moved the sensor to other muscle groups to demonstrate to her that they were also relaxing as she practiced. Her skin resistance continued to drop, and her temperature rose another 3 degrees.

Ellen and I then talked about the problems and crises in her life. Each time she discussed an emotionally difficult subject—her marriage, her relationship with her children, her fear about her deteriorating physical state—her temperature and skin resistance plummeted, and her muscle tension increased. This showed the clear interconnection between her emotional state and her physical response. Thus the apparatus itself documented that when she was upset, her body was creating the conditions—tightness and arousal—for pain to take root.

In the ensuing weeks, Ellen began an extensive program of training, incorporating self-hypnosis, relaxation, and imagery to control pain, and individual and family counseling to help alter the emotionally stressful situations in her life. Biofeedback did not become a crutch, because it was never the center of her treatment. Rather, it was a procedure she could use—hooking herself up and testing the skills she had learned—to evaluate her progress. The readings of hand temperature, skin resistance, and muscle tension provided a numerical measure and objective data about her improvement. It instilled self-confidence in her and verified that the mental procedures she was using were having the desired physiological effects. That, in essence, is the greatest promise of biofeedback.

Rats and Swamis: The Possibility of Self-Control

Of what value is the detailed, continuous information that biofeedback provides? It is useful only if it can help you make long-lasting changes in your body. Two types of medical research prompted scientists to begin seriously investigating whether an individual could voluntarily control his internal body. Not only were there promising studies with rats regarding their conscious influencing of internal functions, but there was also research into some extraordinary human beings who seemed able to perform superhuman feats.

Following the lead of Russian psychologist Ivan Pavlov, Neal Miller and his colleagues at Rockefeller University demonstrated that autonomic functions could be changed via a planned learning process. Working initially with rats, whose voluntary skeletal nervous systems were paralyzed with small doses of the paralytic poison curare, Miller showed that they could alter their blood pressure, heart rate, intestinal contractions, and urine formation to avoid electrical shocks. The curare was used to ensure that the rats did not achieve control by using the voluntary nervous system to tighten the muscles around blood vessels.[2]

The studies clearly indicated that the rats had altered

their internal responses as automatically as Pavlov's dogs had learned to salivate at the sound of the bell. Miller's work proved that autonomic responses could be controlled and modified in response to rewards and punishments. This suggested that by clever manipulation of reward and punishment, patients could also learn to regulate these functions, which are responsible for many common illnesses.

Indeed, biofeedback treatment patterns itself after this simple model (without the curare, of course, since we don't really care if people get help from their voluntary muscles in making themselves healthier). The patient is rewarded—with good health, encouragement, and a feeling of personal power—when he is able to change his autonomic functions in the desired direction. Interestingly, he usually learns to control his responses without any idea of how he did it. Like the rat, he may not even be told what bodily function is being monitored and rewarded, and so the entire learning process can be unconscious.

But conscious control is the ultimate goal of biofeedback. Each patient should eventually be able deliberately and voluntarily to lower his blood pressure, relax his muscles, or change any of the other physical responses that science can clinically monitor: brain waves, heart rate, skin temperature, and skin resistance.

What are the limits of conscious control over internal processes? Some studies have been conducted on extraordinary subjects who have achieved amazing internal control. These individuals are often products of non-Western religious systems, notably the Hindu yogic tradition, which emphasizes not only mind/body unity, but also awareness and conscious control of one's entire internal workings. Certainly you've read about yogis who could sleep on beds of nails, walk across hot coals, turn off their breathing, or live in constant ecstasy. Their feats should lead us to speculate on how they do it, as well as on how we each can learn to duplicate their achievements.

Based on reports that Swami Rama, a Western-educated

Hindu teacher, could stop his heart, control his brain waves at will, and perform various other startling acts, Elmer and Alyce Green invited him to the Menninger Foundation, where they could check these claims. During an array of tests of his physiological responses, Swami Rama demonstrated astonishing control over most of his autonomic functions—heart rate, blood flow, temperature, pain, brain waves, and most internal muscles.

On the final day of Swami Rama's stay, he actually stopped his heart—a dangerous and seemingly impossible maneuver—while hooked up to various monitoring devices. This feat involved making his heart muscle contract so fast (several hundred times a minute) that blood could not flow through it—and it stopped. He did this verifiably for nearly half a minute.[3]

The Dutch-American teacher Jack Schwartz discovered as a child that he had a wide range of extrasensory abilities and powers of internal control. He is able to take a dirty needle and pass it through his arm, without causing bleeding or infection. After the needle is extracted, the wound closes easily, and no scars or scabs develop. At public demonstrations, Schwartz teaches his technique of "focused awareness," similar to meditation. Members of the audience are then often able to perform the needle-piercing on themselves.[4]

Schwartz has been observed by various medical researchers, who conclude that it is clearly possible to control infection, bleeding, and awareness of pain. The significance of this for surgical and medical treatment is obvious.

If a few individuals can accomplish these feats, why can't everyone? It is unlikely that these adepts are genetic freaks, and in the case of Jack Schwartz, he did not experience a long period of arduous training. So can these skills be taught? That inquiry helped initiate the development of biofeedback treatment. Voluntary, internal self-control was potentially far safer, and more powerful, than drugs. So why not investigate the full scope of man's natural abilities?

Some researchers simply asked the adepts how they accomplished their extraordinary feats. Based on responses he received, Erik Peper, former president of the Biofeedback Society of America, noted two common factors in achieving visceral self-control: (1) passive attention, instead of active trying; and (2) an emphasis on the process and their attention to it, rather than the outcome or the goal.[5] Adepts report that they enter a special state of consciousness in which their attention is focused not on some objective end point, but on the present, here-and-now sensations in the body. Neither Swami Rama, Jack Schwartz, nor even Ellen learned self-regulation by trying to do so.

Peper observed that consciously striving toward and anticipating a goal disrupted the process of physiological self-control, since both contributed to self-defeating muscle tightening and the alarm reaction. According to Peper, the desired behavior is a state of letting go and allowing change to take place. This wisdom forms the basis for all relaxation, meditation, and self-management exercises.

Biofeedback as a Learning Phenomenon

Biofeedback apparatus is a sensitive and objective reporting device that should be viewed as merely a tool—a measuring device—which is just one part of an entire training process. Unfortunately, biofeedback is sometimes associated merely with the machines, which is like confusing the surgeon with his cutting tools. The skill, dedication, and commitment of the learner, and the quality of the learning process, are the critical elements.

Just how relevant to permanent healing is sitting in a laboratory, attached to a monitoring machine, receiving rewards (perhaps pennies) for each blip on a machine, which signifies, say, a decrease in muscle tension or blood pressure? Not very. After the electrodes are removed, the patient can leave the office and have a heart attack an hour later if he is subjected to severe stress. So conscious control outside the laboratory is essential, with or without the help of machines.

This is a dilemma that Neal Miller and other experimenters faced as they sought to make their findings clinically useful. While they could teach a person to produce a response in the lab, just as rats could be taught, the change was sometimes only temporary. The individual also had to learn conscious awareness and control in his everyday life.

For example, one of Miller's first human patients was Robin, a young woman who had suffered slight brain damage, which was complicated by essential hypertension (a dangerous increase in blood pressure with no clear precipitating cause). Although she felt no particular discomfort, the chronic elevation of blood pressure could have ultimately led to other serious illnesses, such as heart attack, stroke, and hardening of the arteries. While hypertension is usually treated with medication, the drugs had undesirable side effects. Miller felt that Robin, who was hospitalized and therefore could be placed on a long-term, strict training program, might be taught to decrease her blood pressure with biofeedback.

Robin was connected to a machine which measured the changes in the pressure of the blood flowing through her veins. Initially, the fluctuations in pressure seemed almost random. She experienced rises and falls erratically from one moment to the next. She had no sense of how or why these changes occurred. However, what if she had noticed that whenever she ruminated about her illness, her blood pressure went up? And whenever she thought of relaxing at home and regaining her health, it dropped? Eventually, by following hunches and subtle cues, and becoming sensitive to the instant feedback of how well she was doing, she learned to decrease her blood pressure to an acceptable level. Nevertheless, it took weeks of dedicated work at the machine.

The apparatus Robin used contained a light that flashed on only when her blood pressure was dropping. It would not respond when the blood pressure had leveled off or was rising. Her task was to keep the light on, which signaled that her body was working in the desired direction. Her reward—the bright light and better health—came only when lower blood pressure was achieved.

Because of her success at learning self-control, Robin was taken off medication. Immediately thereafter, her blood pressure rose. But with a few more days at the biofeedback machine, she was able to decrease it again.

Did biofeedback change Robin's consciousness of her internal processes? Or was this merely an unconscious response, as with the rats? Her account of the training suggests that it was a little of both:

> I was determined to succeed. I felt that this was the only part of my treatment that I could do anything about at all, and I am a habitual overachiever. At first, it seemed that lowering my pressure was only a simple muscular trick. I thought it was only a matter of relaxing my stomach, my chest, my breathing, but none of these worked all the time. I found I could drop my pressure quickly by fooling with my muscles, but I could only sustain the drop if I "relaxed" my mind. It all seemed to depend on clearing my mind of all stressful thoughts. It's almost the yoga thing, almost self-hypnosis. . . . Making the pressure go up is a lot easier than lowering it. The best way to get it up is to take a big breath and think angry thoughts—I may remember some real jackass I knew in the past, and get mad all over again at his stupidity. But any kind of mental effort, even adding a lot of big numbers, seems to have a similar effect. . . .
>
> If I pay close attention, I think I can tell when my pressure is up or down, but I can't always hold it there smoothly. What I mean is, when I'm trying to lower it, I know sometimes it goes up and I can detect the change, but my lowering maneuver takes several seconds to work. I'm not sure why this happens. There seems to be some sort of vibration inside my head when my pressure is high. One day just before I left the hospital, I was conscious of the blood rushing to my arteries. I could tell my pressure was high and it frightened me a little, so I called for a nurse. She took it, and it was 112, which was way above

normal for me at that time. So I tried to lower it with the techniques I'd learned, and then I asked her to take it again, and it was down to 90.[6]

Blood pressure, then, is highly variable, responding particularly to life stress. The highs and lows of life were clearly reflected in changes in Robin's pressure. Certainly the biofeedback training process had taught her to decrease her pressure in the lab. But much more important, she had sharpened her awareness of the meaning of subtle internal sensations and inner feelings, which allowed her to continue her control away from the laboratory.

Like many successful biofeedback patients, Robin needed a periodic return to the machines to reinforce what she had learned. She would occasionally find that when stress or negative feelings entered her life, her pressure increased. But now, she was aware of it almost when it happened. Calling upon her long-term training, she was still not always able to bring her pressure back down unless she returned to the laboratory. However, after a few days of review, she was able to lower her blood pressure to an acceptable level. Biofeedback, then, must be an ongoing process.

Many patients ask me for biofeedback as if it were a new pill. They seem prepared to play only the traditional patient role of passive submission and fail to recognize the part they may have to play in overcoming illness. Many believe that they can get hooked up to a machine—and instantly change.

They're wrong. Biofeedback is a lengthy treatment requiring many hours of practice, learning to achieve self-control. After working with the apparatus, the patient must spend many additional hours at home trying to duplicate the success achieved in the laboratory.

This misconception about biofeedback would be cleared up if people understood that it is not medical treatment. Instead, it is a process of education, or skill development. For one to achieve any significant physiological changes, biofeedback training demands more than twenty hour-long laboratory training sessions, plus daily home practice and self-observation. However, the rewards of this commitment to change can be enormous.

Naturally, there are some clear limitations to the value of biofeedback as a clinical tool. Biofeedback will be ineffective if the particular physiological function that needs to be monitored is not easily accessible, without having to, say, place an intravenous needle under the skin. Also, the function must be accessible to control—that is, some physical processes (such as blood pressure) seem receptive to only limited regulation, less than what may be clinically needed.

The internal functions easiest to alter with biofeedback are predictably those closest to consciousness. Muscle tension, for example, is easy to detect at the skin's surface, and because muscles are under conscious control, a person can quickly learn to release muscular tension through a type of biofeedback called EMG (electromyograph).

Typically, biofeedback works best when only a specific localized symptom troubles a person. For example, Reynaud's disease (a blood-flow constriction causing abnormally cold extremities), abnormal heart rhythms, specific muscle atrophy with no organic damage, bruxism (grinding teeth) and other conditions related to chronic tension in one particular muscle group, and some types of headaches are all ailments to which biofeedback can contribute lasting benefits. Some symptoms can, in fact, be permanently altered via biofeedback training.

Bernard Engel taught patients with cardiac arrhythmia (a comparatively mild symptom similar to hypertension, which can have serious health consequences) to recognize irregularity in their heartbeats by watching light signals. After a while, they not only could sense their irregularity but could also control it. In a follow-up study several years later, many of these patients had still maintained their sensitivity and their regular heart functioning. Several no longer needed medication—an impressive piece of clinical evidence.[7]

Generally, the physiological reactions that produce illness

are complex, interconnected, and difficult to measure, and thus not particularly treatable by biofeedback. Yet in some situations, biofeedback can certainly be helpful, especially when combined with one of the other methods of meditation or relaxation.

Because biofeedback machinery is expensive and the training can be arduous, holistic practitioners have often switched to nontechnological training aimed at body awareness and self-control. Some use biofeedback only for diagnosis and for evaluation of their clinical results. Techniques such as meditation, relaxation, and mental imagery can be learned easily and without equipment in only a few training sessions. They offer generalized help in relaxing and modifying the body's response to stress.

A Biofeedback Training Program

A biofeedback training program proceeds through a number of stages (which are also applicable to all holistic health treatments). They are:

1. A clear diagnosis and observation of the problem and its context in an individual's life
2. Selecting a treatment strategy and modality
3. Practicing the new skill, both in the clinic and at home
4. Practicing the new skill in the specific situations in which most problems arise

The initial task is to determine and observe exactly what is working improperly in your body and what functions need to be changed. It also requires an assessment of the degree of tension or stress in your life and the events or situations that cause it. You can use traditional medical approaches for gathering physiological information, or you can apply some introspective, self-diagnostic techniques. You may need to keep a careful chart of your symptoms, difficulties, or habit patterns—from day to day or even hour to hour—in order to recognize fully the changes that are required.

Next, you must choose the proper treatment, followed by training and regular practice of it. During this stage, you might learn and practice internal control in the biofeedback lab, trying to discover ways to carry your success over to your outside life. Homework is absolutely essential, not only with biofeedback training, but also with the relaxation, meditation, or imagery approaches. The goal is to increase your awareness of when your body is functioning improperly, and enhance your ability to immediately reverse an inappropriate or ineffective psychophysiological response.

The final step involves learning to alter your responses in the actual situations that cause the most trouble. The woman trained in Miller's lab, for example, most needed to keep her blood pressure down in circumstances of particular emotional stress. In the end, you must learn to vary your response to the situations in your life that have in the past caused, or may in the future cause, problems that could culminate in a physical breakdown or illness.

Let's examine how this entire process was applied to one of my own patients who suffered from low-back pain. First, I talked with her about health and healing in general, as part of a class on health, which included reading and discussion. This led to an agreement to pursue treatment.

This particular woman then began to explore the factors in her life that may have aggravated her pain. She recognized connections between her pain and her job (which she hated). She also saw a relationship between her pain and the illness of her husband (who she felt was naggingly dependent). She recorded the time of day when her pain was most severe, and her activities, feelings, and needs at those moments. She also noted the various things that made her feel better, such as exercise.

A physical examination and consultation with her physician ruled out the need for traditional medical approaches, because there was no clearly definable lesion in her back. So she was then ready to design a personal treatment plan, which included relaxation training both in a class and in daily practicing at home. She was also introduced to biofeedback training so that she could learn to relax her back muscles. Eventually, she had the skill to relax her whole body, especially her back, whenever she wished. I also explored with her ways to modify her home and work situation, and I talked with her husband about household roles and expectations.

Over the next few weeks, she became adept at relaxation. So did her husband, who also learned the relaxation technique to cope with the stress in his own life. The household tensions decreased, and she also changed jobs.

Whenever she now feels stress, she takes immediate steps to relax or relieve the tension. Instead of working herself into a tension-filled frenzy, she has learned to respond by calming herself down. Her back symptoms have become very rare.

One of the attractive side benefits of this holistic approach is an increased sense of self-confidence and well-being. Before I began working with this patient, she felt helpless in controlling her body and her pain. Indeed, she expected her body to let her down whenever she needed energy or stamina. But that has changed. Now she is able to use her body to mobilize herself to do the things she wants.

As biofeedback researchers have noted, this confidence and power often carries over to many other areas of a person's life. The individual who successfully completes a holistic treatment program incorporating biofeedback often experiences a general increase in positive self-image, and new faith in his ability to achieve what he wants in other areas of life.

For now, it's clear that the medical instrument with the greatest potential for alleviating disease-inducing stress seems to be the same one that has enabled humanity to harness the external world—conscious awareness and self-control. The medical revolution of biofeedback thus represents a turning inward, and a crossing of the artificial mind-body boundary, to help us learn more about our inner workings and become aware of our largely untapped mental resources for maintaining our own health.

15 Seizing Control of Self-Defeating Behavior

Most individuals do not worry about their health until they lose it. Uncertain attempts at healthy living may be thwarted by the temptations of a culture whose economy depends on high production and high consumption. . . . Facing the insufferable insult of extinction with the years, and knowing how we might improve our health, we still don't do much about it. . . . Prevention of disease means forsaking the bad habits which many people enjoy—overeating, too much drinking, taking pills, staying up at night, engaging in promiscuous sex, driving too fast, and smoking cigarettes—or, put another way, it means doing things which require special effort—exercising regularly, going to the dentist, practicing contraception, ensuring harmonious family life, submitting to screening examinations. The idea of individual responsibility flies in the face of American history which has seen a people steadfastly sanctifying individual freedom while progressively narrowing it through the development of a beneficent state. . . . The cost of sloth, gluttony, alcoholic intemperance, reckless driving, sexual frenzy, and smoking is now a national, and not an individual, responsibility. . . . I believe the idea of a "right" to health should be replaced by the idea of an individual moral obligation to preserve one's health—a public duty if you will.

JOHN KNOWLES

Lynn, a married woman just turned forty, had been gaining weight gradually for fifteen years. She entered our clinic

211

after receiving a diagnosis of dangerously high blood pressure. I learned that she had lost several hundred pounds over the years, on various crash diets and at health spas, but had always gained it back. Now, with a serious medical complication partly caused by her eating habits, she was frightened enough to try making a lasting change. She was willing to commit herself to a special diet—low in cholesterol, salt, and calories—that was critical to successful control of her blood pressure.

Like many people, Lynn had developed a complex and emotion-ridden relationship with food and her body. She ate when she was under stress. As her parents had taught her, she considered rich and flavorful food a gift to herself. She felt devoid of all willpower to avoid food. Her body had never seemed good to her; she had always perceived herself as fat and ugly. Except for her finely defined face and hands, her image of herself was round and featureless. Lynn's parents had taught her early that one's body should never give pleasure. Her body awareness was low, and physical exercise was pure drudgery.

We began Lynn with a period of self-observation, aimed at making her aware of her habits, feelings, and behavior patterns relative to food and health. She kept a daily log of what, when, and where she ate, how she felt before and after meals, her exercise, and the stressful events of each day. At the end of the first week of self-observation, she was anxious and depressed at how "bad" she was and how hopeless her plight seemed. The enormity of the process haunted her, and in her own mind, her power of self-control seemed inferior to the task at hand.

In order to create change, a person needs to experience at least some initial success, demonstrating to him that he can alter his habits and life. I decided that Lynn's first task should be to increase her body awareness and control over stress, both of which were indirect contributors to her eating. This task was easy and felt good, and by doing it well, she might increase her motivation for the more difficult undertakings to follow. Because she had such a long history of failure at altering eating patterns, I thought that her food intake should be approached only after she successfully made other changes.

I initially taught Lynn a relaxation exercise with the help of a cassette tape. I suggested that she try to relax during the most stressful periods of the day, particularly at those times when she habitually ate. My goal was to teach her a new response to stress—to substitute the pleasant habit of relaxation for her self-destructive and ineffectual eating.

I also started Lynn on an exercise program, designed to help her find ways to use her body that were easy and pleasant and could fit into her life-style. She enjoyed swimming and bicycle riding, and by doing them with a friend as I suggested, she used her companion to reinforce her own commitment to exercise. Her habitual morning coffee and rolls were replaced by a morning swim and bike ride. After only two weeks of this regimen, she felt better physically, more confident, more alive, and less stressed. Incidentally, during this period I had instructed her to eat what she wanted and not weigh herself, to take her mind off this problem area.

Eventually, we began exploring Lynn's eating patterns, aiming toward easy and gentle changes. Because she was responsible for preparing her family's meals as well as her own, this phase of the program needed the cooperation and participation of her household members, particularly her husband. He was healthy and slim, and not particularly concerned about his wife's weight. He kidded her about her dieting, while always requesting large meals. Her teenage sons, active in athletics, also liked high-calorie meat and carbohydrate foods. These posed direct conflicts if Lynn was going to change.

How could Lynn's family be encouraged to help her change? Ultimately, her health became a sufficient motivator. When Lynn enrolled in a special health-cooking course, lower-calorie alternatives at dinner became more palatable for the others.

Lynn agreed to serve herself smaller portions of food, eat

more slowly, and eliminate dessert. Everyone stopped drinking caffeinated coffee. Her husband began giving her massages and other special rewards for adhering to her diet regimen.

Actually, family meals were not Lynn's major problem. Her most destructive eating occurred primarily when she was home alone—while anxious, bored, or under stress. The junk food she kept in the house fueled this behavior.

Thus, Lynn's behavior-change program required three steps. The first was to restructure her environment. Many types of food were eliminated from the shopping list. She consciously began to avoid the kitchen. Conversations in the family about food and eating were curtailed. When the temptation to eat became strong, she was instructed to do something else besides eat—walk out of the house, call a friend on the phone, or remind herself of her commitment to change and its positive consequences.

The second aspect of Lynn's change program was to explore her deepest thoughts and feelings that she associated with food, weight, health, and her body. Lynn discovered, for example, that she had insecurities about feeling attractive and sexy if she were thin. After becoming keenly aware of the way she connected food with self-reward, she developed a new belief system, resolving that she was rewarding herself by *not* eating, and recalling how much better she felt when she limited her food intake.

Finally, Lynn began to examine her positive, future goals. Concluding that eating had concealed a sense of inner emptiness and a lack of meaningful companionship, she began searching for a career and made some shifts in her marriage relationship.

Lynn lost weight steadily for a year. She joined a health support group, in which others were also making major life changes. Her blood pressure lowered, and consequently she required less medication. She felt better and more optimistic about her future.

Some of the things that Lynn did not do should be noted. She didn't weigh herself regularly or become obsessed about

whether she was gaining or losing weight. Nor did she ad-
here to a strict diet or count calories. Instead, she altered her
basic attitudes—patterns and behavior toward food, exercise, her body, and herself. Food—whether eating it or not
eating it—became less important, as other aspects of her life
took its place. Within a year, her goal of permanently
changing her health-threatening behavior was accomplished.

Lynn had shared a problem with a majority of Americans—automatic, unconscious eating-behavior which had
gradually evolved into a health hazard. Some studies indicate that perhaps 90 percent of Americans will die prematurely from diseases of civilization that stem, directly or
indirectly, from their relationship to food, exercise, and the
environment.[1]

Most of us are aware of the common health-risk factors we
face. Few of us have not attempted to diet, or have not begun
an exercise program. I know many people who seem ad
dicted to trying to change, but never succeed.

Perhaps you've asked yourself why it's so difficult to ad-
here to your well-meaning and important efforts at self-control. One factor, certainly, is the short-term pleasure of
inappropriate behavior and the delayed nature of the negative consequences. It's much easier to become an armchair
quarterback than to participate actively in an exercise program—and the calamitous impact of your sedentary life-
style may not be felt for ten, twenty, or thirty years. Some
people prefer to deal with life like a gambler, playing the
odds that they won't contract heart disease or cancer. West-
ern culture's denial of mortality and its ignoring of the
body's limits and proper care promote this attitude.

Even so, our bodies eventually tell us we must change. We
start to feel the effects of our negative behavior, and consequently we resolve to alter our eating and smoking habits
and to treat our bodies better. We channel our energy
against the strong current of habits and apparent desires.
However, no matter how hard we try, too often we regress
to our old ways.

In such a situation, you need to apply basic, psychologically founded principles of learning and behavior alteration. Rather than trying to force change, you should proceed in slow steps—perhaps with a guide or helper, or a small group, as a facilitating force—in a complete and effective program of behavior change. No matter what habits or patterns you want to modify, the same general principle applies.

Habits and Health

Most daily activities are done automatically and unconsciously. When I wake up, I go about my morning rituals, and sometimes make breakfast and help my children get their day started, without being consciously aware of what I am doing. I drive my car, cook, clean, walk, type, and do scores of other things without telling myself how to go about them. Indeed, my life would be very different if I had to order my body to make every movement and think about it as I carried out each command. But fortunately, the intricate patterns of movement are accomplished by my body without my conscious control.

In effect, then, most of our daily behavior, like our internal bodily processes, takes place habitually outside of conscious awareness, although it is susceptible to modification by conscious choice. Although our habits are our servants, they can also bedevil and hurt us. That is why it is customary to label habits as good or bad. Over time, bad habits can lead to illness and physical damage.

"People know what they ought to do and they don't do it" runs the complaint I hear most often, not only from physicians, but from patients and friends. A society committed to maximum personal freedom has been caught in the dilemma of trying to find the incentives for each individual to behave in a healthy fashion, when our friends and the environment tempt us in the other direction. Unfortunately, it is more difficult to break a habit than to develop one.

Recent research by Lester Breslow, dean of the UCLA School of Public Health, demonstrates the potential benefits of even the most rudimentary health habits. Seven thousand active and healthy older people in California, Utah, and Nevada were asked about their daily behavior and recent medical history. Their health status was then observed over the next six years.

The results indicate that seven simple habits can significantly determine a person's health status and life expectancy. The more these seven health practices are part of a person's daily life, the healthier he is. An individual who practices all seven habits has the health of a person thirty years younger who ignores all of them. Life expectancy is highly correlated with how many of these habits a person follows: a forty-five-year-old man who practices three or less can expect to live to age sixty-seven, while a man of this same age who follows six or seven should live to seventy eight. (Of course, these are not predictions, but statistical correlations, based upon a large number of people's behavior and health histories.)[2]

Here are the habits that can add much time and health to our lives.

1. Three regular meals a day, with few snacks
2. Breakfast regularly
3. Moderate exercise two or three times a week
4. Seven to eight hours sleep a night (not more)
5. No smoking
6. Moderate weight
7. Little or no alcohol

How many of these habits do you, and other members of your family, observe? Most of those in Breslow's research average only two or three.

Make a list of your own habits, routines, and behavior that may interfere with your health. After a few days of self-observation and reflection, some people have compiled lists containing more than a hundred items. Include omissions—

activities you don't engage in that you should—as well as techniques you use to treat or relieve your ailments which merely mask symptoms without exploring or modifying the causes. For example, many people take aspirin to cure a headache, without attempting to understand its source or the stressful situations which caused it and will likely cause it again.

A Five-Stage Program of Behavior Control

In the practice of psychotherapy, two primary approaches to change and control over dysfunctional behavior have competed for attention. The first method, which grew out of Freud's psychoanalytic theory, suggests that such behavior is based on negative, denied, or misplaced feelings. These feelings are thought to motivate negative behavior. Treatment is aimed at changing the underlying feelings, in the expectation that the behavior change will follow automatically.

The second, and newer, approach is called behavior modification. It assumes that all habits, positive or negative, are learned, and that we can be taught to behave differently via certain basic principles. These behavior-therapy techniques are offshoots of the simple carrot-and-stick concept: eliminate the environmental factors that promote negative health habits and replace them with new factors which support more positive behavior. The feelings that lie behind the behavior are irrelevant.

Both schools have attacked psychosomatic illness, with some success. My own work combines these two perspectives, which are both valid and not mutually exclusive. Some negative behavior is simply a bad habit, but it may also relate to deeper negative feelings or indirectly expressed feelings.

There are five stages in my program to reverse dysfunctional habits of behavior:

1. Observe yourself, to become aware of the nature of the habit and the context in which it occurs.
2. Mobilize that vague internal force which comes under the name of "motivation." This is the energy and commitment that will carry you through the change process.
3. Create a change strategy, and a contract for specific action.
4. Practice or learn alternate responses to the situations that usually lead you to respond habitually, building new, more adaptive habits.
5. Discover support in your environment to continue behaving in a new way, in order to avoid slipping back into an old pattern.

This sequence can be used to alter almost any type of bad habit—from sexual impotency, obesity, shyness, and destructive marital conflicts to stress symptoms, headaches, bedwetting, back pain, and insomnia. Each of these bad habits has been inadvertently learned, and treatment consists of modifying the environment so that it demands or supports different behavior.

Let's consider each stage in more detail. First, there should be a careful study of the habit, spending a week to a month observing yourself to discover exactly when, where, and under what circumstances the habit evolved. I suggest that you carry a sheet of paper with you and, as Lynn did, note when certain types of habits or feelings appear. Each day, you will find yourself creating an inventory of the kinds of responses, emotions, and situations associated with your problem.

If, like Lynn, you want to change your eating habits, chart each bite of food you take, noting how you eat it, where you eat it, and what you are doing and feeling at the time and afterward. Patients who have headaches or other pain should chart the degree of their discomfort or stress at hourly intervals (on a scale of 0 to 5), what they are doing and feeling at the time, and how they deal with it, including medication taken.

This chart often makes a person aware for the first time how prevalent pain or stress is in his life. We often underestimate the severity of our difficulties, or fail to see the habitual nature of our responses. Also, clear patterns emerge. For example, some of us have colds or headaches only on weekends and holidays.

A woman I treated had suffered migraine headaches almost weekly for many years, and through her inventory, she discovered that her headaches typically occurred a few hours after doing something she didn't want to do, or after she had been angry. I next asked her to incorporate into her daily inventory the things she did during the day that made her furious or that she disliked doing. The next time we met, she told me she ran out of paper writing them all down. This exercise helped her finally understand the blocked emotional responses that contributed to her headaches.

With weight control, the patterns are clear. In our day-to-day lives, socializing is usually associated with eating. People also eat when they feel anxious, lonely, or frustrated. Thus, eating is often a primitive (and ineffective) attempt at anxiety and stress control. Many people eat so unconsciously that they are unable to order themselves to stop. But if you keep a list, eating becomes a conscious act.

Once an individual becomes aware of the problem, he can then enter a second stage—the search for the elusive "motivation," the energy to carry out the change process. Motivation is usually thought of as an internal force that prompts us to do or not do various things. But behavioral psychologists perceive motivation or willpower as the end result of a number of internal and external factors, many of which are in conflict with one another. If the sum total is positive, we do something; if not, we don't.

When a person speaks of finding, or having, motivation, he may be talking about creating enough incentives, or eliminating enough obstacles, to accomplish a specific goal. For example, if our salaries were dependent on our observance of proper health habits, or if sugar, salt, tobacco, alcohol, and food additives were illegal drugs with punishment for possession, we would probably be healthier. However, we live in a world where advertisements persuade us to buy and eat these substances without limit. Our lives are arranged for short-term convenience rather than long-term health.

To build positive motivation, first list as many reasons as you can for each of your bad habits. The list should contain all the environmental factors that tempt or persuade you to keep the habit, including people, situations, and feelings. It also might include the benefits obtained from the bad habits. If you are ill, for example, you probably receive considerable nurturing, care, and help from others because you are sick. It may be hard to give up back pain—and the accompanying attention—when it means going back to a dreary job.

Next compile another list (usually shorter) of reasons to change. For many people, the first item on the list is "The doctor said I had to." When a person actually experiences the consequences of a bad habit—shortness of breath, difficulty walking, continual pain, etc.—these become even stronger incentives to change.

Incidentally, it is not uncommon to feel a sense of loss when you abandon a habit that might have been pleasurable. For that reason, the motivation and incentives for new behavior must be powerful. Therefore, you need to make a third list, in which you create a new, nondestructive strategy for obtaining each of the benefits which until now you've derived solely from your bad habits. For example, you might ask for attention or schedule a daily rest, instead of complaining about your body.

Stage three of the program is critical. It involves examining your lists of positive and negative incentives and designing a program for change. Many people expect the doctor or therapist to do this for them. But this passive attitude inhibits one's commitment to change.

You and your physician or guide must work together to

create a program to alter behavior. It may involve one master plan, and then small weekly or monthly steps and goals, specifying particular changes. Certainly these goals must be clear and specific. Rather than striving "to lose weight," you should aim toward "losing thirty-five pounds within six months, by modifying eating behavior and adopting a vigorous exercise program." The reasons and incentives for the goals, as well as the obstacles and deterrents, should be specified.

To heighten your commitment, the program should be in writing, and signed by you, your facilitator/physician, and perhaps even a member of your family or a close friend who can help in the program. You may also find it helpful to incorporate specific rewards into the regimen. For example, after achieving your goals for the week, do something that you like or treat yourself to something special. This is a good way to build motivation.

The fourth stage of the change program involves adopting new and healthier habits. As with any consciously selected new habit, there is an initial break-in period during which it seems unnatural. During this time, it has to be earnestly practiced. Soon it will become automatic and easy.

Role playing—or actually trying out new responses in make-believe situations—can be helpful in learning new habits. For instance, why not practice saying no, or even leaving the table, when you are offered food, when others smoke, or when you feel angry? Consider the situations that give you trouble, and work to create new responses.

Controlling your environment is another aspect of learning new responses. We often behave in reaction to our environment. If food is nearby, we may eat it without thinking. Or if we pressure ourselves with unrealistic deadlines or wake up too late to eat breakfast, jog, or meditate, we are setting ourselves up for unhealthiness.

The final step in altering dysfunctional habits is to make sure that you have continuing support for the new responses. Since the ordinary environment does not usually value healthy behavior, you will probably have to actively recruit a group—e.g., your family—to offer such encouragement. Obviously, if you're trying to lose weight, it is helpful to live in a home which does not provide high-calorie foods. If you have just quit smoking, it's helpful if your family and friends do not smoke near you. In fact, it is easier for an entire family (or a couple) than an individual to diet or stop smoking, or to adopt an exercise or relaxation regime. A family that works together to modify its behavior patterns and has fun doing it, praising and coaxing each other along, is the most effective vehicle for change.

Beyond the family, the best way to support new behavior is through a self-help group of men and women with the same problem.[3] One of the oldest of these programs is Alcoholics Anonymous, founded and run entirely by ex-alcoholics. AA has developed one of the few successful ways of persuading people to stop drinking. In recent years, other self-help groups have been formed to encompass almost every type of difficulty and illness. Self-help groups support and encourage adaptive behavior and add to the positive incentives in the environment. It may seem absurd to pay a fee for the privilege of going on a diet and weighing yourself publicly each week, but the applause of your peers and the fear of disappointing them seem to be potent incentives to lose weight and maintain the loss.

As I presume you've recognized by now, I cannot offer any miraculous program to gain control over behavior that threatens your health. I often find that people who seek such magic cures, or easy change, actually want to continue their behavior. Gaining internal control over damaging habits demands hard work to look closely at these patterns, understand their roots, and restructure the environment to create incentives for new behavior and new habits.

16 Freeing Yourself from the Past and Creating Your Future

> To dismiss the most central fact of man's being because it is inner and subjective is to make the hugest subjective falsification possible—one that leaves out the really critical half of man's nature. For without that underlying subjective flux, as experienced in floating imagery, dreams, bodily impulses, formative ideas, projections, and symbols, the world that is open to human experience can be neither described nor rationally understood. When our age learns that lesson, it will have made the first move toward redeeming for human use the mechanized and electrified wasteland that is now being bulldozed, at man's expense and to his permanent loss, for the benefit of the Megamachine.
>
> LEWIS MUMFORD

Irving Oyle, frequently called the family doctor of the holistic movement, espouses a very radical position about illness, derived from conceptions of reality that are the basis of modern relativistic physics. Oyle suggests that as humans, we create our reality from second to second. Just because you were ill a moment, a month, or a year ago does not mean that you are necessarily ill right now. What you need, he counsels, is to free yourself from the belief that your present reality is so firmly connected to your past. Only then can you create a future in the shape you desire.[1]

Many of the contemporary psychological self-help programs echo this perspective. They proclaim that the past is important in defining who we are, but it does not have to be an impediment that keeps us from changing.

When beginning a self-discovery and behavior-modification process, some patients ask questions that can be summed up as follows: "If I am not consciously aware of the original trauma or the early experiences that led to my current stress symptom or discomfort, can I really uncover them? Can I contact my seemingly incomplete and imperfect memory, and rediscover the origins of my physical responses to stress? And if I can remember or encounter a negative pattern that still affects me today, can I then change it, and thus maximize my chances for good health?"

My answer to these questions is yes. By using special techniques such as psychic visualization and imagery, it is possible to remember much of our history that seemed long forgotten. Ultimately, with an understanding of how we got into our dilemmas, we can uncover the information to help us solve our difficulties.

Reexperiencing the Past

I hope by now you're keeping some kind of daily journal of your stress situations, negative habits, or symptoms. In conjunction with this, I'd like you now to try a simple imaginative exercise that will enable you to go back in time—often to early childhood, or even to the moment of your birth—in order to explore past experiences related to your present concerns. This technique is fashioned from the hypnotic process known as *age regression*, which is used to delve into a person's past.[2] But, like other techniques I use, it does not demand a physician or therapist as a guide. It can be practiced at home, by yourself, and in most cases the results can be as revealing as those obtained in the doctor's office.

The first step in this and every imagery exercise is to enter a state of deep relaxation. In the process of relaxing the body, you will also free the mind from attaching itself to specific thoughts and worries. This state of relaxation is identical to a light hypnotic trance, or self-hypnosis. (Refer back to chapter 13 if you need help achieving a state of relaxation.) You can perform this exercise by listening to a recording of the instructions or by reading them over several times and remembering them.

Once you are relaxed, imagine that you are stepping onto an escalator, such as you find in a department store. The escalator is very long, and there are no other people riding it. As you descend, you will find yourself becoming even more deeply relaxed. Feel yourself continuing downward, with your hand on the rail, effortlessly gliding along the moving stairs. With each passing moment, you will be more and more relaxed.

Finally, you are coming to the end of the escalator. As you reach the bottom, you step off into a room. Looking around, you realize you are in a small, private theater. This is your personal magical theater, where you can sit comfortably and, in a state of deep relaxation, discover and reexperience many distant events in your life.

As you quickly notice, the seats in this theater are deeply cushioned and comfortable. Sinking into the seat cushions, you realize that you may never have been this relaxed before. As you sit quietly in this chair, your relaxed state deepens further.

Now, look upward at the empty stage in front of you. In a moment, you will begin to see a scene. It will be from your own past, dating back to a time several minutes before you first experienced your particular bad habit, physical symptom, or pain, or before you responded with the type of behavior that you would like to change. Wait a few moments until the scene appears by itself. Do not try to create it in your conscious mind. If you are patient, it will emerge spontaneously by itself. You won't feel any anxiety, pain, or discomfort when it emerges, because the scene begins before your symptom or habitual behavior was necessary.

Has your scene now appeared? When it does, examine it closely. Since this is a magical theater, and the events are familiar to you, you may find that you can enter the minds and bodies of the characters in the scene, and feel what they are feeling. As you reexperience this picture, try to fill in as many of the details as you can. Who are the people in your scene? What do they look like? What are they doing, feeling, and thinking?

As your state of watchful relaxation continues, let the scene slowly and completely unfold before you. Watch the situation develop. Without experiencing tension, anxiety, or pain, can you detect the moment when you began to feel discomfort (in the scene, not in your chair)? What was happening or what were you feeling that led to your response? Watch yourself closely, as you respond to the situation with your habitual symptom or dysfunctional behavior.

As the scene develops, make certain that you remain relaxed. If you become upset or tense, simply turn off the image for a moment, and concentrate on giving yourself some suggestions for relaxation. Once you are relaxed again, then continue with the exercise.

As the scene nears its end, take a look at yourself within it. How do you (onstage) feel now? What are you taking away from the situation? What have you gained from your response? What is still unsettled or incomplete? Let yourself clearly perceive the entire pattern that has led you to the particular reaction that is harmful to you and your body.

Now, let the image fade from the stage. This scene will be stored in your mind, and can easily be recalled after you leave the relaxation state. There is no need to try to remember it consciously. Once the image has passed from your mind, center your attention on your body and deepen your relaxation.

This exercise can be repeated, going back to another time, to watch yourself create other dysfunctional behavior, pain, or difficulty. As a rule, two or three scenes can be experienced in one relaxation period. After the exercise, when you return to your ordinary state of awareness, write down each of the experiences in your journal, giving it an approximate date. As you describe each one in writing, you can begin to reflect upon it, asking yourself why you felt forced into such a response and what alternatives you had.

If I were counseling you in my office, I would teach this exercise to you and then send you away for a week or two, with instructions to recall and write down at least two past scenes each day. Usually, by the end of the second week, some of the images would date back quite early in your life and offer a large amount of forgotten material to examine. Equipped with a journal that includes not only your present problems and experiences but about twenty past situations, you are then ready for the next phase of work—using imagery, as well as behavior change, to alter your response.

About one-fourth of the scenes that my patients recall during this exercise date back to childhood. Many are dramatic, emotionally liberating, and revealing. However, just as I am reluctant to accept the idea that illness has a single physical cause, I also doubt that these incidents from the past are the sole cause of a habit or symptom. True, by their very emotional power, and the suggestibility of young children, they certainly appear to be important links in the chain that creates symptoms. But I hesitate to embrace them as the only force behind a particular problem.

There is another factor to consider. Some therapists would argue that these events did not occur at all. For example, after hearing many patients describe seemingly incredible experiences of parental seduction, Freud concluded that these events were mere fantasies, wishes, or mistaken judgments about innocent situations. However, whether these memories are real or fantasy, the emotional power of the patient's belief still influences present responses.

I recall one woman who had had several operations, including removal of her gallbladder and many gallstones. In the exercise described above, she returned to an incident in her life that she had not regarded as significant before. She had broken up with her boyfriend of several years and had dropped out of college. After a succession of jobs, having no place to live and being rejected by her family, she decided to call this old boyfriend. They spent a night together, during which he was brutal to her. In the morning, he told her he was getting married the next day. She left in a daze and felt emotionally numb for literally years. A few months following, her series of operations ensued, but she had never before noted the connection between her illnesses and this traumatic event.

Interestingly, this exercise often need not take you into your past more than a few days or weeks. A young businessman discovered that his stomach pains, which seemed to be leading to an ulcer, arose whenever he performed competently in a job he didn't enjoy. Another woman's pains erupted during times of conflict, as when she was enjoying a party which her husband couldn't attend.

As you gain experience in self-observation, you will become less attached to negative responses as the only method of handling your environment. By exploring the past and examining the present, you will discover other ways to react. The purpose of this exploratory process is to gain insight in order to change present behavior.

Rewriting the Script

In a sense, your habit patterns and physical symptoms are a script which your body unwittingly follows whenever certain types of situations arise. As you have probably discovered, there are ways to change that script by reorienting your mind, your body, and your behavior toward new patterns.

You should practice not only new behavior (as I suggested in the previous chapter), but also new thought patterns. You must utilize mental-imagery techniques that in turn tell your body how you want it to react in stressful situations and crises. Thus by consciously selecting and creating positive, health-supporting physiological and behavioral responses, you are rewriting your life script for a more positive outcome.

The exercise in which you reexperienced difficult episodes from the past is a model for the rewriting of your script. You can relive each scene not only as it was, but also as it might have been. You can practice alternative responses in the safety of your imagination.

As I noted in chapter 13, "systematic densensitization" has been helpful in retraining responses to the environment. It requires a person to explore specific situations that cause him anxiety, fear, or other negative emotional or physical responses. He lists them in order, from the least difficult and frightening to the most. Then, while in a state of deep relaxation, he imagines himself in each situation, starting with the least difficult. He pictures himself experiencing the situation calmly and responding to it positively.

Using this technique, people have learned to face situations and crises that once terrified them, by practicing in their imagination a new way of approaching each scene. Once you can experience what you fear in your mind while remaining deeply relaxed, you will be ready to practice new behavior in actual life situations. Typically, you'll be able to deal with the event with diminished muscle tension and fear.

Let's assume that you experience negative physical symptoms in certain types of job or school stress—perhaps facing your boss, taking an exam, or meeting a deadline. Why not imagine facing these stressful events while remaining relaxed, and taking more positive steps calmly, without any physical reaction? After practicing this in your mind, do it in the actual situation. The imaginative work, by creating a physical pattern within the body, acts unconsciously to help you create the change in actuality.

In my healing and stress-management groups, I insist that the situations and the alternatives that are envisioned be as specific and concrete as possible. Vagueness and ambiguity in one's plans and mental imagery can lead to problems in actualizing this behavior later. But if you envision in detail how you will handle a certain stressful situation, what the other involved individuals might say, and how you will respond, you will increase your chances of a positive reaction.

While you can practice and learn this technique on your own, the small group is the ideal vehicle. In a class setting, people absorb the exercises together and then do their homework of daily practice, self-discovery, and alternate possibilities on their own. During each session, they share their progress and use other members of the group to practice their role playing. People also make contracts with the group, promising to try specific changes, and then they report back about their success or failure.

Positive Imagery and Self-Affirmation

Try to become aware of the many ways that you are self-critical. Perhaps you call yourself names, or express frustration at your limitations. Every time you say something containing a negative emotional charge, it has a tiny but measurable negative effect on your body. There is a significant difference between this self-criticism, which can easily lead to self-punishment and self-hate, and a constructive assessment of your mistakes and shortcomings. In the former situation, you can end up inflicting psychic pain—worry, depression, and anxiety—or physical illness upon yourself.

By contrast, what if you periodically took a moment to compliment yourself, to remind yourself of your positive potentiality, your essential goodness, how deserving you are of health and happiness? If you have a negative image of yourself and your body, such apparently simplistic rituals can be very supportive. Repeating positive, self-affirming suggestions to yourself in a relaxed, gentle tone can help mobilize your expectant faith in your future and your inner potential for self-health.

The healing power of prayer probably stems in part from

this ritual of self-acceptance and affirmation. By praying, we acknowledge our inner worthiness and regard ourselves as connected to the wider human community. Prayer can be seen as a process of relaxation and an initiation of positive, self-healing mental imagery, which perhaps can reverse many deep negative mental and physical patterns. In the same way, the power of the physician—and of his ally, the placebo—rests largely in the ability to stimulate positive expectations. In many spiritual and healing traditions, the power of positive mental images has been a major source of healing and change. Today, the new religion is science. Now that we know how the mind affects the body, technical interpretations are available for what was formerly explained as divine intervention.

Consider the experiences around the turn of the century of Emile Coué, a French pharmacist who founded a clinic that utilized positive imagery as a method of attaining maximum health. Coué's famous phrase, which he had his patients repeat to themselves many times a day, was "Every day, in every way, I am becoming better and better." That basic suggestion, combined with specific formulae for various ailments, was aimed at using imagery and suggestion to affect physiological responses. During Coué's time, the germ theory was quite new, and technological advances and wonder drugs were decades in the future, so suggestion and hypnosis were among the most powerful elements in the physician's black bag. One of the major achievements of the new, holistic medicine is the rediscovery and reworking of this ancient tool, combining it with modern advances in medicine and physiology.

The crucial element in the use of suggestion in self-healing is to develop a mental image of a positive future state. This visualization presumably has a physiological effect, stimulating your body, your mind, and your behavior in that direction. By picturing an ideal conception of yourself, you begin the process of creating the kind of future that you desire. A seed is planted which redirects the mind toward a particular goal, and through the mind, the body is influenced.

Whenever you meditate or relax, I suggest that you end each session with some positive images, goals, and messages about your future. For instance, if you are ill, you could visualize a future time when you will have regained your health. Be concrete and fill in as many details as you can, to imagine how you will look and feel. Most important, picture what you will then be doing.

I once worked with a woman who suffered severe chronic pain. When she imagined her future, she saw herself back at work. However, she believed her job was stultifying, and when I pressed her, she admitted that she preferred being in pain to working. I thought it was essential for her to remove this negative future image. She finally agreed to seek a different job after regaining her health.

People who cannot conceive of doing anything pleasurable in the future do not have much incentive, and hence much internal energy, to regain health. It often takes a long time to develop a positive picture for the future. Yet one needs that specific image in order to begin the healing process.

There are many examples of the power of positive suggestive imagery. It can affect our physical capacities dramatically, even in athletics. Timothy Gallwey's "inner tennis" helps people improve their strokes and let their bodies passively do the rest. Through his method, tennis becomes a form of meditation.[3]

Bruce Jenner has recounted how he utilized imagery as a central part of his training for an Olympic decathlon gold medal. Many times a day, he would picture in vivid detail every movement of every event. He knew he could not afford a single misstep or miscue, and so he programmed the correct responses in his body. With imagery, he instinctively performed at his maximum potential.

Athletes in other sports have found that visualization is as much a part of their training as physical conditioning. One study revealed that athletes who practiced shooting baskets merely by imagining the ball going smoothly into the basket improved as much as those who practiced with a real ball and basket. Edmund Jacobson, who pioneered the use of progressive relaxation, has demonstrated that people who visualize their bodies shooting baskets will actually tense the correct muscles.[4]

Whether or not you're an athlete, there are other suggestions that can help you achieve your goals. While trying to conquer illness or stress symptoms, I ask people to create a set of positive phrases or messages they need to remember and write them on a card. They place the card on the bathroom mirror and repeat the phrases to themselves several times during the day, letting them work on their unconscious. These phrases may include "I can get the love I want without having to eat," or "I will feel tremendous, vital, healthy, and breathe freely each day that I do not smoke," or "I will treat my body with love and respect." Such messages serve to counteract negative patterns that may have begun years earlier.

Many people also find it helpful to include affirmative personal statements on their cards, letting themselves know that they are worthy of being healthy, or being loved, or of changing in a positive direction and reaching some of their life goals. It may seem silly, but suggesting something often enough has a powerful effect.

Below is an example of an affirmative-image meditation created by a patient I worked with. He repeats it three times a day, saying each sentence several times to himself. Here is the meditation:

Every day in every way I am getting better and better.
My mind is quiet and still.
My mind is quiet and happy.
I am letting go of my parents.
I am safe and solid.
I am one with all living things.

Every day in every way I am becoming more alive.
I am free of childhood needs.
I use my consciousness to be free of outside forces.
I am filled with energy.
I am letting go of my unrealistic expectations about my work and family.
I am grounded and steady.
I am free of all outside forces.
I have everything within myself to enjoy every minute of every day.
Every day in every way I am becoming more and more healthy.
I accept myself completely.
My body is calm and relaxed.
I am safe and at peace.

Notice that all of these phrases are in the present tense, proclaiming that they are happening now. There is no wishing or hoping involved. There is much repetition, and the statements are simple and direct.

After several weeks, this patient wrote about his experience with affirmative meditation: "I find it very meaningful. I am very aware that never before had I tried to talk to myself in a positive manner."

I am continually amazed at the power of positive images and self-affirming meditations. Imagery has freed many people, particularly those who had never viewed themselves as healthy and worthwhile, of the weight of their negative expectations.

Of course, self-affirmation is not a miracle cure for deep-rooted psychological problems. However, the exercises I've presented can help you to remake your future—first in your imagination and then in actuality. While this is often accomplished under the guidance of a professional therapist, I believe that for most people, a large portion of this work can be realized through self-examination and reversing long-standing self-destructive health habits and stress symptoms.

17 *The Healing Power of Imagery*

To prevent disease or to cure it, the power of Truth, of divine Spirit, must break the dream of the material senses. To heal by argument, find the type of the ailment, get its name, and array your mental plea against the physical. Argue at first mentally, not audibly, that the patient has no disease, and conform the argument so as to destroy the evidence of the disease. Mentally insist that harmony is the fact, and that sickness is a temporal dream. Realize the presence of health and the fact of harmonious being, until the body corresponds with the normal conditions of health and harmony.

MARY BAKER EDDY

Imagine a table set with your favorite foods. Perhaps there's a well-cooked steak, steaming vegetables, and fresh fruit. Allow your mind to create this picture down to the minutest detail of sight and smell.

Now, visualize yourself taking a bite of the most delicious serving. Chew on a make-believe ripe peach, or whatever you've found on your own perfect platter. Feel its coolness (or warmth) permeate your mouth, and taste it as it settles easily over your tongue. Notice your saliva running, as if the morsel were actually in your mouth. Feel your stomach respond expectantly, awaiting the arrival of the food.

Next, try a different picture. Imagine stepping out into the street and suddenly seeing a huge truck bearing down on you. It is roaring toward you at fifty miles per hour, and it probably won't be able to stop before it reaches the crosswalk where you are standing. Can you feel a visceral response—anxiety, shallow breathing, and a tightening of your stomach and other muscles?

Clearly, mental images directly affect your body. The mind has an enormous capability of altering physiological functions.

Let's try one more exercise. This time, you will attempt to alter a specific physiological response—namely, your hand temperature. Here's how you're going to do it:

Create a mental picture of a bowl of ice water, filled with half-melted ice cubes. The water is terribly cold, and condensation is forming on the sides of the bowl. Now imagine slowly placing your hand into the freezing water. Let yourself experience the shock of the cold, and feel your hand shivering and then becoming numb, heavy, and stiff as it remains in the icy liquid. As the image becomes vivid in your mind, your hand will respond by actually getting cooler. Through mental imagery—imagination—you will be able to alter your autonomic physiological responses.

Earlier in the book, I differentiated between voluntary and visceral bodily functions. As you'll recall, the voluntary muscles respond to direct, active will. We tell our hand to move—and it does. We do not have to order each muscle to expand or contract; we simply give the command, and our unconscious automatically knows how, and does the rest.

With the visceral, automatic body functions, which occur largely outside of awareness, we have learned that a different mode of communication must be used—specifically, the language of imagery, suggestion, and passive volition. Instead of directly ordering yourself to relax, go to sleep, cease eating junk food, lower blood pressure, feel more energy, stop experiencing pain, heal a wound, or kill cancerous cells, you can make your visceral body respond by using the language of imagination, mental pictures, and suggestion. In this chapter, we continue our lessons in the grammar and style of this self-communication and self-control.

Pretend that your body has an infection that is threatening to spread. Or perhaps deposits have accumulated on the linings of your blood vessels. Or maybe your body does not produce enough of an important enzyme. Under these circumstances, what can you do to facilitate the necessary changes in your body? Is it possible for you to imagine white blood cells moving even faster to the infected site, or the deposits melting away, or your chemical factories increasing their output of the life-supporting enzyme? Can this influence the actual performance of your body?

If this is possible, you will be using your own powers to achieve what others rely on drugs to accomplish. If your mental state can increase your body's efficiency by even just 10 percent, then you can, in effect, enhance the power of your conventional medical care by that amount. And in the many cases where external treatments are impotent, the use of mental imagery might be the only way to catalyze your body to action.

As a mode of treatment, imagery has definite advantages. It has no negative side effects that may endanger or injure the ill person, nor can it conflict with or jeopardize other therapies. Therefore, an increasing number of physicians and health teams are experimenting with these exercises, adding them to the treatment process.

In many ways, mental imagery seems alien to the treatment that physicians typically prescribe. Imagining broken bones healing, pain disappearing, or white blood cells as knights battling cancer cells—this runs counter to traditional conceptions of medicine and healing. So how could imagery possibly help? As David Bresler, director of the UCLA Pain Control Unit and a prominent researcher into imagery, tells his chronic pain patients, "In this clinic, I am going to ask you to do things that would have had you committed ten years ago."

Yet just as mental exercises can produce a balanced state of relaxation, and biofeedback can help you control specific autonomic responses, so can mental images affect the speed and effectiveness of healing.[1] Once you learn the proper language and style of communication, you have the potential to assist your physician by exercising considerable control over internal healing functions.

Divided Consciousness

Although much still needs to be learned about imagery, and specifically how it affects our body, recent brain research has provided some interesting information that may be relevant to this unique form of inner communication. We know, for instance, that the brain is divided into two hemispheres, which have different skills and specialties. The left hemisphere controls all the activities and sensations of the right side of the body, and vice versa. The left side also governs speech.

Robert Ornstein, among others, suggests that different types of thought take place predominantly in each hemisphere.[7] The left hemisphere is more animated when the brain is engaged in rational, logical, digital thought. The right hemisphere is more active when the person is thinking in metaphorical, pictorial, musical, poetic, symbolic, or analogic terms. In various life tasks, one or the other mode of thought (and hemisphere) predominates. For example, in reading, talking, planning, or thinking logically, brain waves from the left hemisphere predominate, while in activities like fantasy, drawing, playing music, or meditating, the right hemisphere and its attendant consciousness prevails. From my perspective, interacting with our unconscious through the imagery process is clearly a right-hemisphere function. It utilizes a consciousness quite different from our goal-directed, willful, rational activity.

Psychologist and hypnosis researcher Ernest Hilgard has clinically demonstrated that we have two types of consciousness. He worked with several patients who while under hypnosis were not knowingly aware of various sensations (e.g., pain or a loud noise). However, these same individuals, via unconscious mechanisms such as automatic writing or raising a finger, could nonetheless communicate that some other part of them did perceive this pain or noise.

Hilgard concludes that each person has two or more separate, distinct consciousnesses. He thus theorizes that techniques such as hypnosis, and probably also meditation and deep relaxation, shift a person from ordinary consciousness to subtler levels which are typically outside of awareness.[3]

When a person enters the relaxed, receptive, inward-oriented state, he moves to a less dominant type of perception, which brings him into contact with different realities, including what Hilgard calls the unconscious observer. When he practices relaxation, meditation, autogenics, and imagery, he is training himself to utilize the type of awareness embodied in the right brain. While in this state, he can obtain information from himself that is not available to his everyday consciousness, and he can send messages, suggestions, and commands to his unconscious and his body. As Carl Jung pointed out, the unconscious speaks in language that is comprehensible only to the right brain. It communicates through the symbolism of dreams, intuitions, and metaphoric images, not in logical sentences. To tune in to these messages, we must first bring ourselves into that mode of perception.

If two or more separate types of consciousness exist independently, then it seems likely that they may sometimes conflict. In fact, many common ailments may stem from such dissonance. The techniques of healing imagery, however, can bridge this gap, opening a clear channel from our conscious to our unconscious mind. The latter is that part of us that knows why we are ill, how we got that way, and most important, how to make us well again.

Unfortunately, we are educated to exercise primarily left-hemisphere thought. In talking, working, and coping with our world, there is much more demand for and opportunity to use this externally focused mode of thinking. Consequently, many of us neglect, ignore, or minimize the imaginary processes of the right hemisphere, even though they can potentially contact our visceral awareness and affect our internal functions. Most people (with the exception of some artists, dancers, poets, and intuitive thinkers) need remedial education in the use of this half of their brain. With such education they will experience increased physical awareness, as well as an enhancement of their powers of internal self-healing and self-control.

Planting Healing Images

Creating and using healing imagery is so deceptively simple that it almost requires a leap of faith to believe that it can actually promote internal healing. Here's how it works:

First, you enter the deepest possible state of relaxation, using any of the methods outlined in chapter 13. Once your muscles, and your mind, are relaxed, you create an image in your mind's eye of what you want your body to do. This image can take several forms. For the medically sophisticated or the technically minded, it can be a precise representation of specific physiological activities. For example, you might want your body to produce an extra supply of a particular enzyme. Or you might require your immune system to destroy a virus in the stomach. Some people read medical texts to inform themselves about their illness and its cure as preparation for creating their healing picture.

The image, though, need not be technical. It can also be symbolic or fanciful. Some physicians using these methods believe that it is unimportant how realistic the healing image is. So rather than visualizing additional enzyme production, you might imagine rays of light energizing your body. Or you could picture little men with ray guns charging through the body, killing an oozy green virus.

It is important that your healing image feel right and have personal significance to you. In my health groups, after people have practiced relaxation for a week, I spend considerable time helping each person create a satisfying healing picture.

Try this visualization exercise for yourself. While in a

state of relaxation, focus your mind on your body. Let your attention wander to the particular bodily part that is a source of discomfort or illness, or does not function properly.

Direct all your thoughts to this selected area, and allow yourself to experience what it feels like right now. After a moment, allow a picture related to that region to enter your mind. It may be a detailed representation of what you think that part looks like internally. Or it could be more fanciful, reflecting how that bodily region feels to you. Keep your attention there until you are satisfied with the picture you've created.

Now begin to visualize a process taking place within your image, making that part of your body function better, or start healing. You might envision energy flowing into it. Let your imagination judge its appropriateness. A strong healing image could actually cause you to feel better right away.

Next, spend five or ten minutes holding that picture in your mind, using it as a focusing thought for a period of meditation. If you find your mind wandering, gently return it to your healing image. However, if your picture starts changing, simply let it happen, watching the transformation occur. Sometimes, important information about your illness can be communicated in this way.

Over the ensuing weeks, focus upon your healing image for a few minutes twice a day, as part of your regular meditation or relaxation process. Many individuals discover that their images are always with them in the background. From time to time during the day, they find themselves spontaneously focusing upon their healing image, allowing it to remain there for a few moments. While your conscious imagery work will take only a few minutes each day, your unconscious and your body will spend nearly all the time on the healing process, if you do not distract them with excessive stress or external demands.

Think of the marked contrast between this use of imagery and your usual response to pain or illness. Too often, you probably clench your muscles, become angry, or desperately try to ignore the discomfort, hoping that aspirin or a more potent analgesic will ease the pain. Such a response makes you even more tense, creating further obstacles for your body to contend with. But in a healing meditation, you directly confront and assault the dysfunction within you, by mobilizing the positive forces that can aid in the struggle. Instead of passively, or naively, working against yourself, you actively stimulate whatever latent powers of healing lie within. You have nothing to lose and much to gain by joining in this experiment in self-healing.

My own first exposure to the power of healing imagery came from my friend Mark, whose personal account is a vivid example of how visualization can work alongside traditional medicine. Mark was in a head-on automobile accident in which both of his legs were crushed, one of them nearly severed below the knee. That leg was broken in many places and was held together with only some skin below the knee. He was in excruciating pain and was reaching the point at which pain medication would no longer be effective. Physicians recommended that both legs be amputated, because there was almost no chance of their healing. Mark was warned that even if they did heal, he would never walk again, and he could expect a lifetime of severe leg pains. Despite the prognosis, he refused to allow the surgery.

In the ensuing days and weeks, the discomfort in Mark's legs intensified, just as the doctors had predicted. As the pain mounted, the UCLA clinic called in a hypnotherapist/psychic healer, hoping that such treatment might control the pain. The therapist taught him to relax and to spend most of his waking hours telling the leg to heal. Mark would imagine his broken bones joining and his infections healing. He would picture himself walking naturally. Over time, his bones healed, his infections disappeared, and he learned to control his pain so effectively that he stopped taking almost all of his medication.

Within two years, Mark was walking with only a slight limp. His physicians described his recovery as "unprecedented." In Mark's meditation, by relaxing and telling his body that he wanted it to repair itself, he mobilized some innate, latent, and potent healing mechanisms.[4]

There is no reason to believe that Mark is special in any sense or that such powers do not lie in every person. Restorative activities such as tissue repair and regeneration are processes that a body does for itself. Physicians can only adjust a bone into place and try to control pain and infection, but the body must accomplish the healing. Through imagery and relaxation, these natural healing processes can be enhanced.

As the evidence of imagery's benefits grows, many clinics and researchers have begun using it alongside other treatments. They uniformly report better results than when traditional medical treatment is applied alone. At the UCLA Pain Control Unit, at Norman Shealy's Pain Rehabilitation Center in Wisconsin, and in the cancer clinic of Carl and Stephanie Simonton in Texas, imagery is a common tool used to increase the effectiveness of treatment and to control pain and suffering. In countless other clinics, hypnotic methods (which are almost indistinguishable from imagery and relaxation) help where drugs are ineffective.

Orthopedic surgeon Robert Swearingen uses these techniques in his emergency room in Colorado, where injured skiers are plentiful. Several years ago, Swearingen began noting that certain ski-patrol members brought in casualties who were much easier to care for and required less medication than others. Upon investigation, he found that these patrol members instinctively helped their patients to relax as they were carried in, treating them with sensitivity and consideration. Soon, Swearingen was teaching all ski-patrol members how to relax their emergency patients. This resulted in a 50 percent decrease in the use of pain medication by the clinic. Many fractures were set using only healing imagery to control pain. In addition to his orthopedic work, Swearingen takes time to explain to each patient how his broken bone will heal, and he suggests that in the ensuing weeks, the patient visualize this process taking place often.

Swearingen's initial observations indicate that casts can be removed in about 30 percent less time from people who use imagery to influence their mending.[5]

A nurse named Joan offers another vivid personal account of pain control and self-healing. She was born with a congenital hip deformity. Fifteen years ago, as her problem caused her increasing pain, doctors recommended that her hip joint be fused, which would also severely limit her movement. An active and athletic woman, Joan did not want to accept this traditional treatment. As a nurse, she knew that a new treatment—a total hip replacement, substituting an artificial hip—was being developed, and she decided to wait until that operation was available.

In the meantime, she sought treatment from one of the few psychologists who were using relaxation and self-hypnosis at that time. From him she learned to control her pain without restricting her activities. She heightened her body awareness, and when she became sensitive to tension, she systematically relaxed. She was also taught the pain-control methods that will be presented later in this chapter.

Joan also learned to pay attention to the particular needs of specific body parts, especially her hips and legs. She began to "talk" to them, using various imagery and dialogue methods that will be described in the next chapter. When she felt discomfort, she would ask her tight legs or muscles what she could do to take care of them. Whenever something unusual or particularly active was required of her, such as a day of sailing, she might suggest, "If you let me do this without much pain, in return I will take special care to rest you for the next two days. Is that all right?" She would wait for an affirmative reply.

By becoming intimately aware of the needs of her hips and joints, and by catering to them, Joan was able to enjoy many active, relatively pain-free, productive years until the replacement operation was perfected. This was in contrast to the gloomy prediction of pain and physical restrictions made by the physicians who had recommended the fusion operation.

Joan also used imagery techniques to prepare for the hip-replacement operation, which was fraught with medical difficulties. She first talked at length with her surgeon about the operation and studied its procedures and effects. Then several times a day, while deeply relaxed, she visualized the surgery and what would have to occur for it to be successful. She imagined the operation itself proceeding flawlessly. She visualized the surgeons being totally relaxed, and their hands moving efficiently and competently. True, her imaginings may not have had much effect on the hospital personnel, but they helped calm her for the ordeal and increased her optimism about its outcome.

Joan also prepared her own body for the surgery. She asked her blood vessels not to rupture, and told her immune system how to perform. She instructed various organs precisely how to act after the operation. In effect, she conditioned her body for the difficult healing process to come.

Joan's surgery proceeded successfully. However, a complication did arise after the operation. The nerves in one of her legs had been damaged, leaving her with no feeling along the implanted bone. She was frustrated, but decided to do something about her dilemma. She began spending time every day imagining her nerves growing and becoming whole. Her physician told her that they might grow a millimeter a day, and would eventually have to extend the whole length of her leg. But she imagined them growing much faster, and eventually, sensations returned in her limb. Joan's story is a clear demonstration of how imagery and relaxation can become an integral part of traditional hospital medicine and can perhaps increase the chances of success in high-risk medical and surgical procedures.

Pain Control Without Medication

Most requests made of physicians are not for healing, but for relief from the pain and suffering that accompany illness and injury. Pain, which can totally disrupt a person's life, is the warning signal that something is wrong within the organism. Physical pain—from chronic backache to headaches to digestive discomfort—often persists even during an absence of a clear, specific physiological problem. Pain medication can only partially alleviate this discomfort, and over time, may become less effective or cause negative side effects (from stomach upset to drug addiction). I believe that pain control is among the most pressing medical problems facing physicians.

Actually, the medical community has not yet even developed a satisfactory theory of the nature of pain. However, it is clear that pain is both a physiological and a psychological experience. The pain sensation itself is generated within the mind. We are most familiar with it when it results from an injury or external stimulus, such as a hot stove. Receptors through the body—inside and out—register pain when there is damage, intrusion, inflammation, or malfunction.

But messages from the body account for only one aspect of pain. Interestingly, discomfort can persist long after the nerves in that bodily area have been surgically severed. In fact, pain can even emanate from limbs that have been amputated. Discomfort can also exist in a bodily area that is healthy or healed.

We also know that severe pain can be ignored or remain unconscious, as it does on the athletic or battle field, until hours after the injury is sustained. Some will experience severe pain with a particular type of injury, while others feel very little. A person under hypnosis can be pricked with a pin, and the discomfort does not register consciously, although the "hidden observer" in the mind is aware of it at some other level of consciousness.

There are two categories of pain—acute and chronic. Acute pain, which is in response to damage or illness, is an important physiological indication of injury, and signals that healing is taking place, demanding that we stop and rest. Usually time-limited, it is easily controlled by local anesthetics or medication. By contrast, chronic pain persists despite a lack of evidence of an acute problem. Or it accompanies a chronic physical condition or disability that will not heal.

Chronic discomfort offers a very different medical challenge than does acute pain. Traditional medicine treats it with medication, which does nothing to remove its root causes. Its symptoms are usually a response to external stress, which is not alleviated by drugs. And, of course, long-term use of medication creates many medical problems.

If drugs are not an effective answer, then what is? Evidence is growing that imagery methods may be very potent in reducing discomfort, particularly when it is chronic. New pain clinics, emerging in many areas of the country, successfully utilize not only imagery in the treatment process, but many of the other techniques described in this book, like relaxation, suggestion, diet, exercise, and various types of individual and family counseling.[6]

One of the most interesting and effective approaches to the alleviation of pain is glove anesthesia. It has been used effectively for both chronic and acute discomfort. Here is how it works:

Guide yourself into a relaxed state, using the techniques of chapter 13. Then imagine immersing your hand in ice-water, and continue doing that until your hand feels numb. Eventually, by visualizing your hand in freezing water, you should be able to induce this heavy, clammy sensation.

Once you have successfully numbed your hand, place it on the part of your body in pain. Next, imagine that the coldness is moving from your hand to the discomfort. The painful area will eventually become cold, and then numb, just like your hand. Keep your hand there until the entire area of your discomfort has lost all sensation, including pain. As you continue practicing this exercise, you will be able to ease your discomfort more and more quickly.

Another method of pain control uses healing imagery. When a person is in pain—perhaps with a headache—I place him in a relaxed state and have him imagine the pain literally getting smaller and smaller. One woman visualized the pain in her back as a huge claw pinching her, and was soon able to envision it loosening its grip. In the process, the intensity of her pain decreased. Similarly, a woman seeking relief from bronchial pain partially cleared up her lungs—and eased her pain—by picturing the clogged passages expanding and the fluid draining.

An opposite action can also induce pain relief. Focusing on the pain, rather than avoiding it, may be helpful. To try this method, first relax as deeply as possible. Then place your attention fully on the uncomfortable area of your body. Examine the places that hurt in the minutest detail. Learn all that you can about the feel of the pain. Notice that you can tolerate and even accept it. To your surprise, after a while the discomfort will begin to change and some degree of relief will result. Throughout this process, you must remain completely relaxed. If you feel yourself becoming tense, return your attention to your breathing and enter the relaxed state once again.

Why does this technique work? Why does focusing all your attention on a painful area help to alleviate the discomfort? There are several reasons for this seemingly paradoxical situation. First, a large proportion of pain stems not from, say, the injury that was suffered, but from the muscle tension with which we responded to it. But when we relax and focus on a painful area, we do so without muscle tension. This, especially with backache or headache, often is enough to minimize the severity of the discomfort.

Secondly, by centering on the pain, we face it directly, without anticipation or exaggeration caused by our fear. When we focus on every aspect of the discomfort and pay absolute attention to it, it often becomes psychologically less frightening, less intense, and more manageable. By confronting pain through relaxation rather than through fear, anxiety, and tension, we release ourselves from factors that tended to intensify it. Relaxation, then, is a pain-control technique in itself.

Discovering Meanings Behind Healing Imagery

As you produce images in your mind to facilitate the healing process, take the time to examine them very closely. The picture you create to represent your illness and its healing communicates a great deal about what you know or anticipate about your sickness. Also, it is a representation of your inner hopes, fears, expectations, and assumptions about yourself.

In my practice, I give patients a piece of paper and a variety of colored pens and ask them to draw the healing image they have created in their mind. Then we discuss the picture. The images are always revealing, brimming with vividness and emotional truth.

The picture is not interpreted and then left alone. After some discussion, I ask the patient to take it home and look at it regularly during the week. A particularly good time to examine the picture and reflect on its meaning is just before and after a relaxation or meditation period. The power of the symbol may stimulate other images and information relative to the illness and the patient's life. Such drawings continually help people discover new aspects of themselves.

Try this exercise yourself, and visualize your most recent, or most serious, or chronic ailment. One man pictured his hypertension as a huge vise crushing him. A woman drew her chronic bronchitis as a plug in her chest, blocking her breathing. A man saw his added weight as an inner tube, keeping him afloat on a stormy sea. A woman's lymph cancer became a termite invasion. Such pictures offer a glimpse of the psychic reality which is compressed into a symptom, and a pathway to begin to understand what it means.

This imagery exercise can be expanded upon in many ways. A patient of mine with an ulcer had initially envisioned his illness as a stomach being punctured with an arrow. The second time he tried the exercise, he visualized a heart, with a path leading from it to his stomach. When we discussed the picture, he talked about his lack of intimate relationships with others, and his denial of needs for companionship in his characterization of himself as a "loner." He was lonely, and needed to open his heart to others.

Read the description below, written by a patient with cancer. The imagery he selected can be interpreted as a message from his body and unconscious mind concerning how he feels about his illness, and how he sees his body's potential for combating it. Because of its vividness and potency, it is hard not to believe that his battle against cancer will be successful.

> I'd begin to visualize my cancer—as I saw it in my mind's eye. I'd make a game of it. The cancer would be a snake, a wolverine, or some vicious animal. The cure would be white husky dogs by the millions. It would be a confrontation of good and evil. I'd envision the dogs grabbing the cancer and shaking it, ripping it to shreds. The forces of good would win. The cancer would shrink—from a big snake to a little snake—and then disappear. Then the white army of dogs would lick up the residue and clean my abdominal cavity until it was spotless.[7]

After hearing the imagery created by hundreds of cancer patients and learning how they ultimately fared, Carl Simonton, Stephanie Simonton, and Jeanne Achterberg can now predict with some accuracy how successful an individual will be in influencing the course of his cancer. They examine the relative size and potency of the images of the white cells and the cancer. The differences seem to indicate how the real battle in the body will go. Generally, whichever side is stronger in the imagery will prevail. If the cancer is a dangerous animal, and the white cells are puffs of snow or cotton, the situation might not be hopeful.

As an example, they cite the visualization of ants. People who spontaneously choose ants to represent their cancer appear to do poorly, and the Simontons relate this directly to reality. In the actual world, a person simply cannot completely eradicate a plague of ants; there always seem to be a few stragglers that survive. In these clinicians' residential treatment program, they try to help people alter or modify their images (as well as their attitudes) so that the cancer does, in fact, lose the mental battle.[8]

Use the guidelines in this chapter to evaluate the effectiveness of the imagery you have created for your own healing process. Also, talk with a friend about your visualization, sharing your thoughts and your friend's reactions. What do the images make the two of you feel about the process going on within you? Which side of you—the illness or the healing powers—feels stronger, more in command? If you cannot visualize the healing process as more powerful than the image of your illness or symptom, then you have to explore your negative attitudes about getting well. Perhaps you already feel defeated in the struggle against your illness or chronic symptom, and do not believe that anything, especially mental imagery, can have an effect.

In short, your visualization reflects your attitude. It is the route by which you can look at your feelings, expectations, and inner experiences—and evaluate and strengthen your own healing powers.

18 Dialogue with the Self: Using Your Inner Healer

> *It must be admitted therefore that, in certain persons at least, the total possible consciousness may be split into parts which coexist, but mutually ignore each other and share the objects of knowledge between them, and—more remarkable still—are complementary. Give an object to one of the consciousnesses, and by that fact you remove it from the other or others. Barring a certain common fund of information, like the command of language, etc., what the upper self knows, the under self is ignorant of, and vice versa. . . .*
>
> WILLIAM JAMES

If you've ever been in psychotherapy, then you are probably familiar with the following patient/therapist ritual, which almost invariably occurs in the early stages of the treatment process. The patient has told his story, presenting his personal dilemma and his feelings, and then turns needily and expectantly to the therapist, asking either silently or with words, "Well, what do you think I should do?" Therapists are taught to resist this invitation, because patients need to discover their own solutions, and also because the suggestions of therapists are rarely heeded anyway. So instead, the therapist tosses the question back, asking the patient to begin exploring his inner experience more deeply, as the first step out of his situation.

The major premise of psychotherapy is that the wisdom to confront, understand, and resolve such dilemmas lies within each person. In the psychotherapeutic process, the

patient moves from his initial expectation that discovery will
come from the outside (specifically, his therapist) toward
the ultimate discovery that the answers exist within the hidden corners of his own psyche—namely, the unconscious.

In recent decades, much of the theorizing and speculation
in psychology and psychiatry has been directed at the structure and the nature of the mind. How do thoughts and
images become unconscious? How can they be recovered by
the relatively small conscious part of the total psyche?

Already we have explored several methods—relaxation,
meditation, and imagery—that can be used to rescue critical
personal messages from the unconscious. Freud developed
still another method, called free association. According to
Freud, the unconscious contains instinctive, often sexual,
demands for pleasure and gratification, demands of which
our conscious mind is only dimly aware. He also felt that
childhood experiences, fears, pain, and other emotional conflicts are pushed out of our awareness; he used the term
"repressed."

To free-associate, the patient enters a state of relaxation
by lying on a couch, and then he verbalizes any thought or
feeling that enters his mind. In effect, this is a meditative
process in which words are attached to thoughts as they
arise. The patient becomes familiar with his hidden fears,
instincts, desires, and forgotten memories, which underlie
his current conflicts.

Carl Jung, Freud's foremost disciple, broke with his mentor, believing that the unconscious was more than the junk-
yard for feelings and experiences that were rejected as too
frightening for consciousness. Jung wrote that certain universal human patterns were expressed in mythology, fairy
tales, dreams, poetry, art, and religious and cultural rituals.
These universal symbols and patterns were stored geneti-
cally within each individual's nervous system, and they rep-
resented the deepest and highest strivings of individuals.
This "collective unconscious" contained patterns and goals
that all human beings share.

Jung, and other psychologists of what is termed the "humanistic school," thus believed that the unconscious contains not only the negative, frightening feelings that Freud uncovered, but also the positive potentials that enable humans to find fulfillment, to discover the deepest expression of their unique nature, and to experience profound, spiritual truths. Exploring these aspects of the unconscious is an important life task. As people come into contact with their deepest creative parts, they can express them through art, through human relationships, and through their various life activities. The ability of each individual to fulfill his own unique destiny in life has been called "self-actualization"— literally, making oneself real and actual. Nobel Prize winner Albert Szent-Gyoergyi, and other biologists indicate that all living matter seems to contain this drive to perfect itself and to express itself fully.[1]

According to Jung, the psyche consists of many semi autonomous unconscious archetypes, which are almost like individual selves requesting conscious expression. Rather than having one personality, each individual is a collection of different people, with various talents, abilities, and modes of expression.

Some of the exercises presented in this book are based on the premise that we have different, occasionally conflicting desires, personalities, or selves lying within us. Jung himself pioneered many imagery exercises, and his theory of the person, while incomplete and containing many inconsistencies and ambiguities, is the one that is most applicable to therapists like myself who use imagery methods of healing and psychotherapy.[2]

The goal of humanistic modes of psychotherapy, then, is to help an individual realize his potentialities and find a style of life, work, and relationships which seems to correspond most closely with an inner sense of what is right for him. In a period of stress or crisis, an individual often has several conflicting needs or pathways and finds making a choice difficult. Or he may have pursued a path that does not bring him the satisfaction or peace he expected or needed. In such cases, he must discover the right choice and the strength to pursue it.

How can you reconcile the different talents, potentialities, and selves lying within? As with health itself, the key seems to be balance. If you push yourself into too narrow a mold, or deny aspects of yourself that require expression, you will soon discover messages from those parts of you that have been denied. Very often, these messages surface in the form of a physical symptom or ailment. If you seek more than symptomatic relief, your unbalanced life-style needs exploration and change.

I recall a vivid example of how denying one's potentialities can be expressed through a physical symptom. I was treating a young man who had succeeded at everything he had ever done and was beginning a business career with a prestigious firm. However, he was plagued by severe pains—particularly stomach cramps—and haunting fears that he was about to contract a terrible disease. This dilemma kept him futilely seeking a medical cure for his problem. It also prevented him from enjoying his success.

While exploring the patterns and sources of his stress, we discovered that he had attacks of pain primarily when he was doing well at his job. For example, he typically experienced discomfort at meetings and interviews.

In an imagery session, I asked him to try to remember a critical incident in his life related to his symptoms. He regressed back to junior high school, when he had made an almost conscious decision to give up his free-spirited life-style and "really get serious" about his life. His grades improved, but in the process, he gave up satisfying hobbies such as basketball and guitar playing. At that time, his symptoms arose, and they had remained with him ever since.

His pains seemed to be an unconscious reminder that his serious attitude denied an important part of himself—the playful, musical, relaxed side. Somehow, he had developed the idea that both he and his parents demanded a life of unremitting seriousness. His prosperity came at the expense of his other potentialities.

As our discussions continued, the situation became even more complex. He was not really certain that he wanted to be a businessman after all. He had chosen his career largely to please his parents, but as he became more and more bothered by his pain, he constantly let them know he was miserable. When the discomfort was most intense, he was babied by his wife and his mother, thus providing him with some emotional benefits for his discomfort.

As he began to understand the dynamics of his problem, he started to play music again and fulfill his recreational desires. Also, he stopped punishing his parents by continually complaining about his symptoms to them. After a few weeks, his pain subsided, as he learned effective techniques to control it. His fear of serious illness vanished. And he began to grapple with the more crucial and central issues in his life: namely, his own desires relative to his life and his career.

Illness, then, can be the opportunity to begin an exploration of the self and an expansion of inner knowledge. An important message of this book is that illness is an occasion to begin such a positive transformation. Very often, a sickness contains significant information about the nature of a personal crisis and what must be done to resolve it. Illness is an important signpost or message about something taking place in the inner self. It expresses a basic split, and a lack of integration and development in a person.

The Dialogue Process

One of the most effective means of exploring the psychological and unconscious messages and meanings within a symptom, pain, or illness is to build a dialogue between the conscious and the unconscious selves, in which they can share information and work toward the mutual goal of ful-

filling the inner person. Many of my patients have successfully experienced this intimate, shared conversation with
their inner selves, using methods common to other forms of
internal development.

Here's how you can begin this process:

Think for a moment about a particular physical symptom
or illness that has plagued you. While in a deep relaxed state,
imagine it taking a human form, or think of it as having its
own separate distinct voice. In your mind, begin to create a
dialogue between the symptom, or afflicted area, and your
conscious self. Here is an example of such a dialogue:

ME: Stomach, I want to know why you cause me so
much pain.
STOMACH: I want to hurt you, you creep.
M: What did I ever do to you?
S: You work all day in that chair, doing things
you don't enjoy, and even worrying about
them. You're dying in that job.
M: But I have to earn a living.
S: Yes, but you could think about other things.
M: Like what?
S: Well, you could leave your work at the office
when you go home in the evening, and begin to
enjoy yourself more with your family.
M: But that's hard. I'm always worrying.
S: Maybe you need to learn to stop worrying.

As you practice, the dialogue about a particular conflict or
symptom will unfold automatically, much as in free association. People are always surprised at what emerges when
they try this technique, especially when they have initially
felt it is childish or silly. Via this process, they slow down
left-brain activity and speak to their inner selves. Just as in
meditation or relaxation, they come into contact with important information about themselves.

When a person is bothered by a pain or a symptom, I suggest that he enter a relaxed state and ask his pain or symp-

tom why it exists. There is always an answer which has some relevance to his life. The unconscious material which has been crystallized in the form of a symptom surfaces, and can be useful in planning a change.

This self-inquiry does not deny that there are physical reasons for the illness. Indeed, I encourage visits to your physician when you are ill. But this dialogue is another pathway, another source of information that might aid in the healing. Very often, you will discover feelings you have not faced, or a source of anxiety or conflict in your life that made you susceptible to a particular ailment.

Jung cautioned that when we begin a dialogue with our unconscious, the symbols and messages will pop into our receptive consciousness so spontaneously that they will seem to be coming from outside us. We may not recognize them as being part of ourselves, and thus may initially relate to them as if they were from a separate and independent source.

In one workshop I asked the patients to try to eradicate the chronic tension that many carry in their jaw. I suggested they accomplish this by placing themselves in a relaxed state and then moving their jaw until the tension seemed to disappear. Most of them felt inadequate approaching this exercise. One woman said aloud, "My jaw acts like it has a mind of its own."

This woman's sentiments seem, in a sense, correct. Our body, our unconscious potentials, our needs and functions all operate within us as if they had their own minds. They affect our behavior, but not our conscious awareness. To integrate the various hidden parts of ourselves, a long, difficult process is required, which involves discovering and assimilating unconscious material, and joining it with our conscious self.

I have found that in many cases of serious physical illness, the healing process followed quickly after a realization that a part of oneself had been denied, forgotten, ignored, rejected, or despised. This realization is so poignant and affecting that, although I don't understand fully how the disowned

potentiality manifests itself as illness, I am certain that there
is an intimate connection.

I once worked with a man who meditated conscientiously
to the exclusion of everything else, including sexual relationships and the expression of most feelings. He developed an
ulcer, despite the apparent deep relaxation he obtained from
the meditation. Through an internal dialogue, he realized
that he denied and feared the sexual and angry parts of himself. With that insight, he began living a more balanced life,
and his ulcer started to heal. I have known several other
deeply committed meditators who have had physical or psychological difficulties stemming from feelings that they
repressed.

Here is an excerpt from a letter written by a woman who
seemingly influenced her cancer into remission using an internal dialogue:

> I began to write letters to my cancer as a way of communicat-
> ing with it. I have learned that whatever we hate, we give power
> to, and it has the power to hurt us. But when we make friends
> with our problem, it will not hurt us. Besides, we cannot reject
> something and simply turn it over to God. We must first accept
> it, because, after all, we made it happen to us.
>
> I wrote down what I felt about my cancer, and then I wrote
> what my cancer said to me. I managed to discover a great deal
> about myself, and how I keep my real needs inside me and do
> not ask others to help me. I don't think I would have discovered
> these things in any other way than by having cancer. It's too
> bad the lessons of our life have to be so harsh, but at least I fi-
> nally paid attention to things. I hope you will learn to take care
> of yourself as well.

The remarkable insight in this letter was that her cancer
was perhaps the ultimate result of a lifetime of systematic
self-denial. In my therapeutic work, I have learned that no
outside therapist can tell another individual what he is
denying. Each individual has to discover his hidden selves
on his own. The helper can serve only as a guide, perhaps

showing the one who needs help how to look inward and encouraging him to do so.

What you decide to do with the information you receive in the internal dialogue is often a complex matter. When an inner voice says, "Leave your job," or "Leave your wife," or "Face up to your anger and frustration," you are confronted with a real dilemma. In fact, that is probably why the information remained unconscious for so long. In a future dialogue, or in consultation with a healer or therapist, you must begin to find a balance. Dialogue can open windows, but it does not make the process of following up and using the information easy.

Inner Healers, Spirit Guides and Advisers

The healing process, according to the ancient Greeks, required a personal transformation strikingly similar to the one described in this chapter. The sufferer would journey to a healing shrine, where he would share his difficulty with a priest or healer and begin a period of personal purification. During a process called dream incubation, in which he would sleep in a special place in the temple, visions would appear in his dreams, which the priest would later help him unravel. The priest would suggest the nature of his affliction and what he needed to do in order to regain his health.

Psychologist Henry Reed has resurrected this ritual. He travels to various parts of the country, setting up a "dream tent." Patients come to Reed and share a difficulty or problem with him. These individuals offer a gift and then prepare themselves for the healing dream. They sleep in the tent, and when they awaken, they discuss their dream. According to Reed, in most cases the dream acts like the ancient oracle, by illuminating hidden aspects of the problem and suggesting a new perspective on how to overcome it. Reed and other dream researchers (including Freud) suggest that the dream is an easily accessible gateway into the soul's hidden potentials—a repository of wisdom and beauty that we can benefit from knowing.[3]

Dream incubation is a two-way process. By reflecting on the nature of our difficulties, and by removing ourself temporarily from ordinary concerns, we implant a message or concern in our unconscious, directed toward a hypothetical inner adviser who can tap our unconscious wisdom and bring it back to us in usable form. In my work, I have found that every individual has this wise adviser or inner healer living within him. At some level, each of us knows exactly what we need to do to heal, and how to go about it, although sometimes we are unwilling to acknowledge that message or act upon it.

Perhaps the most important task of a health guide is to help an ill person contact his inner healer. This inner adviser is the part of us that actually does the healing, that mends the bones and coordinates the fight against stressors and external invaders. It is the part of us that recognizes self-destructive behavior and can warn us against it. The inner adviser has accumulated all the wisdom and knowledge of our body and psyche that usually escape our more limited, ordinary consciousness.

Your inner healer can be an invaluable resource for your physician because of its direct access to your inner state and physical processes. At the Headlands Health Center in Bolinas, California, inner and outer healers have worked together as a treatment team. Physicians Irving Oyle and Michael Samuels have helped thousands of people make contact with their inner healers and have written extensively about their experiences.[4] David Bresler, director of the UCLA Pain Control Unit, also uses inner advisers as a cornerstone of his pain-control program.[5]

It is easy to make contact with your own inner adviser. Begin by entering a state of deep relaxation or meditation. Spend a few minutes simply enjoying this state, allowing yourself to release not only your physical tensions, but also your external concerns and feelings. When you are fully relaxed and at peace, imagine that you are in a place—actual or imaginary—that you love very much and feel peaceful and at home in. Perhaps it is a park, a beach, or a mountain. Create a vivid image of this site and place yourself there, using as many senses as you can. Examine your surroundings in detail. Feel the air. See, hear, smell, and taste exactly what your special place is like.

What did you select as your magical place? Some find themselves in a lovely part of nature, where they have always felt fully relaxed. Others create an imaginary house which has a special room, full of old, lovely, and personally significant antiques and ornaments. Whatever you have chosen, remember that your mind has guided you there. It represents the place where you feel relaxed and open to a meeting with the special healer that lies within you. Here you will come face to face with a part of yourself that can help you discover and learn about the incredible resources and riches that lie within you.

If you'd like, let yourself relax and experience your special place for a spell before you continue with the rest of the exercise. Do not proceed until you feel calm, peaceful, and at home there.

When you're ready, wait calmly with the expectation that someone or something is about to join you. It might be a person—perhaps a wise old man or woman, a literary character, or a distant relative. Or an animal, a cartoon figure, a plant, or a point of light. If you wait in a quiet and receptive state, some being will eventually enter your consciousness. Whatever its form, it is the unconscious part of yourself that will provide you with the important and vital information on how to live your life with greater health, energy, and vitality.

If no being should appear, you might try to make one up. Sometimes a person needs to feel he is fabricating the process in order to be free enough to experience an inner healer. If you have a shy adviser, another approach is to ask yourself why you do not wish to make contact, and see what answer

you uncover. One woman who had great difficulty in finding
a healer learned that she was not yet willing to try to overcome her illness. Only after I explained that meeting the
healer did not presuppose that she was ready for healing did
she encounter her healer easily.

When you finally encounter your adviser, greet him
warmly. Then begin to talk to him in your imagination, just
as you would to any new, respected acquaintance. You
might ask his name, or something about him. It is helpful to
get to know your healer or adviser before plunging into
leading questions. Sometimes healers—particularly those
who take the form of animals or energy—talk in ways that
are unfamiliar, heavy with symbols or pictures, or even rid-
dles, which you will need practice to understand.

Eventually, your inner healer or adviser will respond to
questions about what is wrong with you, why you are ill,
and what you need to do to overcome your disorder. Unlike
your physician, who deals in the physiology of illness, the
inner healer will tell you the personal significance of your
illness at the present time. He may say that you are ill because of unhappiness over your job or current relationships.
He may even tell you that you are not really sick at all.

Irving Oyle relates the story of a woman who was convinced she had cancer, even though her physicians could not
find any malignancy. Her adviser insisted that she didn't
have cancer. With that message coming from such a personal, inner source, she was able to accept it.

Because your inner adviser is such an integral part of
yourself, he cannot be conned. He is able to recognize things
that you know, but have not yet admitted. For instance, the
adviser might tell you that you are being dishonest with
yourself. Or he might make fun of your pretensions, or tell
you that you really don't want to go on a diet, or you really
don't want to change your job. You can't hide from yourself
as you can from physicians, friends, and family.

Talking to a healer can be mundane, funny, frightening,
emotional, or anxiety-relieving. Interestingly, some find that

over time, the form of the adviser will change, or a new one will visit. A cancer victim who had previously imagined her white blood cells as a polar bear fighting her malignancy found that her adviser was a fierce bear who was protecting her. But several weeks later, the bear had been changed into a domestic animal, which she kept around the house as a companion.

A man suffering from pain in his joints encountered an inner healer in the form of a wise old lady, similar to the ancient women who inhabit fairy tales and myths. He became friends with his adviser, and she told him she would help him get over his pain. Just then he felt tugs at the joints of each of his fingers, and after that, he had more mobility and less pain.

Dialogues with inner healers are usually simple, clear, direct, and explicit. For this reason, when I work with a patient, I often talk directly to his inner healer, in a sort of joint consultation. The healer provides me with information about why the person is ill, and also why he is not getting well. This inner source provides explanations for why an individual may fear starting new relationships, or why he won't diet, or why he works so relentlessly. It is the most aware, direct, wise, and responsible part of each of us.

Identifying and contacting this inner healer through an internal dialogue is a simple and effective way to dramatize and confront the conflicting forces of health and disease that lie within you. There are unconscious positive and negative forces and struggles lying beneath the surface of your psyche. Often an illness is an indication of the ascendance of the negative (which Jung calls the "shadow") forces that you tend to ignore. When neglected, they can assume more power over you than is desirable.

There are other ways you can communicate with these forces behind your illness. For instance, let's assume you have severe facial pain. If you were in my office, I might suggest that you relax and focus your consciousness upon the painful area. Then I'd ask you to give a voice (and perhaps even a shape and a name) to that part of your face, and talk to it. I, too, would talk directly to the area of your discomfort—that part of you which has left the harmonious whole of your person and has set out on its own. In essence, you can look at disease as a force that has captured part of the body.

This mode of healing would consist of asking that part of your face what it wants or needs, and what is being avoided that is causing it to rebel. Often, the reply will be that you do not love that part and have abused or neglected it.

As this process continues, I would suggest that you now ask your inner healer what ought to be done. Often an agreement can be reached. Perhaps your adviser will remove your symptom if you start changing your behavior and paying attention to that need. Many common aches and pains can be alleviated by responding positively to what they are asking for—simple things such as regular rest, exercise, or a good diet. You can be assured that if you continue to ignore your symptoms and the requests from your inner adviser, your pain will only get worse.

After you've experimented with internal dialogues for a while, analyze how you're doing. If you're still finding them difficult after several attempts, you can try communicating in other ways. You can draw your message with colored pencils or paint. Or you can write or, as I do, type questions, and ask for the responses. Let the words just emerge almost automatically on the paper, without consciously choosing them. While most people need complete privacy while talking with their advisers, you may be more comfortable with a close friend or relative nearby.

You must remain relaxed and receptive to this process. You will soon recognize the inner dialogue as an important way to bypass or avoid conventional mental patterns, beliefs, expectations, and everyday reality. By short-circuiting these usual perceptual channels, you will enter what Carlos Castaneda's external guide, Don Juan, and his internal spiritual guide called a "separate reality." The guides and powers that populated the inner world of Castaneda during his spiritual development are examples of how a person's inner selves can become autonomous guiding forces, independent of everyday conventional reality.

The Goal

Your ultimate goal should be to live in harmony with all aspects of yourself. By contacting your inner healer, and other personalities and parts of yourself that you encounter in your dreams, fantasies, and meditations, you will become comfortable, open, and familiar with yourself. Then when you have a problem, a pain, or a crisis, you can approach the resources that will help you find a solution to your dilemma.

As this process continues, you will begin to experience progressive changes. You will start to feel better about yourself and less anxious and defensive about the world. By ceasing to fear and defend yourself internally, you will project fewer conflicts and fears onto the external world.

You will also notice changes in the nature of your internal world. The inner healer will tell you more, and you will experience various messages of wholeness, unity, and completeness. You may also become open to mystical, spiritual, peaceful experiences which have been given various names, from "higher consciousness" to "fulfillment." With this state of unity will come, as a matter of course, greater health. And ultimately, that is what we are all striving for.

Throughout this book, our exploration of illness has led us to investigate our deepest human needs, desires, and purposes. As we have scrutinized the physical breakdown and crisis of disease, we have found that the process of overcoming it frequently demands an understanding of who we are, the nature of our lives, our personal development, and our highest aspirations.

The Socratic injunction "Know thyself" must be applied to the healing of physical illness. A sickness cannot be separated from the rest of your life. It reflects everything about you.

When physical treatments are not effective, then other modes of therapy must be explored. My own search has convinced me that self-exploration, self-care, and training in self-control, are the most effective tools you can use to maximize your health and live more fully. Your physician cannot any longer be expected to do your job and maintain your health and well-being. If you want more from life in the future, then you must increase your awareness and participation in safeguarding your physical body. You will be whole and well only when you've developed a harmonious coexistence with your entire life and environment.

Images of the New Medicine

In the future, I envision a medical-care system more aware of the personal nature of illness and the critical role of self-care and self-regulation in preventing and overcoming disease. When the self-healing powers of the individual are fully recognized, the effectiveness of technological, medical, chemical, and surgical treatments will be enhanced. The areas of personal exploration and self-healing techniques I have presented here will be an integral part of a holistic health-care, and health-promotion, system.

As hospitals and other medical centers have become increasingly receptive to this wider, person-oriented focus on health, I have begun to fantasize about how medical care may evolve. Perhaps my young sons may encounter a combined health/physical education program in their elementary and secondary schools. Not only will they learn to manipulate their voluntary muscles in active sports, but they will be introduced to self-control of their visceral muscles through techniques such as meditation. Their "health lab" might include a variety of biofeedback instruments, with which they will be taught to sense tension and relaxation in each part of their bodies. They will learn to be sensitive to their internal cues and the workings of the various parts of their organisms. They will also be instructed about the best possible nutrition and health practices. By the time each child graduates from high school, I hope he will possess a basic confidence in and awareness of his physical being.

In the future, every individual may undergo a yearly health checkup, but it will not be just a few minutes of poking, probing, and lab work by a doctor. Instead, it will include a thorough assessment of the state of his entire psychophysical system. Each day I encounter more physicians who are taking the time and committing themselves to work in this way.

The entire family will undergo this process together, spending a few evenings evaluating their health status as individuals and as a family, and then proceeding to the health center as a group for their checkups. Upon arrival, they will meet with a health counselor to discuss their self-assessments and areas that they have already pinpointed for further work. They will then individually meet with a physician for the usual medical tests. However, no test will be undertaken without a full comprehension of its significance. When a troublesome area is uncovered, physician and patient will together discuss the possible reasons for this difficulty.

Each person, and the family as a whole, will create a treatment program for the specific problems that have been detected. Each will also set some general health goals, and a plan to attain them within the next year. If very difficult transformations are necessary, the person will begin attending remedial health classes or a health-support group. Many medical practices have already moved in this direction.

On the technological side of medicine, I believe there will be important changes as well. In emergency rooms, I expect that the setting will be designed to lower the patient's stress level and create a positive, relaxed, and hope-inducing environment for healing. A health guide will meet each person upon admittance, guiding him in some imagery and relaxation exercises until a physician can begin treatment. If surgery or other emergency procedures are needed, they will be preceded by a period of psychological preparation, when circumstances permit. This session will be much like a readiness class for childbirth, in which the patient will learn about the nature of the surgery and about exercises to relax his body for the ordeal and to cope with the resulting physical pain. Afterward, members of the family will use their energies to help the healing process in the person they love. The hospital and recovery environment will make allowances for basic human needs—including time with the family, quiet and sufficient rest, and remedial help in self-healing.

I anticipate that future health care will once again become a science for living well. We will take a daily interest in our well-being and recognize that only through our own efforts can we remain at an optimum level of health. By so doing, we can all feel less helpless and more confident in our ability to be well—and remain well.

Notes

CHAPTER 1

René Dubos, *The Mirage of Health* (New York: Doubleday/Anchor Books, 1959), p. 114.
1. Lewis Thomas, "On the Science and Technology of Medicine," in *Doing Better and Feeling Worse: Health in the United States*, ed. John Knowles (New York: W. W. Norton, 1978), pp. 35–47.
2. David Rogers, "The Challenge of Primary Care," in Knowles, *Doing Better*, pp. 81–104.
3. Ivan Illich, *Medical Nemesis* (New York: Pantheon, 1976).
4. Thomas McKeown, "The Determinants of Health," *Human Nature* 1, no. 4 (April 1978): 60–67.
5. Eugene Vayda, "Keeping People Well: A New Approach to Medicine," *Human Nature* 1, no. 7 (July 1978): 64–71.
6. John Knowles, "The Responsibility of the Individual," in Knowles, *Doing Better*, p. 79.
7. John Knowles, quoted in *Time*, August 6, 1976, p. 62.
8. Lewis Thomas, "Science and Technology."
9. Elmer Green, A. Green, and E. D. Walters, "Voluntary Control of Internal States: Psychological and Physiological," *Journal of Transpersonal Psychology* 2, no. 1 (1970):1–26.

CHAPTER 2

Claude Bernard, quoted in *Stress*, Walter McQuade and Ann Aikman (New York: Bantam Books, 1975), p. 3.
1. David Bakan, *Disease, Pain and Sacrifice* (Boston: Beacon Press, 1968).
2. Claus B. Bahnson and Marjorie B. Bahnson, "Cancer as an Alternative to Psychosis: A Theoretical Model of Somatic and Psychologic Regression," in *Psychosomatic Aspects of Neoplastic Disease*, ed. D. M. Kissen and L. L. LeShan (Philadelphia: Lippincott, 1964), pp. 184–202.

271

272 NOTES

CHAPTER 3

Virginia Woolf, "On Being Ill," in *The Moment and Other Essays*
(New York: Harcourt, Brace, 1948).
1. Susan Sontag, *Illness as Metaphor* (New York: Farrar, Straus &
   Giroux, 1978), p. 3.
2. William Osler, quoted in Dubos, *Mirage*, p. 123.
3. Charles Péguy, quoted in *The Five Point Executive Health Program*,
   Research Institute of America, 589 Fifth Ave., New York, NY 10017,
   p. 2.
4. Rollo May, lecture given at Association for Humanistic Psychology
   conference, San Diego, Calif., April 1977.
5. Lawrence L. LeShan, "Some Observations on the Problem of Mobilizing the Patient's Will to Live," in Kissen and LeShan, *Psychosomatic*, pp. 110, 111.

CHAPTER 4

Arthur Guidham, *A Theory of Disease* (London: Allen & Unwin,
1957), p. 91.
1. Susan Sontag, *Illness as Metaphor*, p. 3.
2. Eliot Friedson, "Client Control and Medical Practice," *American
   Journal of Sociology* 65 (January 1960): 374-82.
3. Talcott Parsons and Renée Fox, "Illness, Therapy and the Modern
   Urban American Family," in *Patients, Physicians and Illness*, ed.
   E. G. Jaco (New York: Free Press, 1958), pp. 185-240.
4. Barry Blackwell, "Treatment Adherence," *British Journal of Psychiatry* 129 (December 1976): 513-31.
5. Wilbert E. Fordyce, R. S. Fowler, and B. DeLateur, "An Application
   of Behavior Modification Technique to a Problem of Chronic Pain,"
   in *Pain*, ed. Matisyohu Weisenberg (St. Louis: C. V. Mosby, 1975).
6. Henry Lennard, informal presentation given at American Orthopsy-
   chiatric Association conference, San Francisco, Calif., April 1978.
7. Ernest Becker, *The Denial of Death* (New York: Free Press, 1973).
8. Elisabeth Kübler-Ross, *On Death and Dying* (New York: Macmillan, 1970).
9. Sandol Stoddard, *The Hospice Movement* (New York: Stein & Day,
   1978).

CHAPTER 5

Norman Cousins, "The Mysterious Placebo: How Mind Helps Medicine Work," *Saturday Review*, October 1, 1977, p. 16.

1. Bruno Klopfer, "Psychological Variables in Human Cancer," *Journal of Projective Techniques* 21 (1957): 337–39.
2. Jerome Frank, "The Faith that Heals," *Johns Hopkins University Medical Journal* 137 (1975): 127–31.
3. Henry K. Beecher, "The Powerful Placebo," *Journal of the American Medical Association* 159, no. 17 (December 24, 1955): 1602–06.
4. Reported by Norman Cousins, "Mysterious Placebo," p. 13.
5. Henry K. Beecher, "Surgery as a Placebo," *Journal of the American Medical Association* 176 (1961): 1102.
6. David B. Cheek and Leslie M. LeCron, *Clinical Hypnotherapy* (New York: Grune & Stratton, 1968), pp. 93–105.
7. Cheek and LeCron, pp. 153–172.
8. Robert Rosenthal, "Self-Fulfilling Prophecy," *Psychology Today*, December 1968.
9. Don Johnson, "The Function of Diagnostic Language," unpublished paper, 1978.
10. O. Carl Simonton and Stephanie Matthews-Simonton, "Belief Systems and Management of the Emotional Aspects of Malignancy," *Journal of Transpersonal Psychology* 7, no. 1 (1975): 29–47.

CHAPTER 6

Hans Selye, *The Stress of Life* (New York: McGraw-Hill, 1956), pp. 256–57.

1. Walter Cannon, *The Wisdom of the Body* (New York: W. W. Norton, 1939), pp. 227–28.
2. Alvin Toffler, *Future Shock* (New York: Random House, 1970).
3. Konrad Lorenz, *On Aggression* (New York: Harcourt Brace Jovanovich, 1966); Arthur Koestler, *The Ghost in the Machine* (New York: Macmillan, 1968); Selye, *Stress of Life;* and A. T. W. Simeons, *Man's Presumptuous Brain* (New York: E. P. Dutton, 1961).
4. Selye, *Stress of Life;* Hans Selye, *Stress Without Distress* (New York: Signet, 1974).

CHAPTER 7

James J. Lynch, *The Broken Heart* (New York: Basic Books, 1977), pp. 199–200.

1. Meyer's research is discussed in *Stressful Life Events*, ed. Barbara Snell Dohrenwind and Bruce P. Dohrenwind (New York: John Wiley and Sons, 1974).
2. Thomas H. Holmes and Richard H. Rahe, "The Social Readjustment Rating Scale," *Journal of Psychosomatic Research* 11 (1967): 213–18.
3. Thomas H. Holmes and Minoru Masuda, "Psychosomatic Syndrome," *Psychology Today*, April 1972, pp. 71–72, 106.
4. Richard Rahe, in Dohrenwind and Dohrenwind, *Stressful Life Events*, pp. 73–86.
5. Holmes and Masuda, "Psychosomatic Syndrome," p. 106.
6. C. M. Parkes, *Bereavement* (New York: International Universities Press, 1972).
7. R. W. Bartrop, research study reported in *Lancet*, April 16, 1977.
8. Lawrence Hinkle, in Dohrenwind and Dohrenwind, *Stressful Life Events*, pp. 9–44.
9. Mimeograph sheet furnished by Thomas Holmes, Department of Psychiatry, University of Washington, Seattle, WA. 98195.
10. George L. Engel, "Sudden or Rapid Death During Psychological Stress: Folklore or Folk Wisdom?" *Annals of Internal Medicine* 74 (1971): 771–82.
11. William A. Greene, Sidney Goldstein, and Arthur J. Moss, "Psychosocial Aspects of Sudden Death," *Annals of Internal Medicine* 129 (1972): 725–31.
12. Reported in Lynch, *Broken Heart*, pp. 59–62.
13. Lawrence LeShan and R. E. Worthington, "Some Recurrent Life History Patterns Observed in Patients with Malignant Disease," *Journal of Nervous and Mental Disease* 124 (1956): 460–65.
14. Lawrence LeShan, "Psychological States as Factors in the Development of Malignant Disease: A Critical Review," *National Cancer Institute Journal* 22 (1959): 1–18.
15. Bruno Klopfer, "Psychological Variables in Human Cancer," *Journal of Projective Techniques* 21 (1957): 331–40.
16. Lawrence LeShan, *You Can Fight for Your Life* (New York: M. Evans, 1977).
17. George L. Engel and Arthur H. Schmale, "Psychoanalytic Theory of Somatic Disorder: Conversion, Specificity, and the Disease Onset

Situation," *Journal of the American Psychoanalytic Association* 18 (1967): 355.

18. S. Meyerowitz, "The Continuing Investigation of Psychosocial Variables in Rheumatoid Arthritis," in *Modern Trends in Rheumatology*, ed. A. G. Hill, 2d ed. (New York: Appleton-Century-Crofts, 1966), pp. 92–105.

CHAPTER 8

Peter Marris, quoted at a National Institute of Mental Health conference on relationships between the economy and illness, in the American Psychological Association *Monitor*, July 1978, p. 29.

1. George L. Engel, *Psychological Development in Health and Disease* (Philadelphia: Saunders, 1962).
2. Robert DeRopp, *The Master Game* (New York: Delacorte, 1968).
3. Caroline B. Thomas, Selina M. Wolf, and Marie V. Bowman, "The Study of the Precursors of Essential Hypertension and Coronary Heart Disease: A Program in Preventive Medicine, Book of Population, Procedures and Forms" (Johns Hopkins University Department of Medicine, 1967).
4. Meyer Friedman and Ray H. Rosenman, *Type A Behavior and Your Heart* (New York: Knopf, 1974).
5. David C. Glass, *Stress and Coronary Prone Behavior* (New York: Lawrence Erlbaum Associates, 1977).
6. John L. Lacey, Dorothy E. Bateman, and Ruth Van Lehn, "Autonomic Response Specificity," *Psychosomatic Medicine* 15 (1953): 8–21.
7. Laurence Cherry and Hans Selye, "On the Real Benefits of Eustress," *Psychology Today*, March 1979, pp. 60, 63, 64, 69–70.
8. Irving Z. Janis, *Stress and Frustration* (New York: Harcourt Brace Jovanovich, 1969).
9. James Barrell and Donald Price, "Responses to Stress: Confronters and Avoiders," *Psychophysiology* 14 (1977): 517–21.
10. Reported in *The Five Point Executive Health Program*, p. 10.

CHAPTER 9

Elizabeth Rivers, "The Real Healing," *New Age*, July 1978, pp. 64, 69.

1. Wallace C. Ellerbroek, "Language, Thought, and Disease," *CoEvolution Quarterly* 17 (Spring 1978): 30–38.
2. W. J. Grace and D. T. Graham, "Relationship of Specific Attitudes

and Emotions to Certain Bodily Diseases," *Psychosomatic Medicine* 14 (1952): 243–51.

3. P. D. MacLean, "Psychosomatic Disease and the 'Visceral Brain,' " *Psychosomatic Medicine* 11 (1949): 350.

4. Herbert Weiner, Margaret Thaler, M. F. Reiser, and I. A. Mirsky, "Etiology of Duodenal Ulcer: I. Relation of Specific Psychological Characteristics to Rate of Gastric Secretion (Serum Pepsinogen)," *Psychosomatic Medicine* 19 (1957): 350.

5. Holmes and Masuda, "Psychosomatic Syndrome," pp. 71–72, 106.

6. Grace and Graham, "Relationship of Specific Attitudes."

7. Lawrence Hinckle, Jr., W. N. Christenson, F. D. Kane, A. Ostfeld, W. N. Thetford, and H. G. Wolff, "An Investigation of the Relation Between Life Experience, Personality Characteristics, and General Susceptibility to Illness," *Psychosomatic Medicine* 20 (1958): 278–95.

CHAPTER 10

Margaret Mead, "The Concept of Culture and the Psychosomatic Approach," *Psychiatry* 10 (1947): 68.

1. Salvador Minuchin, *Families and Family Therapy* (Cambridge, Mass.: Harvard University Press, 1974).

2. Sidney Cobb, Stanislav V. Kasl, John R. P. French, and Guttorm Norstebo, "Why Do Wives with Rheumatoid Arthritis Have Husbands with Peptic Ulcers?" *Journal of Chronic Diseases* 14, no. 3 (September 1961): 291–310.

3. F. C. Hoebel, "Coronary Artery Disease and Family Interaction: A Study of Risk Factor Modification," in *The Interactional View*, ed. P. Watzlawick and J. H. Weakland (New York: W. W. Norton, 1976), pp. 363–75.

4. Salvador Minuchin, Lester Baker, and Bernice Rosman, *Psychosomatic Families* (Cambridge, Mass.: Harvard University Press, 1978).

5. Warren M. Brodey, *Family Dance* (New York: Doubleday/Anchor, 1977), p. 20

6. Norman Paul, "The Use of Empathy in the Resolution of Grief," in *Readings in Adult Psychology*, ed. L. R. Allman and D. T. Jaffe (New York: Harper and Row, 1977), pp. 378–88.

CHAPTER 11

Quoted in Henry M. Pachter, *Paracelsus: Magic into Science* (New York: Collier, 1961), pp. 121–22.

1. Joel Greenberg, "The Americanization of Roseto," *Science News* 113, no. 23 (June 10, 1978): 378–82.
2. M. Pflanz, E. Rosenstein, and T. Von Uexkull, "Sociopsychological Aspects of Peptic Ulcer," *Journal of Psychosomatic Research* 1 (February 1956): 68–74.
3. Thomas H. Holmes, "Multi-Discipline Studies in Tuberculosis," in *Personality, Stress and Tuberculosis*, ed. Sparer (New York: International Universities Press, 1956), pp. 376–412.
4. August Hollingshead and Frederick Redlich, *Social Class and Mental Illness* (New York: John Wiley, 1958).
5. Emile Durkheim, *Suicide* (New York: Free Press, 1953).
6. David Bakan, *Disease, Pain and Sacrifice* (Boston: Beacon Press, 1968).
7. Philip Slater, *Footholds* (New York: E. P. Dutton, 1977), p. 182.
8. R. White and S. Liddon, "Ten Survivors of Cardiac Arrest," *Psychiatry in Medicine* 3 (1972): 219–25.
9. Carl Rogers, *On Becoming a Person* (Boston: Houghton Mifflin, 1962).
10. Douglas Boyd, *Rolling Thunder* (New York: Delta Books, 1974).
11. Ross Speck and Carolyn Attneuve, *Family Networks* (New York: Pantheon, 1973).
12. Lawrence LeShan, *The Medium, the Mystic and the Physicist* (New York: Ballantine, 1975).
13. Dolores Krieger, "Therapeutic Touch," in *Body, Mind and Health: Toward an Integral Medicine*, ed. J. Gordon, D. Jaffe, and D. Bresler, National Institute of Mental Health monograph, 1980.

CHAPTER 12

Don Johnson, *The Protean Body* (New York: Harper and Row, 1977), pp. 2–3.

1. Russell Lockhart, "Cancer in Myth and Dream," *Spring*, 1977, pp. 1–26.
2. Seymour Fisher, *Body Consciousness* (Englewood Cliffs, N.J.: Prentice-Hall, 1973), p. 11.
3. Wilhelm Reich, *Selected Writings: An Introduction to Orgonomy* (New York: Farrar, Straus & Giroux, 1973); Moshe Feldenkrais,

Awareness Through Movement (New York: Harper and Row, 1972); Alexander Lowen, *The Language of the Body* (New York: Collier, 1971); Ken Dychtwald, *Bodymind* (New York: Pantheon, 1977).
4. Lonnie G. Barbach, *For Yourself* (New York: Signet, 1977).

CHAPTER 13

Edmund Jacobson, *You Must Relax*, 4th ed. (New York: McGraw-Hill, 1962), p. 90.
1. Herbert Benson, *The Relaxation Response* (New York: William Morrow, 1975).
2. Gerald L. Klerman, "Psychotropic Drugs as Therapeutic Agents," *Hastings Center Studies* 2, no. 1 (January 1974): 8.
3. Illich, *Nemesis*.
4. J. H. Schultz and W. Luthe, *Autogenic Therapy*, 6 vols. (New York: Grune & Stratton, 1969).
5. Jacobson, *You Must Relax*.
6. Kenneth Greenspan, quoted in *Brain-Mind Bulletin* 2, no. 17: 2.
7. Abraham H. Maslow, *Toward a Psychology of Being*, rev. ed. (Princeton, N.J.: Van Nostrand, 1968).
8. Lawrence LeShan, *How To Meditate* (New York: Bantam Books, 1976).
9. Karl R. Rosa, *You and Autogenic Training* (New York: Saturday Review Press/E. P. Dutton, 1976), p. 5.

CHAPTER 14

Elmer E. Green, Alyce Green, and E. D. Walters, "Biofeedback for Mind/Body Regulation: Healing and Creativity," *Fields Within Fields . . . Within Fields* 1 (1972): 141.
1. Barbara Brown, *Stress and the Art of Biofeedback* (New York: Harper and Row, 1977).
2. Neal E. Miller, L. V. DiCara, H. Solomon, J. M. Weiss, and B. Dworkin, "Learned Modification of Autonomic Functions: A Review and Some Further Data," in *Biofeedback and Self-Control*, ed. T. X. Barber et al. (Chicago: Aldine-Atherton, 1970).
3. Douglas Boyd, *Swami* (New York: Random House, 1976).
4. D. M. Rorvik, "Jack Schwartz Feels No Pain," in *Advances in Altered States of Consciousness and Human Potentialities*, ed. Theodore X. Barber, vol. 1 (New York: Psychological Dimensions, 1976), pp. 623–30.

5. Erik Peper, "Passive Attention: The Gateway to Consciousness and Autonomic Control," in *Mind/Body Integration: Essential Readings in Biofeedback*, ed. E. Peper, S. Coli, and M. Quinn (New York: Plenum, 1979), pp. 119–24.

6. Gerald Jonas, *Visceral Learning* (New York: Viking, 1973), pp. 68–69.

7. B. T. Engel, "Clinical Applications of Operant Conditioning Techniques in the Control of Cardiac Arrhythmias," *Seminars in Psychiatry* 5 (1973): 433–38.

CHAPTER 15

John Knowles, "The Responsibility of the Individual," *Daedalus* 106, no. 1 (Winter 1977): 59.

1. Knowles, *Doing Better*.

2. N. B. Belloc and Lester Breslow, "The Relation of Physical Health Status and Health Practices," *Preventive Medicine* 1 (August 1972): 409–21; Lester Breslow, "Research in a Strategy for Health Improvement," *International Journal of Health Services* 3 (1973): 7–16.

3. Alfred Katz and Eugene Bender, *The Strength in Us: Self-Help Groups in the Modern World* (New York: Viewpoints, 1976); Lowell S. Levin, Alfred H. Katz, and Erik Holst, *Self-Care: Lay Initiatives in Health* (New York: Prodist, Neale Watson Academic Publications, 1976).

CHAPTER 16

Lewis Mumford, *The Myth of the Machine* (London: Secker & Warburg, 1967), pp. 75–76.

1. Irving Oyle, *The Healing Mind* (Millbrae, Calif.: Celestial Arts, 1975); *Magic, Mysticism and Modern Medicine* (Millbrae, Calif.: Celestial Arts, 1976); *Time, Space and the Mind* (Millbrae, Calif.: Celestial Arts, 1976).

2. Emmett E. Miller, *Selective Awareness* (privately published, 1977: Menlo Park, Calif.) Cheek and LeCron *Clinical Hypnotherapy;* William S. Kroger, *Clinical and Experimental Hypnosis*, 2d ed. (Philadelphia: J. B. Lippincott, 1977).

3. Timothy Gallwey, *The Inner Game of Tennis* (New York: Random House, 1976).

4. Jacobson, *You Must Relax*.

CHAPTER 17

Mary Baker Eddy, *Science and Health* (Boston: Christian Science Publishing Society, 1903), p. 412.

1. Mike Samuels and Nancy Samuels, *Seeing with the Mind's Eye* (New York: Random House/Bookworks, 1976); Jerome L. Singer, *Imagery and Daydream Methods in Psychotherapy and Behavior Modification* (New York: Academic Press, 1974); David Bresler, with Richard Trubo, *Free Yourself from Pain* (New York: Simon and Schuster, 1977).
2. Robert Ornstein, *The Psychology of Consciousness*, 2d ed. (New York: Harcourt Brace Jovanovich, 1977).
3. Ernest Hilgard, *Divided Consciousness* (New York: John Wiley and Sons, 1977).
4. A full account of this case is published in the first issue of the newsletter of the Unorthodox Healing Foundation, Los Angeles, Calif.
5. Robert Swearingen, "Meditation in the Emergency Room," in *Body, Mind and Health*.
6. Bresler, *Free Yourself from Pain*.
7. Reported in *Quest Magazine*, May–June 1977, p. 113.
8. Jeanne Achterberg and G. Frank Lawlis, *Imagery of Cancer* (Champaign, Ill.: Institute for Personality and Ability Testing, 1978).

CHAPTER 18

William James, in *Scribner's Magazine*, 1890.

1. Albert Szent-Gyoergyi, "Drive in Living Matter to Perfect Itself," *Synthesis* 1, no. 1 (1974): 12–24.
2. June Singer, *Boundaries of the Soul* (New York: Doubleday/Anchor Books, 1976).
3. Henry Reed, ed., *Sundance Community Dream Journal* 1, nos. 1 and 2 (Virginia Beach, Va.: ARE Press, 1976); Russell A. Lockhart, "Cancer in Myth and Dream," pp. 1–25; James Sanford, *Healing and Wholeness* (New York: Paulist Press, 1978).
4. Mike Samuels and Hal Bennett, *Spirit Guides* (New York: Random House/Bookworks, 1974).
5. Bresler, *Free Yourself from Pain*.

Index

accidents, 19, 83, 87-8
Achterberg, Jeanne, 251
acne, 114-16, 123
advertising, influence of, 11
alcohol, use of, 7-8, 173, 217
Alcoholics Anonymous, 223
Alexander, F. M., 164
allergies, 61, 78
anger, 107, 174
  family conflict and illness,
    131-2, 133, 134
  child, 136-41
  marital relations, 134-6
  and illness, 3-4, 12-13, 119,
    120, 123
  illness or death of family mem-
    ber, 48, 49
anxiety, 63, 117, 123
  and eating problems, 220
  and illness, 24, 97, 176
  of family member, 48-9
  and stress, 73, 76, 101, 171, 172
  treatments for, 8, 174
  see also worry
Arbogast, Richard, 141
arthritis, 76
  rheumatoid arthritis, 94, 135
asthma, 24, 122
attitudes and beliefs, 3-4, 21, 61,
    112, 124
  toward age, and longevity, 21,
    76
  emotions and feelings, 57, 66,
    67, 82-3, 118

attitudes and beliefs (cont.)
  depression, 8, 12-13, 19, 76,
    78, 94, 110, 125, 126
  fear, 63, 117-18, 172
  frustration, 12-13, 19, 48,
    108, 119-20
  needs, awareness of, 124-7
  suppression of, and ailments,
    3-4, 12, 21, 34, 35, 43, 44,
    48-9, 108, 114-24
  worry, 8, 25, 41, 63, 73, 76,
    98, 110-11, 171
  see also anger; anxiety; stress
goals and expectations, 112,
    231-5
  discovery of and commitment
    to, 30-4
  of doctor or authority figure,
    patient's response to, 52-63
    passim
  Jung's "collective uncon-
    scious," 240, 254-5
  and placebo effect, 52-63,
    151, 153, 232
  revealed by healing imagery,
    250-2
  and "will to live," 31-4, 54,
    231-5
helplessness and hopelessness,
    18, 19, 92, 93-4, 108, 109,
    112, 113, 119, 123, 149,
    250-2
self-fulfilling prophecies of ill
    health, 60-2

281

A Note About the Author

Born in New York City, Dennis Jaffe received his bachelor's, master's and doctoral degrees from Yale University. He is now a member of the UCLA Department of Psychiatry and is director of Learning for Health, a psychosomatic medicine clinic in Los Angeles. Dr. Jaffe is the co-author of several general and text books in the field of psychology, including *Worlds Apart: Young People and Drug Programs* (1974), *TM: Discovering Inner Energy and Overcoming Stress* (1975) and *Abnormal Psychology in the Life Cycle* (1978).

A Note on the Type

This book was set via computer-driven cathode-ray tube in an adaptation of Janson, a recutting made direct from type cast from matrices long thought to have been made by the Dutchman Anton Janson, who was a practicing type founder in Leipzig during the years 1668–87. However, it has been conclusively demonstrated that these types are actually the work of Nicholas Kis (1650–1702), a Hungarian, who most probably learned his trade from the master Dutch type founder Dirk Voskens. The type is an excellent example of the influential and sturdy Dutch types that prevailed in England up to the time William Caslon developed his own incomparable designs from them.

Typography and binding design by Dorothy Schmiderer.